Complete Course in

# Electronic Piano Tuning

# Complete Course in Electronic

Professional/Technical Series

Nelson-Hall Company nh Chicago

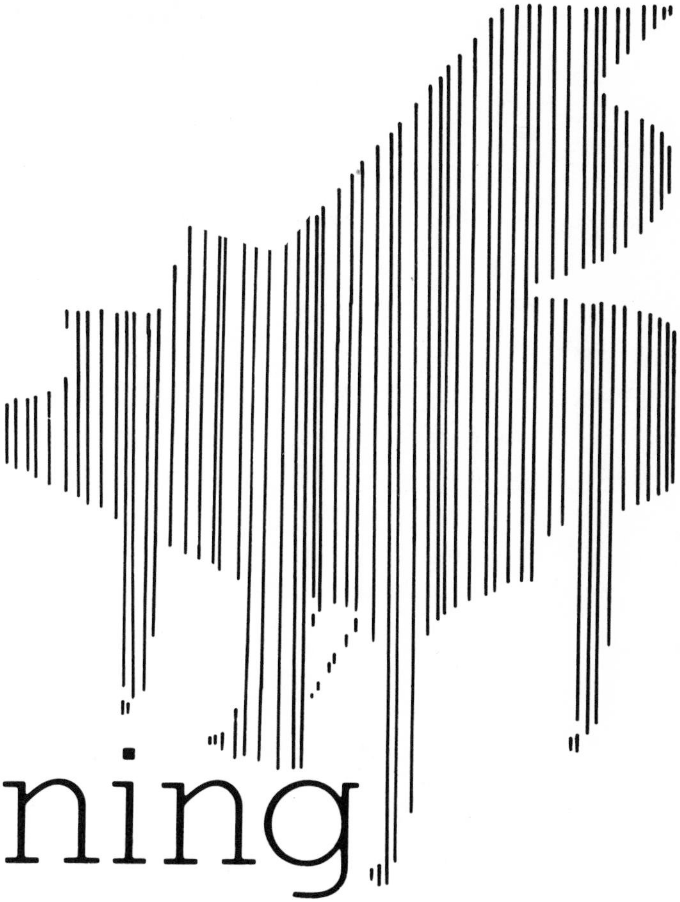

# Piano Tuning

Floyd A. Stevens, Ph.D.

**Library of Congress Cataloging in Publication Data**

Stevens, Floyd A

Complete course in electronic piano tuning.

(Professional/technical series)

1. Piano—Tuning. 2. Tuning—Electronic equipment.
I. Title. II. Title: Electronic piano tuning.
MT165.s8 786.2'3 73-92238
ISBN 0-911012-24-9

ISBN 0–911012–24–9

Library of Congress Catalog Card No. 73-92238



For information address
Nelson-Hall Company, Publishers, 325 W. Jackson Blvd., Chicago, Ill. 60606

Manufactured in the United States of America

This book is dedicated to
Bruce N. Stevens,
who is helping to narrow the generation gap
with music.

And to
Sandra Lee Burnside,
whose mastery of both the organ and the piano
would gladden the heart of any tuner.

# Contents

# Figures

# Illustrations

# Acknowledgments

Without the help of certain individuals, particularly those employed by major manufacturers of electronic piano tuning devices, writing this book may have been impossible. I gratefully acknowledge the contributions of:

William H. Hass, of Peterson Electrical Musical Products, who provided valuable technical information on his company's products, as well as much encouragement.

The Conn Corporation, who granted permission to adopt material on the use of the Strobotuner; and to Dr. E. L. Kent, whose seminars before piano craftsmen have been uncommonly instructional. Conn's laboratory studies of inharmonicity in piano tones offered much clarification on what happens when one tunes a piano.

LaRoy Edwards, Technical Service Manager for Yamaha International Corporation, who provided instruments for testing as well as information regarding the latest developments in electronic tuning.

Willard Sims, Piano Technical Service Manager for Baldwin Piano and Organ Company, who unstintingly gave time and effort to supply important material on proper piano regulation and specifications.

Marvin Masel, President of Berkshire Electronic Industries, who took part in many useful discussions and who generously provided diagrams and instructions on the use of the Tune Master. A physicist, Mr. Masel has devoted years to research in the area of piano tuning.

Opal, my wife, who kept the home fires burning in Ohio while I was in Florida researching, writing, and tuning.

Sandy, my daughter, who cooked meals, taught students, performed in concerts, and still found time to help edit and to type.

Kent, my grandson, "the littlest tuner of them all," who helped me find relaxation with fishing and watching sunsets in Withlacoochee Bay.

Bruce, my son, who often phoned encouragement from Nashville, where he was busy performing.

# Introduction

In my previous book, *Complete Course in Professional Piano Tuning, Repair, and Rebuilding,* I included a chapter on the use of the Conn Strobotuner as an aid to tuning pianos. Since its publication, many readers asked for a book which would deal exclusively with electronic tuning and which would completely survey the techniques and equipment available. With the cooperation of Nelson-Hall and companies which manufacture electronic tuning equipment, I have complied with that request, and this book is the result.

The following chapters will completely cover all useful aspects of modern equipment in tuning pianos, and they are designed to help beginners as well as old-time users.

I hope that the working procedures will encourage young men and women to get started in the tuning business and enable them to tune pianos well right away, thus avoiding years of practice which could restrict their earning power while they learned.

I do not wish to imply that the old method of setting a temperament by ear is outmoded, nor do I cast aspersions on its practice. In fact, I tune both by the aural beat method and with the use of modern electronic tuning equipment. Either way, the tuner can do a fine job. However, modern electronic tuning aids are here, and they are here to stay. There has been a steady refinement in their design and manufacture, and the accuracy with which these up-to-date instruments perform is very high indeed. Every man in the piano service field, whether a novice or an old-line tuner, owes it to himself to become well acquainted with the latest methods of doing his work, especially since they are precise and manageable.

In a recent *Wall Street Journal* article, various aspects of a career in piano tuning were discussed. Although much of what was said merely reflected the opinions of a few tuners who were interviewed, some very salient facts did emerge. They include the point that fewer than 100 persons a year are entering the piano servicing field, and that the deaths of members of just one national tuning organization far exceed this figure. In addition, it was stated that the long apprenticeship required to learn to tune well by using the aural method was in many cases equal to the total time required to earn an M.D. degree.

Since the financial rewards of a piano tuner do not approach those of a medical doctor, few young people were entering this profession. However, piano experts do make good money and this often equals or exceeds the income of most other professionals who require lengthy college training, experience, and a good practice. Yet, the person who considers becoming a piano tuner does not want to wait from two to eight years before he does excellent work and commands top prices. So, few newcomers enter the business.

By considerably shortening the time in which a person

may become qualified to do basic piano tuning and minor repairs, electronic aids can make piano service lucrative much earlier. This should be encouraging to anyone interested in a full-time career as a piano tuner and technician. The way in which one goes about his first tuning with electronic equipment is critical as it will establish the method for all future tunings. Thus, if one follows proper procedures from the beginning, he will become more and more adept at using the equipment and less and less apprehensive of doing the work.

To tune pianos properly by use of electronic tuning methods is relatively easy. In order to indicate this fact, I intend to take the reader through a complete tuning, step by step, using each of the electronic aids available. The matter of tuning a piano is basically an objective matter. That is to say, subjective considerations as to whether another tuner, piano teacher, or musician would like the manner in which one goes about tuning a piano are of no consequence. What does matter is whether or not one tunes a piano with such accuracy and skill that the instrument can be played in all 12 keys and the proper intervals of note relationships are respected throughout the entire instrument.

Electronic tuning makes this possible, without variation, time after time. And it does not require musical ability, nor some "sound" honing of the ear. Neither does it require a mysterious sixth sense as to what sounds good or bad, nor a sense of musical pitch. In short, electronic tuning can be learned by following a simple, systematic method which will tune any piano. False beats, inharmonicities in strings, and other bewildering stumbling blocks that face the newer tuner can be minimized with the aid of electronic equipment.

The resulting sound of music played on the instrument may be properly assessed subjectively, that is, by its appeal to the human musical ear. A musician seldom complains about electronic tuning when he hears the result. Orchestra members, choir directors, horn players, as well as many piano manufacturers, are accustomed to the use of electronic tuning devices for setting accurate pitch. Few public school music departments are without at least one of these aids.

So, not only can the electronic system be learned rather easily, without recourse to special training, but also public acceptance of the result is more than adequate. In all the years I have been tuning pianos, the only complaints I have ever heard about electronic tuning were those from old-line piano tuners who thought it might take away some of their business. Maybe it has done so. No doubt it will in the future if properly executed. However I can think of no other form of piano tuning which will offer a threat to the continued prosperity of the electronic tuner if he does his work well.

A basic knowledge of piano terms and technology will be required for the person who wishes to use electronic methods. No matter how one wishes to tune a piano, he must understand something of the dynamic forces at play during tuning, as well as the physical changes that take place in a piano. Furthermore, some regulating and adjusting of piano parts are often a necessary part of the tuning process. For this reason, this book will include enough basic piano technology to enable a person to feel at ease when he sits down in front of a piano to tune it. (A more comprehensive treatment of the field of piano technology, including rebuilding and detailed regulating procedures, may be found in my earlier work, which was previously mentioned.)

The basic tools of the trade will be listed herein because you will need good tools to do good work. Some of the necessary devices you can make yourself, if you want to. But all the tools essential to a master tuner will be listed and sources for their purchase will be given. In short, if you have never tuned a piano before, but want to learn how, this book will furnish the methods and information. If you are presently in piano service and want to learn more about electronic tuning methods, this text will help you cover the field of available equipment and tell you how to use it on the job. There will be enough theory to explain these units but the emphasis will be on how to tune electronically. Further, you will discover that electronic tuning aids are priced reasonably, most of them costing less than a good set of tires.

You will be trained in establishing a profitable tuning business. Sales methods and techniques, records required, methods of securing and holding clients will be discussed. There is little left to chance when you set out to become a scientific piano tuner if you apply modern methods of doing your work. You will also get the most in pay for what you do.

I have found the servicing of pianos to be a most rewarding profession for a man or woman who does not want to punch a time clock or take orders from others. Prestige, financial security, and a sense of self-respect are the rewards of the piano professional who does every job well. If these are what you are looking for and if you really want to learn to do your work so well that few could improve upon it, the training outlined in this text is for you. And electronic tuning is the method that will put you securely in the field.

In the course of servicing pianos, most of us are called upon to tune electronic instruments such as the organ, Chordovox, etc. In fact, I have often been asked to tune a guitar. While methods of tuning pianos may differ and still get results, the only proper way to tune an electronic instrument is by use of modern electronic tuning aids. Temperament cannot be beat out on most electronic organs. So, the piano service man who can also tune organs is due for some additional income from his business. Rather than being a man of mystery, an image so many old-time tuners like to convey, the electronic tuner can be the man of accuracy and efficiency. His earning power will show him which is the better means for gaining and holding a client's loyalty.

You can become a better tuner sooner with electronic tuning if you will conscientiously set out to learn electronic methods and to become well acquainted with the action and tensions of the piano. The finest concert grand, the lowliest short keyboard spinet, and all their smaller and larger sister pianos must have regular care. Pianos go out of tune frequently. They are made in such a way that all the parts of the sounding system work together, and when there is a significant change in one of their components, the tune of the piano as a whole changes. Humidity and temperature both work havoc in changing piano tensions and tuning. Strings expand and contract. Sound boards move their crowns in and out, although the movement is not visible to the owner's eyes. But the swelling of wooden parts under conditions of great humidity changes the tensions and pressures placed by the bridges upon the strings, and thus the overall tune of the strings is changed.

Most manufacturers agree that all pianos should be tuned at least three or four times in the first year of use, and not less than two times a year thereafter. Pianos in constant professional use should be tuned weekly or monthly, depending upon the frequency with which they are played. It must be remembered that pianos were designed to have the stresses most evenly placed throughout the instrument when the instrument is in tune. When out of tune, unusual stresses happen at points within the framework. The result of these non-designed stresses can range from splitting of the sound board to loosening of the bridges. Out-of-tune pianos are always in the process of going bad.

Since a conservative estimate of pianos in use in America today is 10 million, and the largest estimate ever given as to the number of piano tuners (including the elderly, the students, the part-timers, and the professionals) is about 8,000, you can see that even if all tuners worked all day every day of the year, they could never keep all the pianos in tune. Probably fewer than 3,000 persons are full-time professional tuner-technicians in America today.

For many of these experts, the job of tuning a piano takes as long as two hours. When confronted with certain pianos, some tuners spend more than half their tuning time just trying to get a good temperament. With electronic tuning, the temperament is set at once, with little fussing. The tuning time can usually be set at one hour, and a good job can be done during that time.

The person who does a first class job in two hours does not deserve one cent more pay than the one who does a first class job in one hour or less. You charge for the tuning, not for the hours. So often tuners think they will get more business by charging less. This is ridiculous. Charge the full price, like a master tuner in your area, and do a first class tuning job.

We live in a land where pianos swell and expand in the Northwest while they dry out and crack in the Southwest. In the Midwest, the changes from high humidity to low humidity can cause both effects. A piano is made largely of wood. What isn't made of wood depends on wooden parts to make it work. Wood swells with high humidity, even the best processed kind. It shrinks with dryness, too.

So it is that pianos tuned to A-440 in a normally dry climate will rise in pitch and go out of tune as soon as the humidity increases significantly. Winter heating in the home will cause pianos, which were tuned to proper pitch, to dry out and sink in pitch throughout the center section of the piano, thus putting them out of tune.

Generally speaking, pianos which are kept in any one part of this country will go up and down in pitch as the humidity rises and falls. Thus, a piano in Oregon, when tuned to pitch in normal humidity for that region, will fall in pitch when dryness occurs and will sharpen in pitch when humidity rises. This is so in Florida, Maine, and Arizona. Pianos tuned in these climates will rise and fall with the rise and fall of humidity in the respective area.

I am acquainted with one small piano manufacturer who

moved his business to Utah because he felt that no matter where he shipped his pianos, they would swell and get tighter since most places in America were damper than his location.

Time and tide are on your side to give you tuning business. Further, every real change of weather develops some other business for you in piano service. This is one of the better reasons for becoming a good technician.

There is a special security in life which most people find hard to achieve. That is the security of knowing that no amount of nit-picking or ups and downs in personal affairs will rob one of a sense of self-worth. If you will learn to tune pianos well—and you can learn to tune them well electronically—you will have that security. There are few things left in this world in which a man can take full credit for his work and give a full measure of craftsmanship to what he does.

Kids will play better when the piano is tuned; the A's sound like A's. The teacher will give more A grades, too!

One of the great truths of life is that you must, if you are to succeed, find a need and fill it. Just such a need exists today for piano tuners and technicians. The need is genuine, the pianos are out there in millions of places, the things are going out of tune. You can fill the need to tune them. Once you have mastered the art of tuning, you can feel more creative and constructive. Initially you will be seeking the business; then suddenly, as you tune every piano right, the business will start seeking you.

Because this book will be read more by individuals who want to become tuners than by those who have been tuning for years, I would like to quote a few paragraphs about this profession from my first book:

Someone asked me, "What makes a good piano tuner?" After some thought, I came to the conclusion that the vision of craftsmanship is what makes a good piano tuner. It isn't charm, or college degrees, or certificates, or right connections that makes a qualified craftsman. Only a vision in a man's mind of himself as a craftsman and an excellent practitioner of his skill will do it!

There are people who possess degrees and certificates to prove that they are one thing or another. Unfortunately, we often find that they are not what the certificates say because they don't do what the certificates claim they can do. Or at least, they can't do well what they are supposed to do. Piano technology has only one aristocracy, and that is the aristocracy of achievement. Either you can tune, or you're not considered to be a piano tuner. Your competence, or lack of it, will be revealed as soon as someone sits down to play a piano you have just tuned. That is the moment of truth!

Piano tuning is the key which opens doors to homes of the musically cultured and financially able. You will enter those homes as a qualified craftsman who renders a valuable service. People will respect your skill, once you master it well enough to respect it yourself. With men and women who work in this field, you will share a secret knowledge and a fine sense of self-worth. Money will follow as surely as night follows the day. But first, you must see yourself as a piano tuner, and approach the art with the vision of craftsmanship.

With the greatest respect for the integrity of the aural methods carefully explained to me over the years and with kindness toward those who cling steadfastly to the aural method, I offer the reader of this book a new method, as well as a combination method, which should make better tuners of us all. Listening, testing, and learning each new thing in our craft are certainly the highest marks of a good craftsman. And, with fuller understanding of the tools now available for supremely accurate work, we can all become master tuners.

# 1
# Piano Construction and Operation

I recommend that the person who is going to tune pianos, by whatever method, review from time to time the major features which are common to all pianos and which have a great deal to do with the proper ways in which one may tune. Major changes and shifts in tensions take place when a piano is allowed to stay in an out-of-tune condition, and likewise, major tension changes occur when a tuning is in process. For that reason, knowledge of piano engineering and construction is an integral part of a good tuner's information if he is to understand what is happening while he is tuning.

All pianos are built in about the same way. The upright is constructed much like the spinet and console, and the grand is basically the same as an upright laid on its back. The back structure of a piano is the foundation. Usually it consists of large posts of wood, or, in some foreign pianos, of a large rim which is cast integrally with the plate to handle the tremendous strains imposed upon it. About 18 to 20 tons of pressure are exerted by the string system when the piano is in tune to concert pitch.

The top of the back and the lower section must be in good condition, and all glue joints and bearing stress bolts should be tight if a piano is to take and hold a tune properly. The sound board, usually made of close-grained spruce, is placed from edge to edge of the back and from the bottom to slightly below the tuning pin holes at the top of the back frame. There is a slight crown in the sound board which causes it to push forward (in the case of a spinet) or upward (in the case of a grand). Across this crown run the bridges, which accept the down bearing and the side bearing of the strings as they course from the lower plate hitch pins upward to the bearing bar and agraffes and from there to the pins.

Ribs of wood hold the crown in the sound board and somewhat stiffen its response, avoiding major changes in its shape during tuning and playing. Above the sound board, the pin plank, or wrest plank, extends completely across the top or forward surface of the piano. Each pin hole is drilled approximately .025 of an inch undersize before the tuning pins are driven in. The friction which occurs between the tuning pins (which are slightly serrated) and the end grains of the many plies of the wooden, laminated pin plank tends to hold the tuning pins in position and to prevent their release. The greatest number of possible contacts between the end grain of the laminated pin block plies and the serrated pins themselves offers the greatest possible number of adhering points. For this reason, it is probably not good practice to turn tuning pins unless absolutely necessary, since constant wrenching and turning will wear away the end wood fibres which assist in solid tunings.

Not a small amount of trouble which many encounter in tuning pianos is due to their forgetting about the basic functions of the structure of the piano and their subsequent failure to go along with these functions. The scale of a piano is designed so that full advantage is taken of the resonance built into the sound board and its crowned area. A glance at a violin or cello will show you the basic principle at work in the piano sound board and bridge structure. The tension of the string vibration is passed through the bridge to the curved surface of the sound board and from there to the air with its sympathetic movement around the crown of the sound board.

As one tightens the strings which exert a strong pressure on the bridge (called down bearing), the sound board crown moves somewhat. While the movement is small, the 7 lbs. of down bearing per string when multiplied by the 231 strings in the piano cause a considerable change to the overall pattern of the sound board; also during the tuning operation, a certain sequence of operations is required so as to control the movement of the sound board and to avoid sudden areas of strings which drop or rise after you have just finished tuning another area.

When you consider that the cast iron plate, which has the hitch pins to which the lower string ends are fastened, must bear the full 20 tons of tension, it is obvious that a good tuner will securely fasten all bolting points before beginning tuning. Plates are overstressed in their design and will stand about one and a half to two times the pressure they normally must bear. However, if a section of the plate is not securely fastened to its moorings, the excess movement possible when great tensions occur during tuning can cause plate breakage and an explosive situation.

Bridges, made of hardwood and fastened to the sound board, are capped with a graphitic surface. The lubrication is put on the bridge cap so that the strings, in their coursing from the lower hitch pin and over the bridge, will not adhere to the wood during tuning. The strings pass from the hitch pin over the bridge (which is slightly higher than the string level at the hitch pin); continue upward to the bearing bar (sometimes called capo d'astro bar); pass over the bearing bar; are depressed in their level by the capo d'astro bar; and, finally, from that point, continue at an inclined level downward to the coil of the tuning pins. Agraffes, when used in a piano, serve the same function as the bearing bar and capo bar, in that they alter the course of the string and initiate a basic friction point through which the string does not easily move.

Place that term firmly in your mind. Basic friction points are the points designed within the string course which have the greatest amount to do with tuning a piano. These are the basic friction points in a piano involved in tuning: at the agraffe (or bearing and capo bar) or at any hump or protruding surface between the agraffe and tuning pin; at the point where the string bears down upon the bridge; and at one more point, the place where the string is deflected sideways by the bridge pins. This is the side bearing of the string.

All these basic friction points must be satisfactorily controlled if one is to tune a piano properly and to have it stay in tune for any length of time. The string must be excited by the impact of the hammer in such a way as to cause the most possible free movement of the string across and through the basic friction points. Otherwise you will end up with an insecure tuning, subject to radical alteration the moment the piano is played or the slightest temperature change takes place in the room.

In addition to these points, the inner torque of the pin must be relieved. Let me explain: tuning pins are held by compressed fibers of wood within the pin block. When one moves the outward section of pin in any direction while tuning, he turns the string coils around the pin. At the same time, he sets up a slight torque *within* the tuning pin, because the portion he moved, which was outside the pin block, did not move the portion within the pin block in the same degree or to the same extent.

There is a lag between pin tip movement and pin shaft movement. This tension which the tuner has built up within the length of the pin can slowly unwind by itself and let the string down or raise it (depending on which way he left the pin) and destroy his tuning shortly after he has completed it. He must relax the inner tension within the pin if he expects to satisfactorily tune the piano. Methods for doing this will be given shortly.

Fortunately, I believe I have an integrated method which will neutralize all friction points and "set the pin" in one sequence as one tunes the piano. But for the tuner, whether he be new or experienced, the basic considerations which are being dealt with in this chapter must be handled properly or there is little sense in learning anything else about tuning. Your tuning must be firm. It must last as long as possible. And it can if you will get the picture of these basic friction points clearly in your mind and then think along with me on these matters.

On some new pianos, with their extremely tight pin blocks, it appears to the experienced tuner that the pin stays just where it was put at the factory. But those who tune in with the belief that the tuning takes place by turning the tuning pins are creating a mental problem. If one thinks about the layout of a typical piano string as it proceeds from hitch pin to tuning pin, he might conclude that the string is what needs to be tuned. Therefore let us place the tuning pin just where it belongs: classified as just one part of the system which puts a piano in tune. Further, let us consider the segment of string between hitch pin and bridge. Surely, when the string is pulled to its specified tension at the distant end from the hitch pin, the small segment between hitch pin and bridge is likely to be under a slightly different tension than the longer part between bridge and bearing bar, or agraffe. Now consider the small segment of string between the upper bearing bar, or agraffe, and tuning pin. One might safely conclude that the small segment between these two points is likely to be under different tension than the long portion between the bridge and bearing bar.

In fact, the design of string travel is such that it would seem impossible for the tension to be equal between these different points. The sound of a piano depends upon the vibrations of the speaking length of the string being transmitted through the bridge to the sound board, which in turn moves the air so that sound arrives at the human ear. The tune of a piano depends upon equalizing the distinctly different portions of the piano string so that tensions are left nearly in balance; or if not, regulated so that the speaking length will not be materially altered by the playing of the piano or other factors after tuning.

Up to this point, we have considered the strange and shifting effects of uneven tensions applied to the sound board during tuning and the vagaries which can occur as the result of upper plate wobble. The tuner and technician must know that, having minimized these variables, he can control the mysteries of piano wire as it courses on its way from hitch pin to tuning pin and excites the bridges.

There are ways to have control of this extremely variable component of the piano. Perfecting these ways means perfecting your tuning. And fine tuning depends upon a constant consideration of the factors which, taken all together, can work with the tuner or against him. Working intelligently with the things that are built into a piano can make all the difference. That's the way to make every piano sound its best. Not only does "the tuner alone preserve the tone," he usually improves it!

### *The Tuning Hammer and Its Application*

Tuning hammers (actually levers) come in various systems and styles. For the best tuning it is better to have a tuning lever with a short tip. In tuning a piano, the tip of the tun-

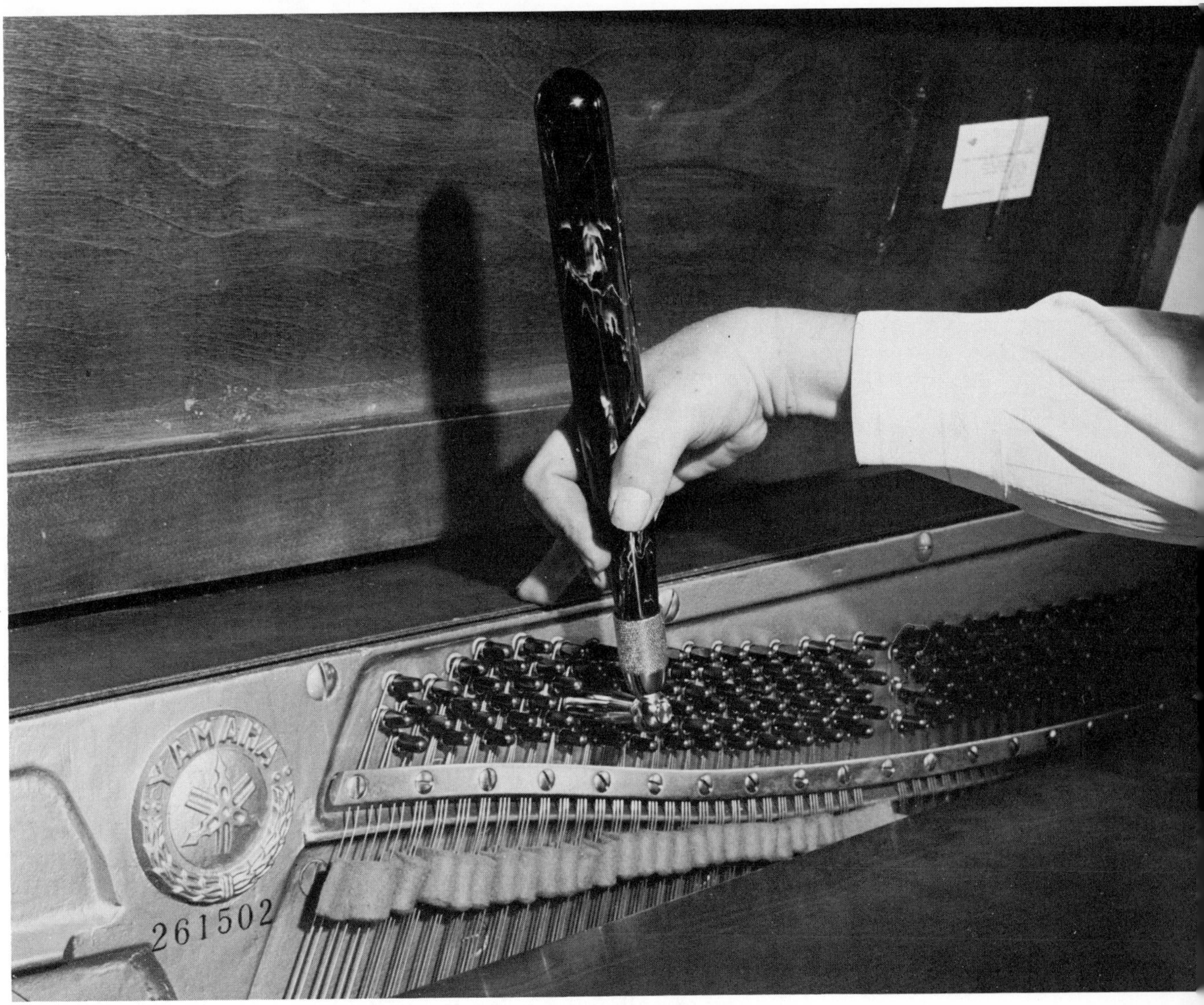


The proper placement of the tuning lever on a pin in a vertical or upright piano allows maximum control without pulling against the tension of the string. Notice that the little finger is resting on the upper surface of the piano, while the tuning lever is gripped lightly with the fingers, which allows you to gently push and pull the lever.

*Figure 1.1*

ing lever exerts pressure upward and downward upon the exposed section of the tuning pins. Too long a tip on the lever will lead to bending of the tuning pins. The handle length should be about 10 in. and, if the tool used is extendable, it should not be extended over an inch or so, but to where it feels comfortably balanced in the normal tuning position. The normal tuning position is one with the tuning lever pressed firmly down as far as it will go on the tip of the tuning pin, and the hammer held at a position of roughly 11 o'clock in relationship to the piano as one sits or stands before it. On grands, this means that the hammer is held at about 2 o'clock.

There is a reason for placing the lever in this position. Since the string is coiled three times around the pin, you will find that an 11 o'clock hold places the hammer in line with the string line, if not at the beginning of the pin movement, at the close of the operation. Since the pin is being pulled toward 6 o'clock by the tension of the string, a hold at 11 or 12 o'clock offers the most responsive feel of the string movement and tensions and permits lifting the string slightly in the direction you want it to go while tuning. This avoids enlarging the tuning pin holes, and because it offers a more sensitive feel of the string, it also avoids too much pin movement in the pin block. Furthermore, it offers you the chance to lift or lower the tension without turning the pin unless absolutely necessary.

If you should have to turn the pin, you would not be wobbling it to the side and enlarging the hole. Whether you use the left hand to tune with, while striking the keys with the right hand, or the right hand to tune with, while striking the keys with the left hand, makes not the slightest difference, as long as you keep the lever in the position described above and lift up on the string as you tune, and allow the normal downward pull of the string to assist you in any downward tuning you have to do. I have heard tuners agree on both left-handed tuning and right-handed tuning. The controversy boils down to using whatever hand enables you to get the most sensitive feel of what you are doing with the pin and the string as you tune. So don't worry about it. Our job is not to perfect a left-handed or right-handed method. Our function is to perfect a tuning method which fits our physical configurations and does a fine job on the piano.

Now I will offer a simple technique with few imponderables which will enable you to set the pin, position the string, and know that the tensions are relieved and in harmony in the piano. This method, even when I first learned it, proved highly satisfactory and was worth more than the price of all the books I ever read on piano tuning and technology.

With the tuning lever in the 11 or 12 o'clock position, bring the string up to one beat per second above the pitch desired. Do this by lifting slightly on the end of the tuning lever, but not hard enough to bend the pin. If the string cannot be lifted to the pitch you desire by this light lift, turn the pin slightly in the direction you wish to go and allow it to lower itself to 1 beat per second sharp. While doing this, strike the note with a firm blow; this will enable the string to flex across the basic friction points. It may go a lot sharper than you expected. And it may go a lot flatter than you thought it would. No matter. Get it up to 1 beat per second sharp when all firm blows are done. Now, with a slight pressure of the little finger or the thumb, bear outward (or toward you) on the lever to lower the string tension to where you hear the beat stop; then go 1 beat per second flat. Release the tension on the hammer. You should be on pitch.

***To Test***

Strike the tone with a 5 to 8 lb. blow. If the string stays put, you have equalized the tensions at the basic friction points. Then lift the tone by thumb pressure on the hammer until it is 1 beat sharp per second. Release of the pressure should allow it to drop to absolute pitch. Lower the tone by thumb pressure on the hammer by 1 beat per second flat. Release of the hammer tension should allow the note to come up to absolute pitch. If the same amount of upward or downward pressure will alter the note by 1 beat per second either sharp or flat, you have released the tension in the pin. Don't touch it. You've got it right, and it will hold.

All the operations outlined above are done in the sequence given and the time spent on one tuning pin is fractional. Total tuning of a piano in this way need not exceed one hour from start to finish, and it usually takes less time than that. The strings don't shift, and the tones don't change.

There has been much written in the past in technical journals as to what is the best way to set the pin, etc., but from my experience it is definite that the pin is set, the string is right, and the problem of creeping strings is completely under control when the tuner can make the string creep in whatever direction he seems to desire and when he is managing the torque in the pin for his own purposes. That is what this method of tuning and pin setting does, and this is the one sure way to know you have a solid tuning which will not go out quickly. It will work on new pianos with good pin blocks, on old pianos with good pin blocks, and even on some pianos with bad pin blocks.

It should go without saying that if there is something wrong with the fit of the pin in the pin block, and the block is worn and old, you should either treat the pin block with chemicals or replace it before attempting to tune the piano. Also, the tension with which the capo bar presses downward upon the string should be sufficient to hold the string in line, and not so great as to interfere with its moving past this basic friction point upon proper application of tension to the tuning lever. But, for all intents and purposes, on a good piano in good shape, this is the tuning method that works best. Practice this method regularly, since you will use it on every string in the piano, and no tuning frequency standard is of any use whatsoever if you can't make the string stay where you want it to.

## *The Piano Action and Usual Minor Repairs*

It may well be that many readers of this book have never tuned a piano in their lives. With that in mind, I will now discuss what piano actions are like and the most common troubles a tuner is expected to repair. If you are going to tune pianos, it would not be wise to attempt doing so until you have familiarized yourself with piano actions and their related repairs.

Most people expect the tuner to fix anything that goes wrong with the piano. While it is neither necessary nor possible within the framework of this book on modern tuning methods for me to give a comprehensive treatise on piano technology, I will offer some general aids.

By all means, if you are going out to tune pianos, don't wait until you're in trouble to buy a book on piano repairs. Since there are from 6,000 to 11,000 parts in the average piano, you might as well go buy a book on piano repairs now. My previous work, *Complete Course in Professional Piano Tuning, Repair, and Rebuilding,* covers repairing in depth. It should prove extremely helpful for those who wish to pursue piano tuning and repair with confidence.

As you read the instruction that follows, refer to the accompanying illustrations of the various piano actions.

In all piano actions, the finger never makes direct contact with the string. Although a properly regulated action will seem to almost reflect the tuner's fingers, the fact is that the action builds up and then releases energy, impacting upon the string, but without a direct chain of contact between the playing end of the key and the string.

When the key is depressed, the downward leverage from the front of the key is transposed into upward motion at the point where the key is pivoted on the center balance rail pin. Attached to the key, and moving upward, the capstan screw, or its related sticker arrangement, causes an upward motion of the wippen, which is pivoting on its flange. At the same instant, the far end of the wippen, pivoting downward,

*Figure 1.2* **Baldwin Grand Regulation Standards**

1 Set key frame buttons paper thickness above key bed with keys removed.
2 Center hammers under strings.
3 Space repetition levers.
4 Square, level, and space keys. (Be sure that hammer shanks clear hammer rest rail first.) Height of keys 1 and 88 to be set as follows: Baldwin Concert Grand, $2\frac{9}{16}$ in.; all other Baldwin and Hamilton Grand pianos, $2\frac{1}{2}$ in.; Howard Grands (Style 474), $2\frac{3}{8}$ in.; all sharps to be $\frac{1}{2}$ in. above ivories.
5 Set touch depth $\frac{3}{8}$ in. measuring $\frac{1}{4}$ in. back from front of natural key.
6 Set end hammers of each section $1\frac{7}{8}$ in. from strings.
7 Set surface A of jack in line with surface B of knuckle insert by adjusting screw.
8 Regulate repetition lever so that it is $\frac{1}{64}$ in. above top of jack at C.
9 Set "let-off" $\frac{1}{16}$ in. from string.
10 Re-check hammer stroke to be $1\frac{7}{8}$ in. on end hammers of each section.

11 Set hammer rest rail 1/8 in. below end hammer shanks.
12 Set hammer line 1 7/8 in. from strings, lining up on end hammer of each section.
13 Set "drop" to 1/16 in.
14 Set back checks to catch hammers 5/8 in. from strings.
15 Regulate repetition spring so that hammer will rise without a jump.
16 To set repetition lever stop hook, press hammer down 1/4 in. below its checking point on back check. The stop hook should then come into contact with the felt. Concert Grands need no adjustment. (Stop hook not present in all actions.)
17 Set key strip so that front of a natural key can be raised 1/8 in.
18 Damper should start to lift when hammer is 7/8 in. from strings.
19 Have 1/16 in. clearance between felt on damper lever board and damper levers.
20 Set sostenuto rod lip to clear 1/16 in. between it and damper lever lip, viewed from front; set sostenuto rod bracket so that sostenuto rod lip projects 1/16 in. under sostenuto lever lip with pedal depressed (viewed from above).

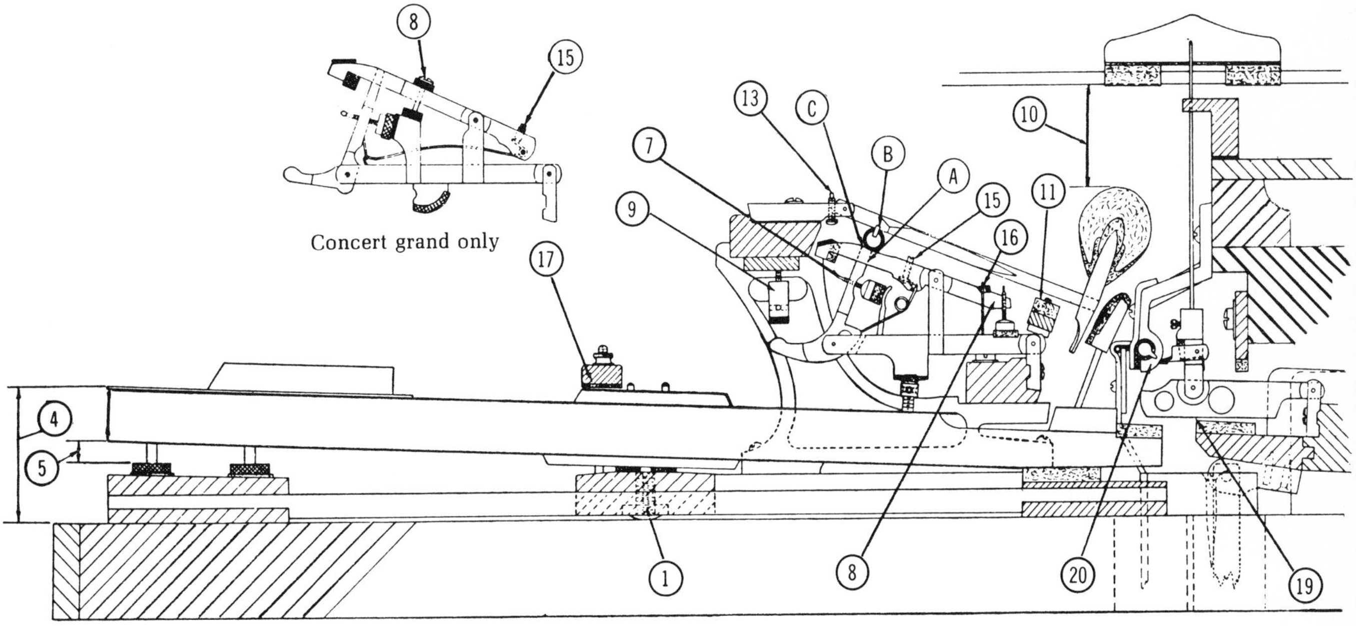

causes the damper spoon to move toward the damper lever. As the front of the key continues downward, the wippen continues upward, raising the jack, which is pivoting on its flange, and compressing the jack spring. The top of the jack pushes upward on an inclined plane, which is the bottom surface of the hammer butt, until such time as the let-off button contacts the forward tail of the jack.

At this moment, the jack leaves its upward motion and proceeds toward the face of the piano. The back end of the wippen meanwhile has advanced during this process to the point where the spoon is in contact with the damper lever, which in its further pivot lifts the felt damper from its position against the strings, preparing the strings to sound.

Immediately upon let-off, the hammer, continuing on its propelled path to the string, impacts against the string or unison of strings. The forward motion of the hammer is reversed by its impact upon the strings, and the hammer moves backward toward the hammer rail. But with the key still depressed, the back check, which has risen at the same rate as the wippen, is now so positioned that the extended end of the hammer butt contacts the back check surface. This stops the rearward motion of the hammer until the key is released. At this time, at the moment of key release, the hammer returns to its rest position upon the hammer rail, the jack returns to its position under the hammer butt, the wippen returns to its rest position, and the damper lever again pivots the dampers against the strings. This is the basic sequence of operations of all upright, spinet, console, and drop actions. It does not vary.

The necessary clearances required to keep this flow of motion working may vary from piano action to action. This sequence is of great importance. Study it over and over until it is clear in your mind. Much of what seems to be big trouble in a piano will be a matter of arranging the action clearances to match what must take place during playing. Minor repairs

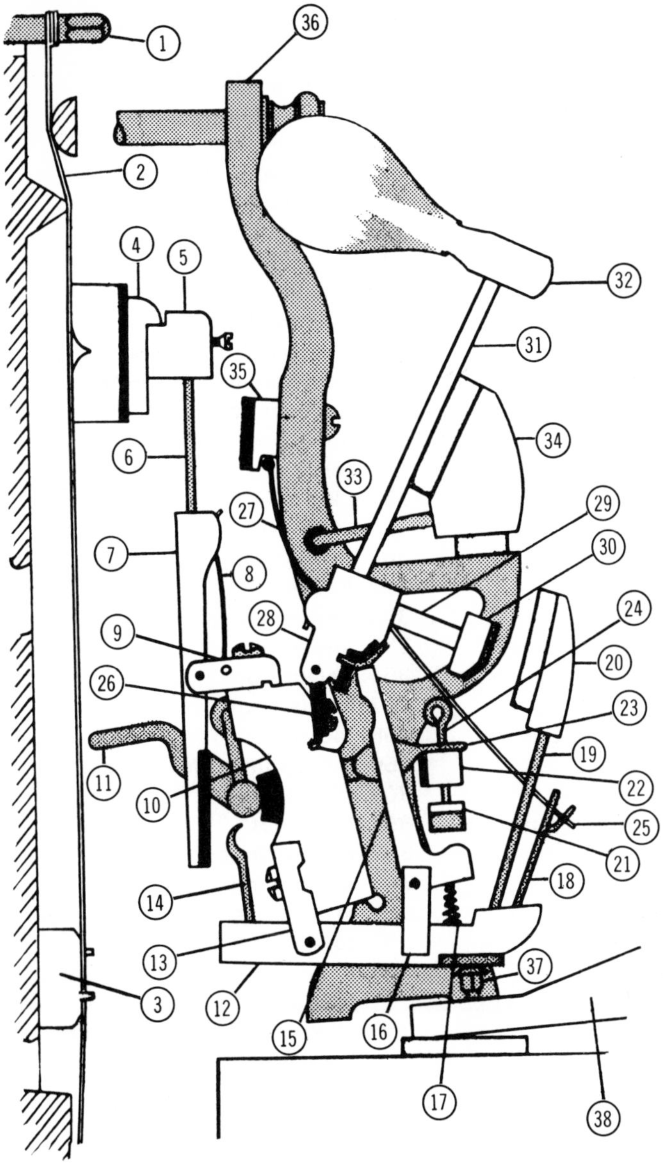

1 tuning pin
2 string
3 bridge
4 damper
5 damper head
6 damper wire
7 damper lever
8 damper spring
9 damper flange
10 action flange rail
11 damper rod
12 wippen
13 wippen flange
14 damper spoon
15 jack
16 jack flange
17 jack spring
18 bridle wire
19 back check wire
20 back check
21 let-off dowels
22 let-off rail
23 let-off rail support
24 regulating screw
25 bridle tape
26 butt flange
27 hammer butt spring
28 hammer butt
29 back stop shank
30 back stop
31 hammer shank
32 hammer head
33 soft pedal level rod
34 hammer rail
35 hammer butt spring rail
36 action bracket
37 capstan screw
38 key

*Figure 1.4*

301 damper block
302 treble damper backing and felt assembly
303 treble damper felt
304 damper wire
305 damper block set screw
306 damper lever
306a damper rod (all dampers)
307 damper lever spring
308 damper lever flange
309 flange attaching screw
310 damper spring cord
311 center pins
311a center pin bushing cloth
312 damper lever felt
313 damper lever spoon
314 wippen
315 action bracket
316 wippen flange
317 main action rail
318 hammer flange
319 regulating rail bracket
320 regulating rail attaching screw
321 regulating screw eye
322 regulating rail
323 regulating button
324 regulating button punching
325 jack
326 jack flange
327 jack spring
328 back check wire
329 back check
330 back check felt
331 bridle wire
332 bridle strap
333 catch skin
334 catch
335 catch stem
336 jack bumper felt
337 hammer butt skin
338 hammer butt cushion felt
339 hammer butt felt
340 hammer butt
341 hammer butt spring
342 hammer butt spring rail
343 hammer butt spring rail attaching screw
344 pickup finger
345 key cloth
346 keyboard back rail
347 keyboard cross rail
348 keyboard balance rail
349 keyboard balance rail punching
350 keyboard front rail
351 keyboard front rail punching (cloth)
351a keyboard front rail punching (paper)
352 front rail pin
353 key (natural)
354 key covering
355 key front
356 balance pin
357 key (sharp)
358 locknut
359 pickup finger felt punching
360 key fork
361 grommet
362 pickup finger bushing
363 action strap
364 attaching screw (action strap to support rail)
365 attaching screw (action strap to bracket)
366 lockwasher (action strap to bracket)
367 hammer rail blocking felt
368 hammer rail
368a hammer rail hook
369 hammer rail felt
370 hammer shank

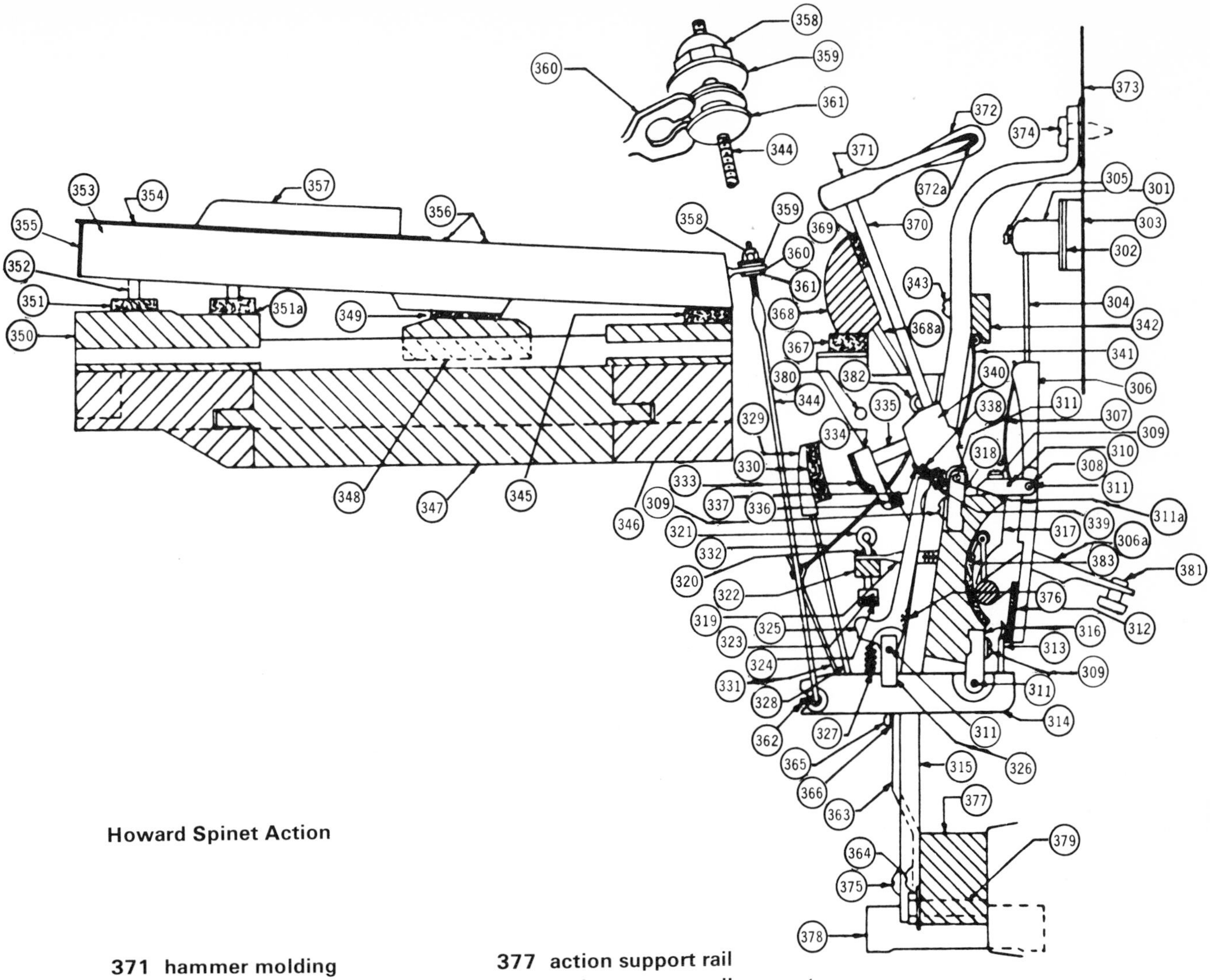

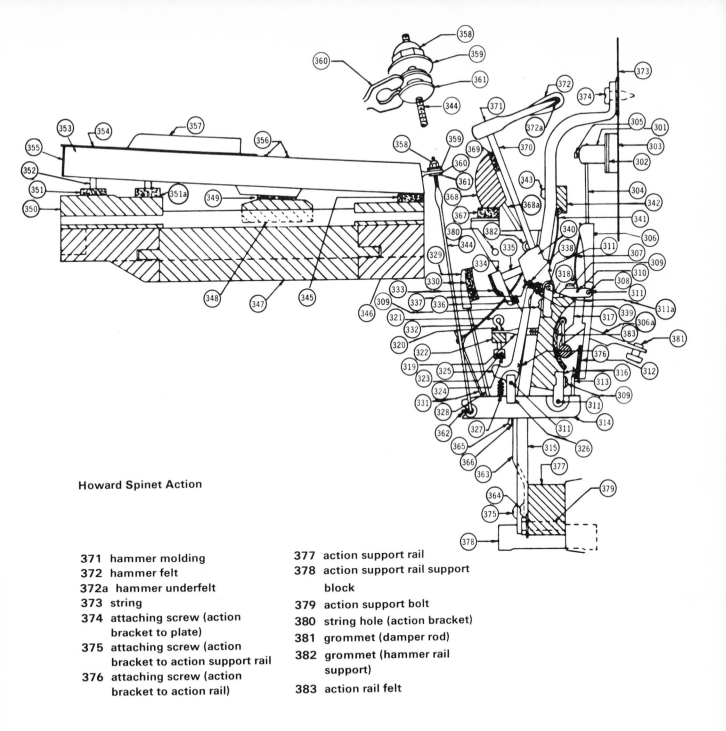

Howard Spinet Action

**371** hammer molding
**372** hammer felt
**372a** hammer underfelt
**373** string
**374** attaching screw (action bracket to plate)
**375** attaching screw (action bracket to action support rail
**376** attaching screw (action bracket to action rail)
**377** action support rail
**378** action support rail support block
**379** action support bolt
**380** string hole (action bracket)
**381** grommet (damper rod)
**382** grommet (hammer rail support)
**383** action rail felt

require as complete a knowledge of the action sequence as major repairs do. Remember this point.

For instructions as to removal of actions and other matters, I refer you to my earlier work.

### *An Overall Inspection of the Piano Prior to Tuning*

Look at the tuning pins. They may be rusty if the piano is old and sometimes if it is not so old. They can be cleaned with a wire bristle brush and also with a patented tuning pin cleaner device which piano supply houses sell. The pins can be reblued with tuning pin bluing or a gun bluing stick (felt tipped). Take care not to touch or damage the strings. Keep oils or lubricants away from the strings, pin block, and tuning pins. Do nothing which will adversely affect the friction between tuning pins and the pin block.

Place the tuning lever on the pins. At first, just one or two pins in each section will do. Using a tuning lever 10 in. in length from end to top, it should take about 20 lbs. of pressure to move the outer end of the tuning lever. You can easily measure this with a torque wrench. However, it can be measured just as well by tying a string from the end of the tuning lever to a small fisherman's scale (which is much cheaper). If the pressure needed to move the tuning pins falls below 10 lbs. at the end of the lever, the pins should be made tighter. To tighten pins without replacing the complete pin block, there are three possibilities:

1. On an upright, you can take a small punch and drive the tuning pin farther into the pin block, provided there will still be room for the thickness of a nickel between the string coil and the surface of the block or plate. When you hit bottom, you are pounding on the back beam of the piano, and you can easily break the pin block loose and ruin the instrument.

2. You can apply pin block restorer, which will take from one to two weeks to set up properly. Follow the directions on

the bottle, and tune the piano later. Also, there is a Quick Set restorer which is a little more expensive but sets up in from 30 to 60 minutes. It works, too. And you can tune the piano sooner.

3. If there are not too many loose pins, you can back off the tuning pin a turn or two, lift the string eye from the center of the pin carefully, lift the coil, and remove the pin. Then drive in the next sized larger pin, or bush the side of the pin with a small piece of veneer, and drive it back in. Some tuners use brass bushings, and some use sandpaper as a positive bushing. The quick way is to use veneer.

If you attempt to do any of these repairs on a grand, you must remove the action. Then block up the wrest plank securely, using a small jack with a piece of wood on top of it. Otherwise, you will probably split the pin block.

Fluids such as those mentioned will cause damage to any piano keyboard or action. To remove the grand action, remove the keyslip under-screws which will be found about ¾ in. in from the outer edge of the front of the piano. There will be three to five screws.

Remove the fall board, which will be either hinged at each end or fastened to the cheek blocks at either end of the keyboard. The cheek blocks can be removed by taking out the screw which goes through from the top (often cleverly hidden under a rubber button in the middle of the cheek block) or comes up from underneath the key bed into the cheek block. On shifting actions (where the soft pedal moves the action sideways), the keyboard will be held by two small wooden fasteners (one at each end) secured to the key bed with wood screws.

Be very certain that no keys are depressed. Then carefully slide the complete action toward you and the front of the grand. When it is 8 in. out, stop and look under the pin block to make sure none of the hammers will hit it. If necessary, tilt the action up from the front at this point so as to clear the pin block with the hammers. Place the action on a smooth level surface. When you get ready to put it back later, clean out the key bed and sprinkle talcum powder on the area where the action rests and slides.

Uprights must be laid on their backs for pin blocks restorers to penetrate and to be effective. The supply houses sell one-man folding contrivances which will enable you to tilt an upright easily onto its back and up again. You can also have one made. While you have the piano on its back, check the casters and sockets. They usually need tightening. This is a good time to tighten the bottom board screws, too. They'll be loose. (That noise you may have heard when you tilted the piano was caused by hairpins and other things such as coins, crayons, etc., falling from under the keys into the strings. Look inside.)

While you are looking inside, examine the sound board. This one component of the piano makes many sales for unscrupulous tuners and dealers. They tell people that a piano with a split sound board is ruined. Perhaps in olden days, when modern glues were not available, they had a point. But split sound boards can be repaired. Often the real complaint is a buzzing which happens when a sound board, whether split or not, has one or more ribs which have come unglued from the back. To fix sound board cracks, if they are small, one can apply pin block restorer to swell the wood and to stop the edges of the crack from vibrating against each other.

Of course, if the ribs become unglued, you must drill a small hole from the back to locate the rib center, then drill a larger hole from the front of the sound board through to the rib. Place glue between the sound board and rib. (Modern White Glue, Evan's Welsh Glue, or almost any aliphatic glue will do.) Place the wooden washer or sound board button on the wood screw and tighten from sound board into the rib. When you find a piano that buzzes, check the sound board and ribs carefully. Also, on uprights, look between the bottom beam and back of the sound board. Chewing gum wrappers, candles, ping pong balls, and jacks will often be found there rattling merrily.

If the crack seems large, take a sharp chisel and make a wedge-shaped trough the full length of the crack. Often it helps to drill a small hole at the ends of the crack to stop its spreading farther. Make a wedge-shaped piece of spruce the length of the trough (or wedge-shaped shim from a supply house), put glue on it, and wedge securely into the crack. Smooth off the repair level with the sound board front, carefully hand sand it level, and then varnish or space spray with plastic clear seal.

Look at the bridges. When the piano string passes over the bridge, it is angled by two bridge pins. Often in old pianos, and even newer ones, the pins will work loose because the bridge cap splits slightly. If the split is minor, epoxy filler will fix it. If it's bad enough for the pin to come out with finger pressure alone, the quickest repair is to buy bridge repair plates from a supply house and to follow the simple directions found with them.

If a complete bridge cap is bad, remove it carefully, and, following directions in a supply catalog, send it in to supplier; a new cap will be made to fit exactly. Carry some bridge repair agraffes with you. They are inexpensive and usually install easily.

Sometimes bass bridges work loose. Usually you will see this at a glance, but whether you see it or not, suspect it when the bass strings all sound dead. To repair, loosen the bass strings, place wedges between the bass bridge and sound board, fill the space thus created with an application of glue, and remove the wedges. Carefully place the bridge in the position it was when the sound board varnish was new, and drill through the ribs into the bridge at each end and center. Use wood screws to hold it tight to the sound board. After the glue has dried, remove the screws, and fill the holes with wooden dowels.

To increase the side bearing on a string, get the bridge

pins where they belong, or use a bridge repair agraffe. To increase the down bearing so as to give vibrant tone in older pianos, some tuners shim behind the bridge. This is difficult and gives no better improvement than simply lifting the strings and placing thin veneer on the top cap of the bridge (notching the veneer so that it follows the contour of the top cap of the bridge), thus adding to the height of the bridge.

Sometimes a dull tone in the bass will not be improved by these methods. Bass strings are wrapped strings. The wrappings often get loose in older pianos. To fix this, let off the ten-

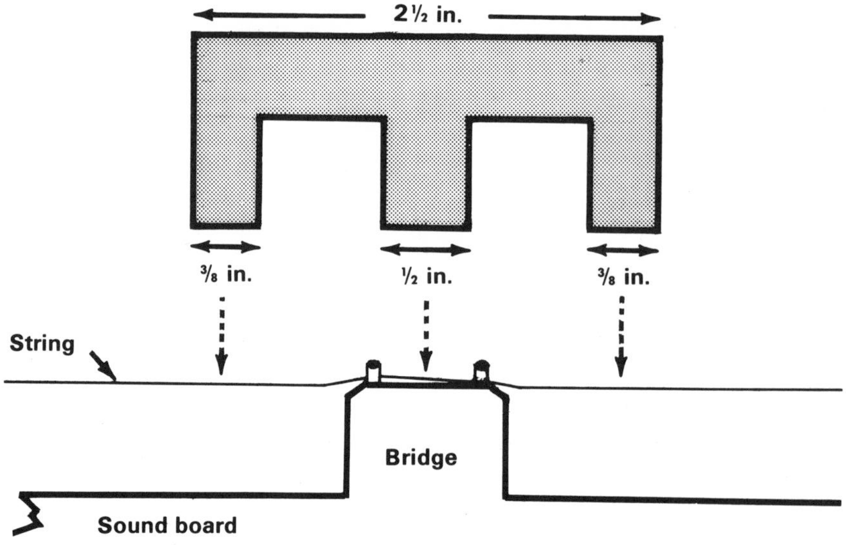


*Figure 1.5*

A down bearing gauge can be made from ¼ in. aluminum stock or harder metal. To use it, place the center foot of the gauge on a string where the string crosses the bridge. Rock the gauge so that the side legs of the gauge touch the running length of the string on either side of the bridge. There should be "rock," as the string should be lower on either side of the bridge than it is on the bridge.

sion on strings so that the end can be removed from the hitch pin. Remove the loop from the hitch pin and turn the string one and one-half to two times in the direction of the copper winding, and replace it on the hitch pin. This really makes an improvement in an old piano.

To check the down bearing, use a bearing gauge. Buy one or make it by following the instructions given in the illustration. Place the gauge with its center foot resting on the string at its highest point in the bridge. Rock the gauge so that the two outside feet touch the same string in the segments toward the hitch pin and toward the speaking length. The rock should be about the thickness of a dime in the treble and the thickness of a nickel in the bass. Some modern pianos use almost no bearing on the bridge. The company which makes this well-engineered piano will send you specifications for the bearing upon request.

A word to the beginning technician: almost all pianos are made in the same manner, and learning these practical common troubles and repairs pays quickly and handsomely. Just a word of caution for beginners and veterans alike: when in doubt, check again. In bridge repairs, as in all piano technology, let your watchword be, "Do no harm!"

Ten minutes spent in careful measuring and gauging will often save you three hours of hard work. There is always an easier and more practical way to fix anything. Remember how the piano works in making sound and how the tension of the string is controlled; be careful and methodical.

## *The Basic Tuning Kit*

It is wise to buy the best equipment available. And it would be good to include everything I mention in order to do good work while tuning. All repair items and tools are available from various piano supply houses listed at the end of this chapter.

First, you will need a piece of chamois leather about 2 ft.

*Figure 1.6*

Note the placement of the muting strip along the center section of the piano. This allows accurate temperament setting and proper control of octave unisons, as well as testing of intervals.

long by 1 ft. wide. This leather is convenient to spread out on the music shelf of the piano once the face is open for tuning. Not only does the cloth keep your tools from causing scratches on the fine finish of the piano, but it also will keep you cleaner, since it protects your hands and arms from dust which may be present.

You will need at least four rubber mutes in these sizes: 6 in. long by 5/8 in. wide, 3 in. long by 7/8 in. wide, 3 in. long by 5/8 in. wide, and one which is 2 in. long by about 1/2 in. wide, and not wider than 1/4 in. at its thick end.

These tapering mutes are used as follows: The first mute is placed at the last string going down in the treble, just where the bass strings begin to overlap, so as to quiet the last treble string (which cannot easily be muted with a muting strip). The second wide mute is ideally suited for muting the bass strings as one brings the unisons to pitch. The last two are used while moving up through the treble after removal of the muting strip. In addition to the above, it is convenient to have a split rubber treble mute for muting close-set strings too short for two mutes, and a felt or leather-tipped mute for sticking into places where other mutes will not go.

Also get one or two felt strips, tapered at least 50 in. long, for complete muting of the outside strings of the unisons throughout the center section of the piano and for inserting as far down into the bass and up into the treble as they will go. With two strips, you can mute almost the entire piano and tune entirely on the center strings; bring in the side string unisons one by one, thus laying an even tension on the whole piano with all center strings; add one-third more by bringing into pitch each left-hand string; and finally, finish up by ''chunking in'' all the right hand strings. The Papp treble mute, made with a spring-open idea, is a great help. Not only can it be inserted between hammer stems adjacent to the note you are tuning, but it works well as an action tool when you are in need of something which will hold the jack and jack spring in

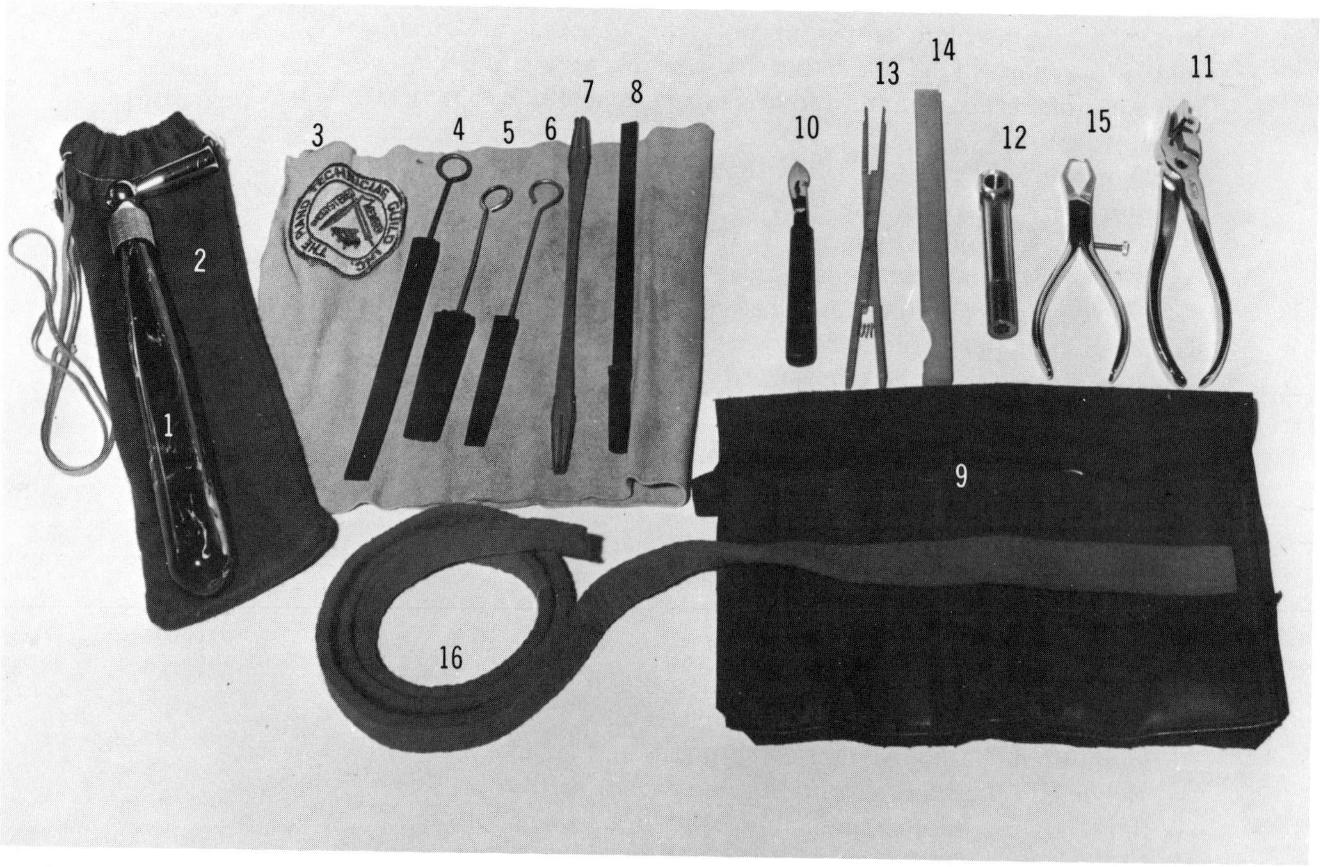


*Figure 1.7*

A basic tuning kit: 1) tuning hammer, extendible, with short head; 2) hammer pouch; 3) light-colored chamois field cloth; 4) long mute for bass end of treble section; 5) wide mute for bass strings; 6) short mute for tenor unisons; 7) wood leather-tipped stick mute for treble; 8) split mute with steel handle for treble; 9) tool roll; 10) trimming knife for felt and shank work; 11) key-easing pliers; 12) alternate longer head for hammer; 13) Papp treble mute, with tips slimmed for clearance; 14) mute case; 15) voicing pliers; 16) 52 in. muting strip of soft felt.

*Figure 1.8*

Regulating kit with associated instruments: 1) damper spoon bender; 2) screw holder for flange screws; 3) tool handle which fits all tools, with short screwdriver blade; 4) long blade for damper screws; 5) short, slimmer blade; 6) grand regulation screwdriver with slotted head; 7) long, flat blade; 8) Phillips blade; 9) heavy case screw blade; 10) front rail pin and key spacer adjuster; 11) back check and bridle wire adjuster; 12) tweezers; 13) scissors for felts; 14) capstan regulating tool; 15) parallel pliers for back checks and flanges; 16) bearing gauge; 17) surgeon's locking straight pliers; 18) surgeon's locking curved-nose pliers; 19) pliers; 20) hammer head for tool handle; 21) let-off regulator with slotted end; 22) curved shaping file; 23) flat mechanic's ignition point file; 24) chrome veterinary syringe with 5 in. needle; 25) tool roll.

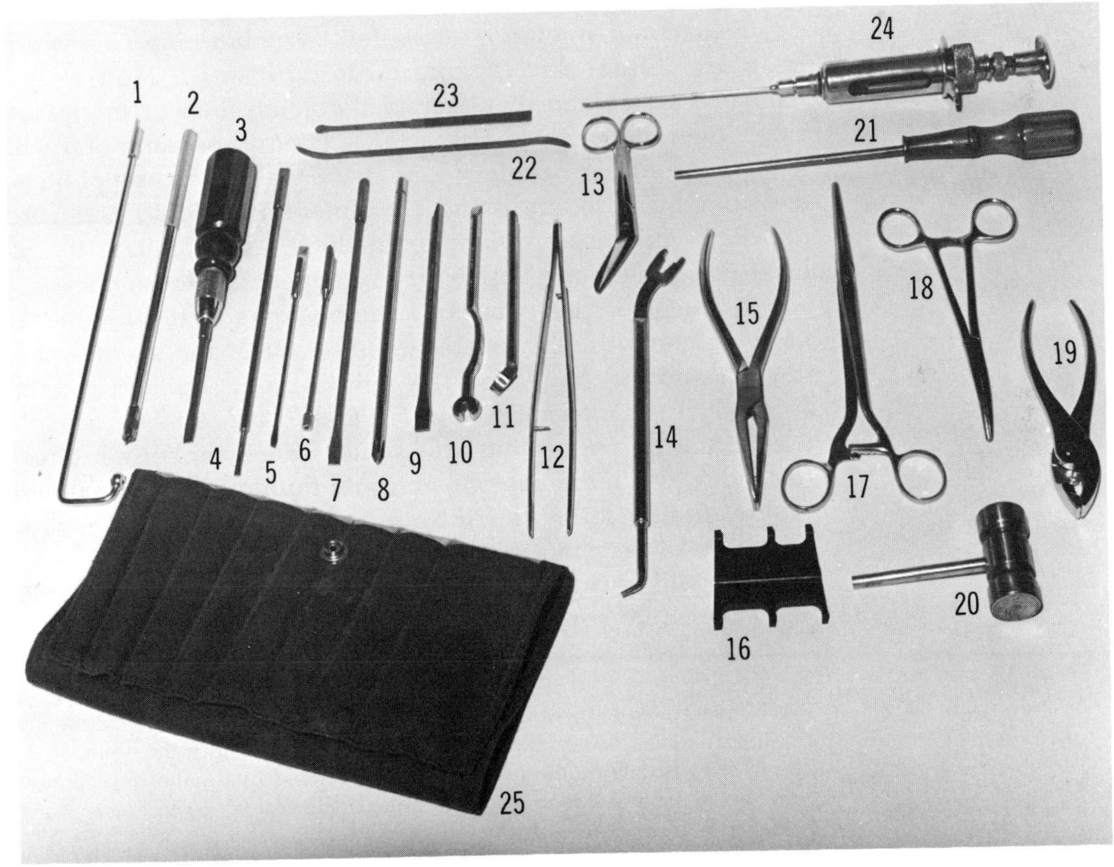

a depressed position while you are removing or inserting butt felts and hammer butt flange screws.

There should be a set of key-easing pliers in your basic tuning kit. Quite often the humidity will cause keys to become sluggish, and your job of tuning certainly will include making sure that all keys play in the piano. These pliers are equipped with a broad face which swivels on one jaw, and which compress the front bushing felts under the keys. Used carefully, they will also compress other bushings in the key action.

Voicing pliers, if desired, may be included in the tuning kit, although the single needle tool should be used before any drastic hammer voicing is attempted. Voicing piano hammers is an art. Great skill is required to do it well. More piano hammers are ruined by attempts at voicing than by any other single operation. But you must learn to do it, because you will want that singular beauty of tone that a well-voiced set of hammers can bring to any piano. Chapters on voicing hammers appear in my book on piano technology. Also refer to the illustration of the basic tuning kit that appears on these pages.

If you like, you can carry tuning forks in the four most used frequencies. These are: A-440 cycles per second (today's standard);* C-523.3, which is also concert pitch; C-517.3, or old international pitch; and A-442, a modern pitch used much by performing artists and some symphony orchestras today. With the use of electronic tuning aids you will not require tuning forks, but they are useful for checking your work and for learning to set an aural beat temperament.

You will very shortly need a basic repair and regulating kit. This should consist of:

*The term A-440 will be used frequently. This means the frequency of pitch at which 440 cycles of sound per second signify the tone of A. This A is key No. 49 on the piano. It is determined by numbering the keys from lower bass end to top treble, counting the lowest left-hand key as No. 1 (which also happens to be A).

One screw-holding device (either an auto mechanic's unit, or one with flexible jaws at the end of a long shaft, not less than 9 in. long).

A screwdriver handle with a selection of blades, including a Phillips head. Always use round-shafted screwdriver blades. The ones with a square shaft tend to strike other parts of piano actions and damage or bend them.

Back check wire-bending tool, and if possible, one which will also fit other applications such as bridle strap wires and various linkages within the piano.

Front pin adjusting or turning tool.

Long pair of tweezers.

One double-ended capstan turning tool, with point on one end and a gradual ''v'' on the other end for square capstans.

One small hammer head, to fit a universal handle.

One let-off button screwdriver or blade (also useful in string repairs).

One pair of good scissors, preferably angled, so that you can see what you are cutting.

One pair of regular pliers.

One bearing gauge.

One small curved ''riffler'' file.

One flat ignition point file.

One pair of long-nosed parallel pliers for back check work, also useful for repairs involving loose jack flanges when they must be reseated and reglued.

One pair of Kelly surgical forceps with curved nose, locking type. These are often sold in surplus stores and in electronic supply houses. If not available there, your dentist or doctor can order them for you. These will be used as pliers for 60% of your action and repair work. Get into the habit of using them instead of your fingers, since they will go where finger tips will not. They also lock in any one of four positions and thus can serve as a small pin vise, or a third hand while you are trying to complete some operation; and they are excellent bridle tape inserter tools. Try to remember when buying and using tools that you are a professional. A professional in any field uses his tools, not his fingers.

Naturally, there are tools for string repairs, music wire, and many other purposes. These are listed in my previous book. This book is concerned principally with only those tools and techniques required for tuning and making minor repairs. With the kit described, and an electronic tuning aid, most piano service required in the average home can be performed.

Chapters on regulating, restringing, and like subjects will be found in my other book and need not be repeated here. With an overall sound understanding of the sequence of piano action and the application of common sense in regluing hammer heads, etc., the beginner can move on to electronic tuning. He will need the technological information on complete regulating standards provided by leading manufacturers; and step-by-step procedures for key leveling, action regulating and tone voicing, which appear in the aforementioned book. Nevertheless, he can learn to tune with this book. And that's what this book is all about.

There follows a list of supply houses and manufacturers of electronic tuning aids. The chapters that follow will describe electronic tuning instruments and how they are to be used.

## Supply Houses

American Piano Supply Co.
Box 1005, Clifton, N.J. 07014

Ford Piano Supply
166 East 82nd St., New York, N.Y. 10028

Pacific Piano Supply Co.
11323 Van Owen St., North Hollywood, Calif. 91605

Schaff Piano Supply Co.
2009 N. Clybourn Ave., Chicago, Ill. 60614

Standard Pneumatic Action Co.
855 E. 141st St., New York, N.Y. 10037

Otto R. Trefz, Jr., and Co.
1305 N. 27th St., Philadelphia, Pa., 19121

Tuners Supply Co.
94 Wheatland St., Sommerville, Mass. 02145
1274 Folsom St., San Francisco, Calif. 94103
761 Piedmont Ave., Atlanta, Ga. 30308

Classified telephone directories may also list suppliers under "Pianos: Supplies and Parts."

## Manufacturers of Electronic Tuning Instruments

Conn Corporation
616 Enterprise Drive, Oak Brook, Ill. 60521

Yamaha International Corporation
6600 Orangethorpe Ave., Buena Park, Calif. 90620

Peterson Electro-Musical Products
Worth, Ill. 60482

Berkshire Instruments, Inc.
170 Chestnut St., Ridgewood, N.J. 07450

Tuners Supply Co.
94 Wheatland St., Sommerville, Mass. 02145
1274 Folsom St., San Francisco, Calif. 94103
761 Piedmont Ave., Atlanta, Ga. 30308

# 2
# Audio Generators

The professionals who tune pianos are a versatile lot. Their search for a foolproof method of setting temperament and perfecting tuning has led them down many avenues. One of the most common attempts in the past to arrive at a solid frequency standard has involved the use of multiple tuning forks. The reasoning behind this method was fairly sound. The tuner reasoned that if one tuning fork can enable a man to set middle C, then 13 tuning forks—each individual fork for a single note of the temperament—would allow him to set the full temperament and be right on pitch for each note. Some still set a temperament that way. But there are some drawbacks to this method.

First of all, the variation of temperature within a room will throw the frequency of a fork off by a number of beats per second. And this variation will have more effect on a light fork, which is designed for higher frequencies at the top of the temperament, than it will have for a thick fork, which is designed for lower frequencies. For example, a variation of 5% on a fork set for 523.3 is 26.165 cycles per second; the variation of 5% on a fork set for A-440 is 22 cycles per second. Of course, it is rare for a fork to vary by 5%, but the larger error is exemplified here to show the disparity within the temperament when the frequency change is somewhat less. And unless each fork is at exactly the same temperature, there will be disparity within the temperament when set by 13 single tuning forks.

Furthermore, the striking of the tuning fork against various substances will alter its angles at times and often nick small particles from its tines. The slightest change in density and amount of material in a fork will alter its pitch frequency by a number of beats per second.

I was present at a meeting of piano tuners at which a frequency standard was set up electronically. All who were present tested their forks by this standard. Eighty percent of the tuning forks being used daily by these professional tuners were off at least 2 beats per second from middle C, and 90% were off when compared to A-440. At least two of the forks that were off by 2 beats per second had recently been calibrated by the factory.

The third disadvantage of using 13 tuning forks is that the response time during which the tuner can clearly hear the beat of the fork and compare it to the note he is attempting to set on pitch is just a few seconds. Even placing the handle of the fork upon a resonant surface, such as the piano music rack or desk, will not cause the tone to continue much longer. With a large tuning bar, mounted for maximum length of sound propagation, the time allowed for the tuner to compare and set the string is around 7 seconds. In other words, the tone just doesn't keep coming long enough.

Should the tuner find an older piano whose strings will not allow tuning to concert pitch, or should he encounter a piano which is to be set at slightly higher than concert pitch (some musicians like them that way), he must have, in either case, a complete set of 13 forks for the desired pitch standard. Otherwise, he judges by beats per second, and increases the individual notes by their particular needed increases, when using the standard forks he has with him. If he attempts to do this, he had better be an excellent mathematician indeed, since each note must be altered by a slightly different number of beats per second.

I am well aware that one could set a temperament to any of these standards using the single fork for any note and then using the beat method aural temperament to complete the bearing or temperament of the piano. But I am confining my discussion to methods of tuning a piano which do not require a beat method of tuning and honing a temperament.

Some tuners have attempted to learn this craft and set a temperament by listening to a recording which is furnished by some schools. The fact that variations of as little as ½ beat per second can completely nullify the fine work desired on a temperament makes the use of recordings valueless. The motor of the playback machine must be an exact replica of the motor used to cut the record if we are to avoid errors much greater than 1 beat per second. Furthermore, the reproducing equipment used to hear the recording must be of the highest quality if we are to hear with complete accuracy the individual tones in their pure form. Unless one wants to set a temperament by using the interaction of beats between the notes of the temperament, a recording is useless. If one wishes to set a temperament and use the beat intervals for honing it up to par, he does not need the recording.

Tapes, tape casettes, and tape cartridges have the same limitations as the recording, with the additional drawback that their speed is even less controllable, and their flutter and wow make an impossible situation for accuracy in setting temperament.

Not to be forgotten in connection with any of the methods mentioned is the vast error factor which arises as soon as the tuner goes outside the temperament and begins to set his octave intervals. The most unreliable interval in the piano, insofar as human hearing is concerned, is the octave.

None of these methods gives a clear and infallible way for obtaining octave intervals. In addition, there is no way, outside of the beat method, by which a tuner can adjust his intervals going up the piano so as to allow a slight stretch upward while still staying musically on pitch. Nor is there any way outside of using beats by which he can allow for the stretch required for the individual piano in the bass. For the above reasons, the methods just given do not measure up to the standard of tuning excellence. These have only been steps on the way to something better.

When a tuner considers all the material just covered, it is clear that an accurate audio standard with which to tune the temperament and the remainder of the piano should embody the following features:

1. It must be extremely accurate, without being affected by temperature.

2. If there is any variation, it must be uniform within the tones provided by the audio generator.

3. The variation should be controllable by the tuner so that he may confidently stretch the octaves going up and down the piano.

4. The stretch must be calibrated in extremely small units of a tone.

5. The basic frequency of the first note of the temperament must be alterable by the tuner so as to make possible tunings to any desired standard of pitch, and all other frequencies must then automatically change by their respective required amounts in relationship to the basic note on which the temperament was begun.

6. The audio generator must be light, practical, and portable.

# 3
# Using the Peterson Chromatic Tuner Model 320

In the light of these desired features, let us examine the Peterson Chromatic Tuner Model 320, an outstanding audio generator.

All of the pitches are controlled by a single oscillator circuit of unusual design using components of the highest stability. The pitch is not affected by changes in power line voltage. Experience has shown that these instruments will maintain their accuracy over a period of several years, there being practically no aging characteristics to the tuning constants. A tuning adjustment is provided for each of the 12 semitones. It is set at the factory and recalibration is easily made if it ever should be required after an extended period.

Since there are no heat-producing parts in the solid state circuitry of the Model 320 tuner, no warm-up is needed. The effect of ambient temperature is almost immeasurable and can

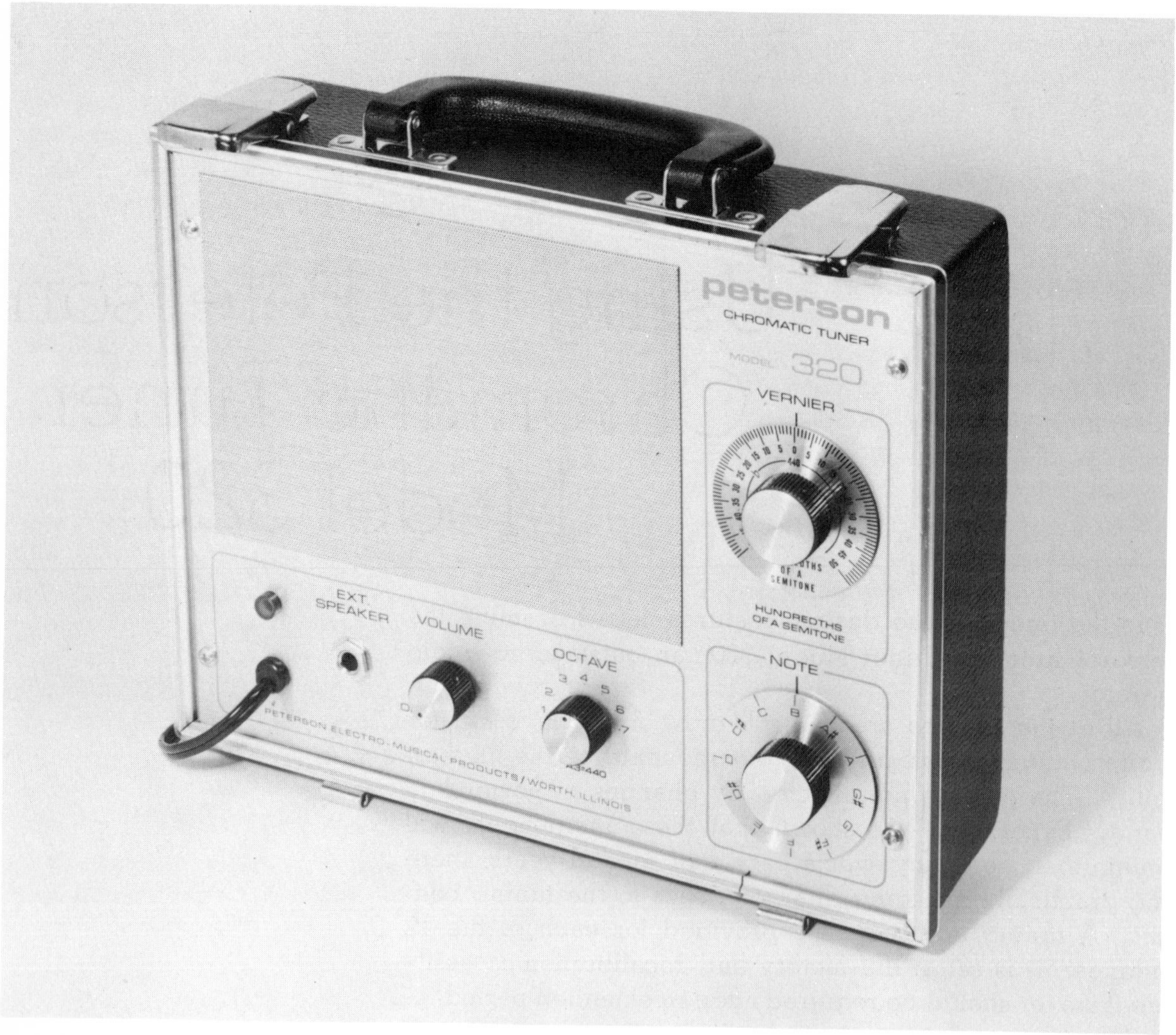


*Figure 3.1* **Peterson Chromatic Tuner Model 320**

be neglected except in extreme cases. When an instrument has been exposed to freezing temperatures or has been stored in the trunk of a car on a hot day, it is a good idea to wait 5 or 10 minutes before beginning tuning.

This is a precision instrument for supplying tones of the equitempered scale to a high degree of accuracy (to within .01 of a semitone). The instrument has been designed specifically for tuning musical instruments, but it may also be used as a laboratory audio frequency standard or wherever a source of a wide range of highly accurate tone frequencies is required.

Two rotary switches and two potentiometers control all functions of the instrument. To turn on the instrument, turn the control marked "volume" clockwise until a click is heard. A tone will be heard. Adjust the volume to a suitable level. The knob marked "note" is for the purpose of selecting the desired semitone of the musical scale. The knob to the left of the note switch is marked "octave." This switch determines which octave will be sounded. If this switch is set to No. 1 turning, the note switch will produce a series of tones that correspond to the pitches produced by the lowest manual octave of a pipe organ when an 8 ft. stop is drawn. If the octave switch is set to No. 2, tones an octave higher will be produced, and so on through octave 7, which is one octave above the highest octave produced by a 4 ft. stop. In other words, this tuner encompasses the range of piano tones for a piano tuner.

The remaining control is for the purpose of transposing the range of the instrument above or below the standard pitch of A-440 cycles per second. If it is desired to tune to standard pitch, simply set the vernier control at 440.

It is sometimes desirable to tune to a pitch other than the standard pitch of A-440 cycles/second. With the Peterson Chromatic Tuner Model 320, it is possible to shift the pitch of all the notes up to ½ semitone sharp or flat, still maintaining the exactly correct interrelationship or temperament of the scale.

To tune to a pitch that is sharp of A-440, turn the vernier control counterclockwise until the desired pitch is obtained. Similarly, to tune to a pitch that is flat of A-440, rotate the control clockwise. You will notice a stiffness in turning this control. This has been incorporated to hold the control at any desired setting and to make it insensitive to accidental movement.

The calibration marks are hundredths of a semitone (commonly called "cents"). This control is accurately calibrated and may be used to measure frequency by zero-beating the unknown to the instrument and adjusting the vernier control and then reading the calibration marks. For example: C#5-21 cents flat. A cents to frequency conversion chart is available at a modest cost from the Peterson factory.

To tune older instruments that were built and tuned to A-435 cycles/second, set the vernier control to a position .20 of a semitone flat of A-440. Frequently it is necessary to tune a pipe organ at a temperature slightly above or below normal temperatures, and in this case the vernier control can be used to compensate. Most organ pipes change pitch about .02 of a semitone per degree Fahrenheit, in a positive direction. That is, an increase in temperature causes a rise in pitch.

In the case of pianos, the steel wire operates oppositely. An increase in temperature will cause expansion of the wire and lower the pitch; obversely the decrease in temperature will sharpen the piano, all other factors being equal.

Obviously, the Peterson Chromatic Tuner Model 320 fits our outlined desired specifications as to pitch alterability, accuracy, close control, and portability, since the case measures 11¾ × 9½ × 4½ in. The covering is a black simulated leather. It weighs 8 lbs. It is available from leading piano supply houses and from the Peterson Electro Musical Products Co., Worth, Illinois.

Additional features: The jack in the lower left of the panel is for the purpose of connecting the tuner either to an oscilloscope or to an extension speaker. (I use a single stereo headphone plugged into this jack for tuning.) You can use a 16 ohm permanent magnet dynamic speaker and connect to an ordinary phone plug, using lamp cord. Up to 100 ft. of cord may be used without loss of volume.

This is a unit which will provide continuous tone on any pitch for as long as a tuner needs it, and at the volume he desires. In addition to that, with the use of a headphone the tuner is able to tune with both hands free, and others cannot hear what he is hearing. The chart mentioned before, which converts cents to frequency, is more than enough to cover every frequency encountered and could be used in stretching octaves, but will properly be used for calibrating unknown harmonics.

Peterson also makes a smaller version of this instrument, but it has less adaptability. For the aural tuner, this would be a better frequency standard than his tuning forks. The smaller tuner, Peterson Chromatic Tuner Model 70, is 6½ × 4 × 3 in. It would fit into any tuning case easily. Battery operated and transistorized, it produces one full octave in the temperament center, ranging from A-440 to G#-830.609 cycles/second. Accuracy is also with .01 of a semitone, and the weight is 1½ lbs. It is not variable. Manufacturer's illustrations are included in this text. Over 100,000 pianos and organs have been factory-tuned with the Peterson Chromatic Tuner Model 320.

### *Tuning Procedure*

After moving the necessary woodwork on the upper front of the piano to effect a clear field of effort, we mute the center section by inserting the long, felt muting strip.

Remember there are three strings per note (or "unison") on the piano, ranging from the top of the bass to the extreme

*Figure 3.2* **Peterson Chromatic Tuner Model 70**

treble. By using the felt muting strip, we can refer from a previously tuned note to instrument without having to stick in wedges for checking purposes. Also, the partial tones, which are a necessary part of piano tone, will not be so likely to sound out from the muted strings.

Beginning at the first treble string (which is the first three string unison above the wrapped bass section), we place the long rubber wedge mute on the left-hand string so as to deaden it. Now, using the handle of a rubber mute, or a fine-bladed screwdriver, we begin pushing the widest portion of the muting strip between the outside strings of each unison as we move up toward the treble end of the piano, leaving a small 1/8 in. loop standing out in front of each center string. We continue doing this until we have used up the entire muting felt, with the thinnest section being in the high tenor or treble on the piano.

We gently push the last hammers which would touch the tenor strings forward, and by lifting the muting strip, we make sure that the hammers will touch the strings and rebound.

Let me introduce some reasons for this method. It is easier to differentiate between two sounds when the random overtones of strings are at their minimum. To try to set a pitch with the use of a rubber mute stuck on each side of a unison, and then to tune the side strings to center string, would mean that we would have three open strings beating against any single string that we are trying to tune up or down the piano.

At the end of the muting strip we use a rubber wedge mute on the right string of the last unison. Now, as we bring all the center strings of the center section up to pitch, we will be stressing the sound board and bridges in this most easily moved section, and since we have worked on center strings only, while placing additional load on the bearing area, we should be readily able to tell if a note falls and what pattern of note shifting occurs when we have finished the temperament area. Then we can correct, if necessary.

We strike the notes in this temperament section all the way from the bottom to top. If we should hear any especially sour notes, we will make note of that string and corresponding pin by marking the pin with chalk.

Placing the Peterson unit on the bench and to our left, we turn the knob to whatever note corresponds to our lowest muted string. In this case, the lowest muted string happens to be F (the 33rd key up from the bottom of the piano), which is the F below middle C. We turn the tuner to F, octave 2, and turn on the volume. When the note sounds, we adjust the volume to our liking.

Placing the tuner lever on the pin corresponding to the string we want to tune, and in the manner previously outlined, we lift slightly upward on the tuning lever. Since the string is nearly on pitch (this being a rather recently-made piano, and regularly tuned), we hear a slight beat between the tone of the Peterson and the sound of the string we are tuning. To those who have not tuned before, we should explain that the string is a few beats per second out of tune with the electronic tuner. One sound is overtaking the other twice per second, so we have two beats per second sounding in our ears. With the tuning lever held as nearly straight up and down as possible, we move the pin slightly to the left. The beats now change, since the string is moving flat in relationship to our audio generator.

Now as we move the string slightly to the right, the beats slow down, stop altogether, and then begin to increase in frequency as we move further to the right. The point at which the beats stop altogether is zero beat, or perfect resonance.

If you have not tuned before, practice this quite a few times until you not only can hear it clearly, but also, by a light lift or light downward pressure on the end of the tuning lever, stop the string at this precise point. There is no way more accurate to tune than by zero beat. Often, when you release the pressure on the tuning pin, the beats will appear again. This means you have not set the pin and string properly. Go back and review the concise instructions given in Chapter 1 as to how to control these matters. The procedures given are fundamental to all good tuning and you cannot tune a piano without following them.

We now zero beat the string to our frequency standard of F. Next we move up one octave to the next F, and switch the tuner to octave 3. We now zero beat the string to the sound from the tuner. We turn the volume down on the tuner and play the two F keys just tuned together. There should be no beat between them. If there is, something is wrong. Either one of the strings has moved, or a slight discrepancy in the piano design causes a rolling beat. Then turn the tuner knob to E.

We zero beat the E above middle C to the tuner; then the next note down, which is D#; then, in order, D, C#, C (at which point we reach middle C, where we switch the tuner knob to octave 2 again), B, A#, A, G#, G, F#, and finally, end on our lower F, which we first set.

Now we play the middle C and the lower F together. We should hear a slight "rolling beat" here, very slow; about three times in 5 seconds. If the beat is not present, check middle C and make sure it is zero beat exactly to the tuner. Then lower the F until the slight roll is heard. In almost all spinet pianos, this will mean that you tune the lower F to .5 cent flat from zero on the tuner. When this is required (and the better the piano, the less likely will it be required), you will usually find that you should also tune F# next, and also G, to this ½ cent flat deviation.

Now we play middle C and the upper F together. The beats will be double in speed as compared to the middle C, lower F combination. If they are not, we tune D#, E, and upper F to 1 cent sharp. The beats should be right.

To continue, play the lower F and A# together. We will hear 4 beats in 5 seconds. Upper F, played with this same A#, sounds the same.

We play lower F and A together. We will hear 7 beats per second.

We play F# and A# together. We will hear a beat just slightly faster than the last beat. (F and A sound like "From Chi-ca-go to New York.")

We play G and B together. There will be 7.8 beats per second.

We play lower F and G# together, then play G# and upper F together. Both beat the same.

We play F and D together. We hear 8 beats per second.

We play E and G together. We hear 8.9 beats per second.

We play E and middle C together. We hear 10.4 beats per second.

We play A# and D together. We hear a pleasant tremolo which is 9.2 beats per second.

We play A and C# together. We hear 8.7 beats per second.

We play A# and D, and the beat rate increases ½ beat per second.

We play G# and C together. The beat rate sounds at 8.3 times per second.

We play F# to D#. We hear a rate of 8.4 times per second.

We play lower F and A and move up through the temperament to the top F, playing all the while in thirds. The beat rate progresses at about ½ beat per second faster for each next third played toward the treble.

Our temperament matches every test used by aural tuners and basically has been set on the same pattern. However, we have avoided using fourths and fifths to set it, and we can, in the future, test only what we want to on the next piano, since we know that if we get the middle C right, and get the two F's in proper relationship (and tune for the slight rolling beat between lower F and middle C) we alter F# and G by exactly the same amount as lower F. This is usually ½ cent flat. We know that the beat between upper F and middle C should be double that between lower F and middle C. If not, we alter upper F, D#, and E by 1 cent sharp. When we do this, our temperament will pass every test for musical accuracy.

It may seem that I had promised not to use the beat method of tuning, but to confine myself to electronic methods, and that I reversed my position and proved my point by using the old aural temperament and the system of checking by thirds for accuracy. Such may seem to be the case, but actually it was done in order to reveal that the tuner who tunes electronically can, if he wishes, match precisely the beat rates demanded by tuners who tune aurally. It also was done so that aural tuners who wish to familiarize themselves with electronic methods will be convinced that the ear plus an electronic device make for good tuning.

Incidentally, I have not claimed that all these tests are necessary when one uses the audio generator as, in this case, the Peterson. In fact, once it is proven that you may alter the few notes of the temperament according to the beat ratio you wish, it would not be absolutely necessary to test if it would work out right. On balance, if one were to tune the complete temperament octave with no alteration to compensate for the piano scale, he could do a decent job on a temperament and might suit most customers. But, assuredly, if he were to use the generator to set his pitches, then also alter those few notes necessary to make his temperament match the aural temperament, he could do a superb job of tuning, and all would be happy. Either way, the Peterson unit makes the setting of a temperament on any piano a much more rapid and certain thing. And that's what tuning is all about.

Our temperament octave is set, and set good enough to

please anybody. But since we found that the scale of this particular piano forced us to alter at the fringes of the temperament, we shall bear that in mind as we begin to tune "out" from our center bearing or temperament.

We now lift the mute which we had inserted near the left end of the treble and tune the outside string to the lower F. Beatless.

Now, using the wide, short mute, we mute one string of the first bass note and tune that E to our upper E. Since our upper E was altered to match the piano temperament, we must stretch accordingly. So we set the audio generator at ½ cent flat, as we did for the lower F, and zero beat the lower E to it. From this point on, we use a method which will tell us how much to stretch the intervals between octave notes as we go up and down the piano.

First, a word of explanation. Since the human ear can hear a perfect octave when an actual octave is slightly sharp and/or flat, there is not much sense in tuning by octaves. We need a more consistent interval by which to tune out of our temperament. The fifth does this job extremely well and can be amplified in lower and higher frequencies by being added to an octave. In other words, the beat we hear between middle C and lower F can be duplicated between B next to middle C and the E below our lower F. Since our lower F is set, unless the string shifts, and our middle C is also presumed to be dead set, we can hear this readily recognizable interval anytime we want to and compare it with a new interval we are working on.

So we set the tuner ½ cent flat, tune the E, and, sure enough, the interval of a fifth between E and B sounds the same slow rolling rate as the interval between F and C. We move our tuning lever to the next string not muted, which is D#, leaving the tuner set as before, and tune the string to the sound from the tuner when it is turned to D#. We check F to

C, E to B, and D# to A#. All have the same rolling rate of less than 1 beat per second.

While it is possible to tune on out through the piano, making adjustments to the tuner according to a predetermined plan or table of changes in the vernier dial, most tuners might find it faster to tune on out through the bass, then from the temperament up through the treble, by simply using this method of fifths. This is good and rather easily learned. When you come to a place where the fifth cannot be heard right, add the span of an octave between your test notes and play, for example, G, the 11th note from the bottom, and D, the 30th note. Then you are using a seventeenth. And you can hear more clearly.

Of course, we also have the choice of finishing the tuning of the center strings by a couple of other methods which utilize the features of the Model 320. First, though, let us remove our rubber mute from the E and D# bass strings and tune those two strings to the ones we just tuned. That being done, we turn our attention to an electronic method of tuning out through the piano.

### *Using the Model 320 to Complete Fifths and Seventeenths*

Always bearing in mind our slight alteration of the temperament octave in the matter of notes F, F#, and G, plus notes D#, E, and upper F, we change the knob to the next note we want to set in the bass, which is D. With the outside string muted, we match this note with the A on the tuner so that we get a slow rolling wave. Since we are heading into the bass, our rolling wave must be on the flat side of perfect resonance; this means that we play the top note of our fifth (which, in this case, is the note A, No. 37) on the tuner; then we strike the bottom note of our fifth (which, in this case, is D, No. 30); next, we move the string to zero beat, then drop the note just enough to get the rolling beat with a rate of about 1 beat per second or less. Continuing, we check by playing the octaves downward to our note just set, and listening to the even progression downward into the bass. Also, once the bass is set, we can check by the use of double octaves, going both up and down, and listening for smooth deepening and rising as we go down and up. If a note sounds sharp when we play double octaves, it *is* sharp. If it sounds flat, it *is* flat.

In the manner just outlined, we can use the tone from the Model 320 at the same setting we used for setting the temperament as the top note for our fifths going down. Once beyond the point where the bottom note of our temperament would be the top note of our fifth, we keep using the notes of our temperament as the top notes of our seventeenths, as we tune on down. It would be next to impossible for the human hand to reach a seventeenth; and yet, by using the audio generator, set at the temperament section, we can have a steady tone on each note we need for the top note of our interval. This we do, and the fifths must slow down slightly in their beat rate with each four notes going down. (They also will increase slightly in the beat rate as we go up.)

### *Reasons for Tuning as We Do*

At this point, nothing has been said which will surprise the experienced piano tuner, but much has been said that may puzzle the apprentice. Perhaps an explanation of the theory behind this tuning method is appropriate.

Tempering is the process of altering the intervals of a pure scale so that the instrument may be played in all possible musical keys without using more than the twelve steps to the octave. All keyboard instruments must be tempered, or have the steps between the notes shaded, in order to seem to be in tune in all twelve musical keys. In fact, all tempered instruments are slightly out of tune in every key, but musically they sound well when played with the scale within the octave properly tempered.

If you were to place a long clothesline between two posts, tighten it, and then pluck it, you would notice that the vibrating body of the line would have various movements. There would not be just one simple movement. The complete line would move in the form of an arc between the bearing points. In like manner, a piano string moves in this same arc and gives forth the fundamental tone. However, one would observe there were other movements which occur at various points along the line. In the case of a piano string, these moving portions set up different notes called harmonics, depending upon the portion of the string which is moving. Some tuners call these sounds "overtones."

With this in mind, let us take the example of C, the 16th note up from the bottom end of the keyboard, and contemplate the series of "partials," which work out as follows:

C 16—First partial.

C 28—Second partial (one complete octave, or twelve keys up from the note being sounded).

G 35—Third partial (five keys up from the second partial).

C 40—Fourth partial (middle C, a fourth up from the third partial).

E 44—Fifth partial (a major third up from the fourth partial).

The primary note usually sounds out the clearest, and this is a help.

However, we must constantly keep in mind that all these notes are sounding when we play a given note on a piano. Even more important to remember is the fact that there are inharmonicities in piano strings. These inharmonicities cause the second partial to be slightly different than a mathematically accurate doubling of the frequency of the fundamental. The third partial is not exactly three times the frequency of the fundamental, and so on. Partials in piano tones are almost always slightly higher (sharp) than the whole number multiples or harmonics. This is important when one begins to tune out of the center section in a piano.

When we hear two piano tones an exact octave apart, the second partial of the lower tone will be sharp with respect to the fundamental of the higher tone. This will cause audible beats to occur and the listener will not consider the tones to be truly an octave apart, even though the fundamental frequency of the top tone is exactly twice the fundamental frequency of the lower tone. In order for an octave on a piano to sound in tune when the two notes are played at the same time, it is necessary to stretch the interval either by lowering the bottom tone (as we go downward in the bass) or by raising the top tone (which we do as we go upward in the treble).

We set the temperament in the center section of the piano because inharmonicity is smallest there. But even in this area, we must compensate somewhat for the inharmonic partial tones. And tuning out from this area, we must not disturb the temperament, but instead, we stretch the bass and treble so as to compensate for these inharmonic factors and arrive at a tuned piano which sounds in tune to the musical listener. The better the piano, the less stretch will be required, generally. But we cannot gauge how much stretch will be required by looking at the price tag on the instrument. Instead, we use the fifth, or classic method, which will notify our ears of the amount of stretch required on any piano as we tune it.

For the reasons given, it is clear that we cannot make a chart of suggested settings for each note on a piano, since the partials and rough harmonics will vary from piano to piano. What we can do is to devise a foolproof temperament method, using electronic equipment, which will give us a speedy and accurate bearing base from which to proceed to tune out the rest of the piano. Also, we can utilize the steady output of the Peterson Model 320 to serve as the immovable top or bottom tone of our fifth interval, and thus save a lot of time.

The Model 320 audio generator was not intended to be

used by a robot. In the hands of a thinking person, it offers the most accurate standard for setting temperament possible for use in the home and at the same time becomes a third hand in tuning intervals outside the temperament area. The knowledge and skill of the tuner-technician are constantly required in adapting the fine accuracy of this instrument to the inaccurate partial harmonics of various pianos.

It seems to me that the Model 320, if intended exclusively for tuning pianos, registers more octaves than are required. For all intents and purposes in the field of piano tuning only, this instrument needs to have the center temperament octave available, with the present vernier control, speaker jack, and volume control. Beyond the temperament octave in a piano, the additional ranges could only be used if one wanted to step up or step down the proposed frequencies generated according to the arbitrary decision of the individual tuner. However, everything else about this fine instrument helps make tuning accurate and speedy. That it will help you do the job well is obvious. The fact that it also includes some other octave ranges than you might need is a bonus factor and does not interfere with good tuning.

Continuing down through the bass, muting each side string, our fifths and our seventeenths, then pulling into resonance the remaining strings, we find that our confidence increases. First, the distant intervals which are impossible for the human hand are now helping us tune accurately in the bass. Second, we know that we will be able to draw a complete chart of the amount of stretch we have established by beating the tone of any piano string against the tuner, then turning the tuner dial until zero beat and discovering the number of cents we have dropped a tone. If we have dropped F 21 by 2 cents flat, we shall expect that a note a fifth lower will be 4 or 5 cents flat, and that the flatting will increase as we go deeper into the bass, providing that we have been using our fifths and seventeenths correctly. Making a quick check, we pattern the bass, according to the calibration of the Model 320 as:

| | | | | | | | | |
|---|---|---|---|---|---|---|---|---|
| C | 40 | 0 | C | 16 | −4 | A | 37 | 0 |
| C | 28 | −.6 | C | 4 | −16 | A | 25 | −1 |
| F | 45 | +1 | F | 21 | −2 | A | 13 | −7 |
| F | 33 | −.5 | F | 9 | −11 | A | 1 | −24 |

Checking all the notes as we go downward, one note at a time, shows a steady deepening of the bass on this piano, with a precise increment added of −1 cent for each note farther down than D 18. The bass is thus smooth. The fifths get less and less roll to them as we go lower. Arpeggios played in this bass section are clear and not muddy. The bass is in tune.

We now proceed to pull the temperament muting strip and, inserting a rubber wedge mute on the right-hand side of our lower F in the temperament, recheck the two strings tuned so far on that note. All is still O.K. Then we tune the right-hand string to match the other two. We tune the third string to match the other two. The reason for this is that we shall never be able to hear how the unison will sound unless we actually hear it as a three string unison. Then we will be able to tell very quickly when all three strings are right, and to compensate for any spurious beats which may arise between the two outside strings.

If the two outside strings are tuned alone to the center (by muting the already tuned left string while tuning the right one), there will probably be every reason to expect that unison to have a slight beat in it. Further, while pulling into resonance the third string we may increase the tension at the bridge in such a way that we disturb the set tuning of the other one or both. So, it is best to tune the last string of the unison with all three strings open and sounding.

Now, to tune the next unison, let's place our mute between the right-hand string and one left-hand string higher above it. We set the left-hand string (of F#) and then the right-hand string. We move onward up through our temperament octave until all unisons are completed. Just at this point we stop and recheck the temperament, setting the Model 320 at its original settings for our temperament. All is well. No changes have occurred in our temperament octave as a result of "chunking in" the unisons.

At last we have finished the bass and the temperament, with all unisons beatless. We are faced with two ways possible to finish up the treble. The better way is to mute the outside strings of each treble unison and to set the center strings to the pitch we desire. The second way is to mute each unison as we come to it either by using the Papp treble mute or by inserting a split rubber mute, which mutes the center and right-hand string at the same time we set the pitch on the left-hand string. Since the left-hand string usually gives the most false beats, this latter method is a good one, too. Placing the treble muting, a long felt strip, is sometimes a problem on smaller pianos, but no problem at all on a grand.

Let's use the second method. Since this piano is in good shape and close to proper pitch, with no sudden dropping having occurred in the temperament when we brought in the outside strings, we insert the split rubber mute in F# above the temperament and set F# by using B as the bottom note of our fifth. We hear a slow rolling wave of about 1 beat per second. Checking down one full octave, we find the octave beatless. From this point on we can either use the temperament notes to give us our lower tone for our next fifth or use the Model 320 as our lower note. Since we have just finished checking the agreement between the Model 320 and our fully tuned temperament, we decide to use the audio signal put out on this instrument as our lower tone for each fifth as we go up.

We pull in the center string of F# to match the left string which we have just set. Then we pull in the right-hand string to a beatless unison with the other two. When we remove the split mute from F#, we place it in the center and right-hand string of G above it. This leaves our hands free for more important work and mutes the next note. We set G to a perfect beatless fifth with middle C and then lower G till the slow beat just begins to be heard. We set the string and pin at this pitch. Then we complete the tuning of the unison. G# is given the same treatment.

At A, we notice that a slow rolling wave similar to F and F# will produce an octave which beats when the A is sounded with the A a full octave below. In this particular piano, it is time to stretch a little, until we have lifted the pitch of the top A so that the octave is not beating. Checking with the Model 320, we observe that we have an A in the top tone which is 2 cents sharp as compared to our temperament A and that the notes F, F#, G, and G# leading up to this top A are 1 cent sharp each. The stretch has begun, and the fifths will now progress a little sharper with each additional four notes or so, if past experience is a guide.

We proceed to tune up through D with the same cents sharp increment. At D# the stretch is increased, because we find that the octave has a slight beat in it when the fifth has the same roll as previous fifths. Thus, we sharpen the upper tone to eliminate the beat in the octave, and then check the fifth to establish the roll which we will be using in the next notes. The fifth is now almost beatless.

Upward throughout the treble we go in this manner, and when we finish we calibrate the treble stretch to see how uniformly it increases with each additional group of notes. Results are as follows:

| | | | | | |
|---|---|---|---|---|---|
| C 40 | 0 | F 45 | + 1 | A 37 | 0 |
| C 52 | + 2 | F 57 | + 3 | A 49 | + 2 |
| C 64 | + 5 | F 69 | + 6 | A 61 | + 4 |
| C 76 | + 13 | F 81 | + 18 | A 73 | + 9 |
| C 88 | + 32 | | | A 85 | + 26 cents. |

Now we play chords on this piano, starting with E 32,

below middle C, and play the major chord of E all the way up the piano while holding down the sustaining pedal. Then we play E major arpeggio all the way up, finishing by dropping in the bass E's as the arpeggios are sounding. Musically this is exhilirating. The treble is crisp; the bass is smooth and resonant. Then we finish our testing by playing arpeggios starting with F major below middle C all the way up the piano, dropping in the bass F, and so on, through all 12 musical keys. The piano is tuned.

### *A Simplified Method for Using the Peterson Chromatic Tuner Model 320*

Mute the temperament octave selected, either from C to C, or from F to F, and continue the muting strip as far as possible up into the treble. (This method is based on muting the outside strings of each three string unison, leaving only the center string open to sound when struck by the piano hammer.)

Set the Model 320 to A-440, or the desired amount of deviation from concert pitch desired, and make a note of the setting used. (This will be the prime reference point to which you will later want to return for checking your work on this particular piano.)

Begin at the C above middle C and tune the open string to the note put out by the Model 320. Then tune each successive note downward toward the bass in this octave to the proper note on the Model 320. Continue downward until you have reached the end of the muted unisons.

Now, set the Model 320 so that it produces the tone for middle C. At the same time, strike the C one octave above middle C so that the two notes sound together. If there is no audible beat between these two notes, no change will be required. If there is an audible beat, raise the upper tone until the beat disappears. Make a note of the amount of cents you have to move the vernier control to produce a tone which will not beat with the upper C you have just set.

Set the Model 320 to sound B just below middle C. Again, using this tone as reference, sound the B one octave above it on the piano. Again lift the upper note to remove any audible beat between this piano tone and the Model 320. This is the amount of stretch required to the top of this C octave. Make a note of the amount of cents you have to move the vernier control to produce a note which will not beat with the note you have just set on this upper B.

Continue down the octave, doing A#, A, G#, G, F#, F, E, D#, D, and C#, checking each one against the standard setting for that particular note on the Model 320. You will note that the vernier needs to move less and less to match the beatless octave you have set. And, by keeping a record of the amount of cents deviation required for each note above, you will have a pattern of stretch which will serve as a general indication of the increase in cents required for each succeeding note going upward from the middle octave.

Now, set the Model 320 on middle C again. Strike the C one octave down from middle C and see if there is an audible beat between the note produced by the Model 320 and the tone one octave lower being played on the piano. If there is, lower the bottom tone until the beat goes away. Play this bottom tone, and turn the vernier control until you find out how many cents flat it is. Record this. Next, set the C# below middle C by producing the C# above middle C on the Model 320, and make the interval between the piano note and the tuner note beatless by lowering the piano note. Record this stretch also, then continue with this process gradually moving upward to middle C, and note the smaller and smaller amounts of cents required to make a beatless octave to the lower note. Usually the larger the piano and the better constructed, the less deviation will be required.

The technician may now either continue with this method, and use the Model 320, setting the vernier control for each note of the temperament, or center octave, the required deviation for each note, and beating the next higher and next lower octave against these settings; or adjust the vernier control so as to increase by the same *additional* amount in each successive octave upward and correspondingly, to flatten by the same additional amount for each successive octave going downward into the bass.

For the convenience of those who desire an average deviation table for the average piano, the following table is supplied. This table will not fit any one piano perfectly, although it was compiled by recording the deviation required for 20 different pianos of various shapes and sizes. It should be remembered that each piano varies slightly from this standard.

***Average Deviation Required to Satisfactorily Stretch a Piano Using the Peterson Chromatic Tuner Model 320***

| | | | | | | | | | | | |
|---|---|---|---|---|---|---|---|---|---|---|---|
| A1 | −25 | A13 | −7 | A25 | −1 | A37 | −0 | A49 | +1 | A61 | +4 |
| A#2 | −23 | A#14 | −6 | A#26 | −1 | A#38 | −0 | A#50 | +2 | A#62 | +4 |
| B | −21 | B | −5 | B | −1 | B | −0 | B | +2 | B | +4 |
| C | −18 | C | −4 | C | −1 | C | −0 | C | +2 | C | +5 |
| C# | −16 | C# | −3 | C# | −½ | C# | −0 | C# | +2 | C# | +5 |
| D | −14 | D | −3 | D | −½ | D | −0 | D | +2 | D | +5 |
| D# | −13 | D# | −2 | D# | −½ | D# | +½ | D# | +2 | D# | +5 |
| E | −12 | E | −2 | E | −¼ | E | +½ | E | +3 | E | +5 |
| F9 | −11 | F21 | −2 | F33 | −¼ | F45 | +½ | F57 | +3 | F69 | +6 |
| F# | −10 | F# | −2 | F# | −¼ | F# | +1 | F# | +4 | F# | +7 |
| G | −9 | G | −2 | G | −¼ | G | +1 | G | +4 | G | +7 |
| G# | −8 | G# | −1 | G# | −0 | G# | +2 | G# | +4 | G# | +8 |

The notes past G# (which is key No. 72 on the piano, counting up from the bottom) should definitely be beat against notes two octaves down and be made beatless. Here is the average stretch compiled:

| | | | | | | | |
|---|---|---|---|---|---|---|---|
| A73 | +9 | C#77 | +13 | F81 | +17 | A85 | +24 |
| A# | +10 | D | +14 | F# | +19 | A# | +26 |
| B | +11 | D# | +15 | G | +21 | B | +28 |
| C | +12 | E | +16 | G# | +23 | C | +31 |

### *Tuning Organs with the Peterson Model 320 Tuner*

No trouble is encountered here, since all that is required is that we match, tone for tone, the frequencies as produced by the Model 320 and tune the oscillators of the organ to this precise mathematical source. Since no stretching is required, we simply set the standard frequency we desire, and without touching the vernier control, proceed to tune the octaves of the organ.

On most electronic organs, the tuning of the one oscillator "can" effectively tunes all oscillator divider circuits in that key. For example, if we tune the C oscillator can by depressing a key and blocking the C key down with a rubber mute, we have tuned all the C's on the organ. However, it should be remembered that the oscillator can you are tuning is the highest C on the organ. For that reason, use the highest stop tablet (such as a 2 ft. flute) and depress the highest C key, while clicking the Model 320 octave switch to the highest octave. Then tune the C can to zero beat with the audio note given by the Peterson. If testing other C notes lower down reveals that one of them is off pitch, there is some trouble in the electronic divider circuits within the organ itself, not in the tuning.

On the type of organ described, there will be only 12 oscillator cans to tune. Tune these and you tune the organ. On some of these, you may think that tuning is such an easy job that you should not charge much. Remember that it is only because you have bought an intricate instrument of precise accuracy that you can tune this organ at all. Charge about what you would for tuning a piano. It is worth it. The Model 320 isn't a pitch pipe. Remember too, that without this instrument a piano tuner cannot approach an organ with any hope of tuning it right.

The idea behind the oscillator divider circuit in the Model 320 is good. If we were to tune the lowest C on the organ, and then have the circuitry of the organ multiply that frequency for some six succeeding octaves, any error in tuning the first oscillator would be multiplied and multiplied with each succeeding octave. By having the tuning take place on the highest note of any series, and then electronically dividing the tone into its next lower harmonic, and so on down the line, the organ manufacturer cuts any tuning error in half at each succeeding divider. So, when you use the accuracy of the Model 320 to tune an electronic "formant circuit" form of organ, you tune an instrument precisely.

Some organs on the market today feature a separate oscillator for each tone produced. Of course, in this case, you have to individually tune all 60 or 84 or possibly any number of oscillators in between. This means you can start at the lowest note on the keyboard, put on the lowest stop tablet for that keyboard, switch the octave switch on the Model 320 down to that frequency, and then tune the oscillator to it.

With each succeeding octave up the scale, you must switch the Peterson to the next highest octave, and so on. But there is little to bother you in this respect, since the organ does not have partials like a piano which might interfere and need compensation. Tune the oscillators to the Peterson without touching the vernier control once you have set your basic frequency standard. All will be well.

As you go up the scale, you will find that you run out of keys before you run out of oscillators to tune. Shut off the stop tablet you have been using, and use the next one voiced higher. For instance, if you start with 16 ft. tablet on and after tuning 4 C's, discover you are out of keyboard, just turn off 16 ft. and turn on 8 ft. Start at bottom C on the keyboard again and you'll be able to tune the next higher C, and so on.

Despite the extra work in tuning one of these organs, you can't charge the owner for all the extra time you spent on it. You must charge everyone the same price for organ tuning, whether it's a formant or individual oscillator type. Make your charge high enough for all jobs so that the easy ones compensate for the tough ones. After all, a customer, when calling for service, doesn't know the difference between one type of organ circuit and another.

Organ tuning tools are simple plastic wands usually clipped inside certain organs; and if not, they are available at local electronic supply houses because they are similar to TV alignment wands. Some require octagon-shaped heads, some flat screwdriver blades.

Be careful when tuning organs not to run the tuning slugs in or out rapidly. Only enough motion is required to move the slug a few slight turns. Otherwise you will push the slug through the channel it rides in. You will then have a real electronic repair job on your hands, and you will be dealing with delicate wires around the tuning coil which may be thinner than a human hair. Again, *be careful.*

In conclusion, the Peterson Chromatic Model 320 Tuner (audio generator) is an accurate and easy-to-use instrument which will tune organs and pipe organs and serve as a highly professional device for the careful piano tuner. In no way can a piano be harmed by its use. In many ways it would make better tuners out of many aural tuners practicing today, because it would increase their ability to gauge with precision. In the hands of a newcomer to the tuning field, this instrument would offer the means, used properly, of setting a faultless temperament and masterfully bringing the proper stretch to the piano in a professional way. It can make anyone a better tuner sooner.

# 4
# Using the Peterson Strobe Tuner Model 400

***Preparation for Use***

Remove the power cord from the inside of the cover and plug it onto the AC connector at the right side rear of the case. Plug the other end into an outlet supplying 105–125 volts, 60 cycle alternating current. (If this instrument is connected to any other source of power than mentioned above, damage may occur.) Next, remove the microphone from the inside of the cover and plug it into the signal input jack located alongside the AC connector on the right side of the tuner.

The on/off switch is located in the lower right-hand corner of the front panel. Slide this switch as far as it will go to the right to turn on the power. The red pilot light and the strobe lights behind the strobe disc will light immediately, and the strobe disc will start to turn.

Since the Peterson Strobe Tuner uses all solid state circuitry and does not have tubes to warm up, it is possible to begin tuning immediately. For maximum accuracy it is best to allow the instrument to run for a few minutes. This is particularly important if it has been subjected to extreme temperatures, either hot or cold.

During operation of the instrument, it is important that the ventilating grills on the top and bottom are not blocked, since air must circulate freely through the unit. While there are few heat-producing parts in the instrument, blockage of the ventilation could cause an excess build up of heat during operation and result in damage.

Since the pitch of this instrument is determined by a highly accurately tuned inductive-capacitive circuit, which is voltage and temperature compensated, it is not necessary to calibrate the instrument.

## *Description and Operation of the Model 400*

### *Vernier Control*

The vernier control is located on the right-hand side of the front panel. The purpose of this control is to enable you to raise or lower the reference pitch of the instrument from the standard of A-440 cps. This control is calibrated in hundredths of a semitone (commonly called "cents"). If the control is moved one division of the scale, the pitch will have been raised (or lowered) .01 of the distance between adjacent semitones. If, for example, the note selector was turned to the note E and the vernier control was set to 25 cents sharp, the pitch of the instrument would be raised ¼ of the distance between E and F. Thus, it is possible to tune to any frequency in the entire eight octave range of the instrument. Moving the vernier control does not affect the temperament.

### Note Selector

To set the instrument for tuning a particular pitch, rotate the note selector so that the desired pitch on the dial lines up with the dot alongside the letter C on the panel at the top of the dial.

The other letters, E♭, F, B♭, around the note switch, are used to automatically transpose the range of the tuner for

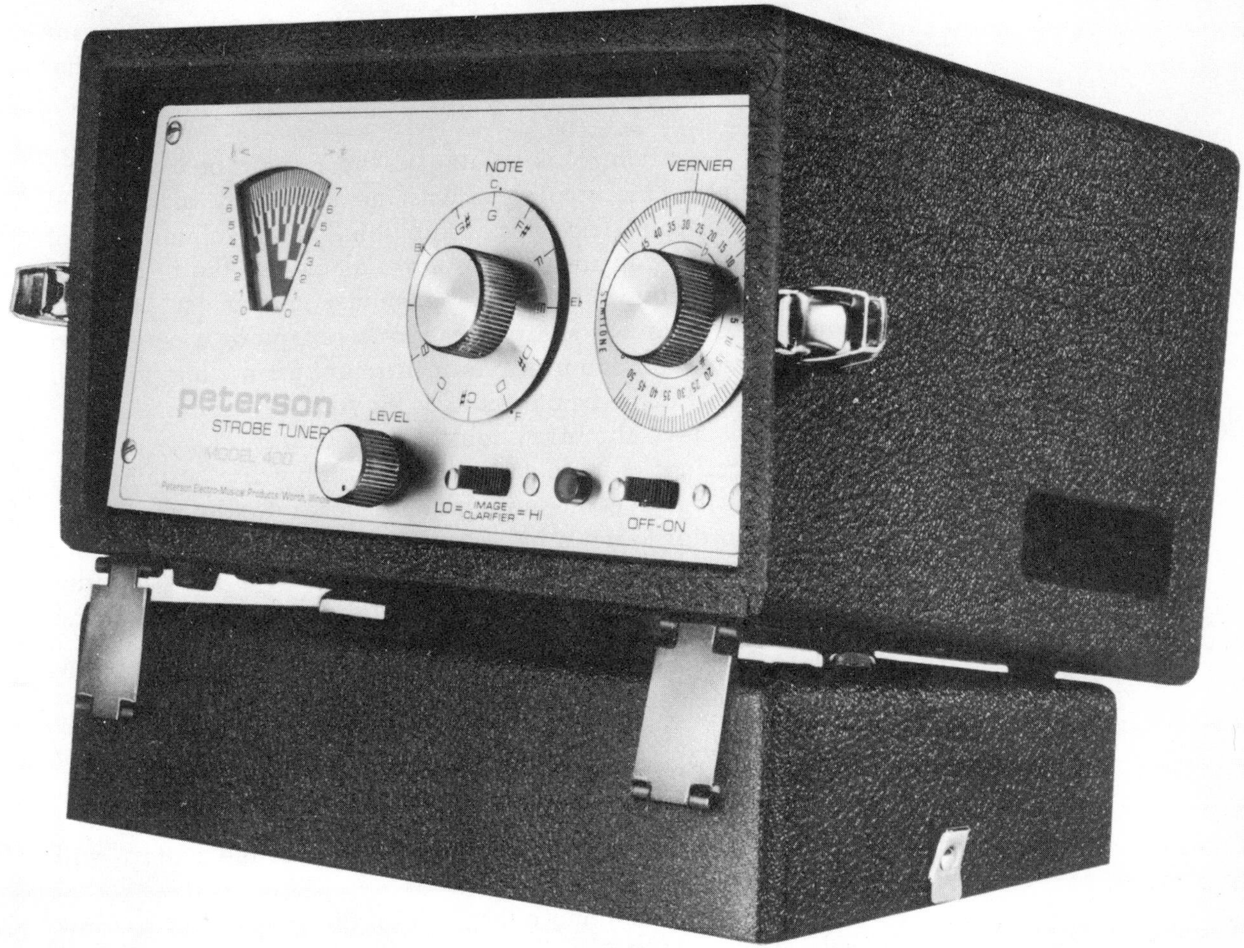


Peterson Strobe Tuner Model 400 *Figure 4.1*

tuning instruments that play in these keys. For example, if you want to play the note C on an E♭ instrument, rotate the note selector so the C on the dial lines up with the dot alongside the E♭ on the panel.

Pianos, organs, harpsichords, and similar keyboard instruments are tuned in the key of C and accordingly no transposing is necessary.

### Level Control

The level control is located at the center bottom of the front panel. This control adjusts the sensitivity of the light behind the strobe disc. It is used much like the volume control on a radio. As you rotate the control clockwise the brightness increases. In this position the sensitivity is greatest, but with some types of tone a sharper image is obtained at a reduced level. After you have used the instrument for a while you will determine what the best position is for you.

If you have the level control turned fully clockwise and you still cannot get a pattern on the strobe disc, it might be necessary to move the microphone closer to the source of sound in order to get a better signal level. Occasionally, the microphone will be located in a null point of the standing wave pattern set up by the tone. In this case the microphone may need to be moved a few inches.

### The Strobe Disc

The sharp and flat signs located above the strobe disc window indicate the direction the strobe pattern will appear to be rotating if the note sounding is sharp or flat. If the pattern rotates clockwise, the note is sharp; if counterclockwise, it is flat. The more off pitch the note is, the faster the pattern will rotate.

The numbers along either side of the strobe disc window indicate the octave bands. The range of frequencies in each octave are as follows:

| | | | |
|---|---|---|---|
| 0—C— | 32.703 cps | B— | 61.735 cps |
| 1—C— | 65.406 cps | B— | 123.471 cps |
| 2—C— | 130.813 cps | B— | 246.942 cps |

| | | | |
|---|---|---|---|
| 3—C— | 261.626 cps | B— | 493.883 cps |
| 4—C— | 523.521 cps | B— | 987.767 cps |
| 5—C— | 1046.502 cps | B— | 1975.533 cps |
| 6—C— | 2093.005 cps | B— | 3951.066 cps |
| 7—C— | 4186.009 cps | B— | 7902.133 cps |

## Image Clarifier

The image clarifier switch is located directly below the note selector. The circuitry controlled by this switch is incorporated in the instrument for easier tuning of pianos, chimes, and other instruments in which the upper partials may not be in tune with the fundamental.

It is a characteristic of the tone produced by strings that the overtones (harmonics) are frequently not integrally related to the fundamental frequency, or to each other. This is true to some degree in all pianos but is more apparent in small pianos with short bass strings. The image clarifier is a sharp cut-off filter which eliminates the upper partials from the display on the strobe disc so that the lower partials are more clearly displayed. In general, the LO position should be used when tuning the bass strings up to about middle C. The HI position should be used above this point. Each tuner will use this feature a little differently so it is best to try several cross over points and determine which one best suits your tuning style.

If a piano note is tuned on the LO position and later checked on the HI position there will, in all probability, be a sharp indication on the strobe pattern. This is because the upper partials are indeed sharp. It should be emphasized that this is not a defect in the tuner but that the tuner is accurately displaying the harmonic components that the string is actually producing.

## Microphone

A sensitive ceramic microphone is supplied with each instrument. A contact microphone can also be used. When you tune electronic organs, it is also possible to use a patch cord and to couple the speaker output directly to the input of the tuner.

## *Service Information*

### Accuracy

The exceptional accuracy of the Peterson Strobe Tuner Model 400 is due to the fact that all of the pitches are controlled by a single oscillator circuit of unusual design using components of the highest stability. The pitch is not affected by changes in power line voltage and experience has shown that these instruments will maintain their accuracy over a period of several years, there being practically no aging characteristics to the tuning constants. A tuning adjustment is provided for each of the 12 semitones. It is set at the factory and recalibration is simple if it ever should be required after an extended period. Recalibration should not be attempted in the field if an accurate standard is not available.

### Guarantee

All Peterson tuners are guaranteed for a period of one year from date of purchase. Any tuner that is returned to the factory prepaid within this period will be repaired or replaced free of charge if, in their opinion, it is defective in material or workmanship. Instruments that require repairs due to accidental damage, abuse, or operation on power sources other than those specified, will be repaired and charged for at current rates.

### Returning an Instrument

Should it become necessary to return an instrument to the factory, observe the following instructions:

Use a shipping carton that will allow at least 2 in. of packing material around the entire instrument. Crumpled newspaper works very well for packing. Mark the carton "FRAGILE, DELICATE INSTRUMENT."

## *The Principles Behind the Operation of a Stroboscopic Tuning Device*

Stroboscopic tuning devices are among the most highly accurate of all instruments for gauging the speed of moving objects. In this case, the compacting and expanding of the air itself are registered upon the diaphragm of a sensitive microphone and then amplified and fed into the circuits of the measuring device. Since the response of electronic circuits utilizes the speed of around 186,000 miles per second, time lag is not much of a problem.

Various psychological studies conducted by many agencies of the United States government have verified the fact that the human nervous system reacts more rapidly to visual stimuli and flashing lights than to sound itself. Theoretically, therefore, a piano tuner should be quicker to respond to a stroboscopic indicator than to the matching of sounds in his ears. So we should find that a stroboscopic tuning device makes for great accuracy.

This instrument is a comparator in that it compares a frequency being fed into the microphone with an internal frequency standard and shows the result, either sharp or flat, on a whirling disc. When frequencies within a stroboscopic tuning device are impinged upon by a like frequency fed into the mike, the pattern on the disc will seem to stand still.

Quite a number of articles have been written which speak in various terms of a "meter" which will make aural tuning of pianos obsolete and enable a deaf man to tune a piano. If such a meter exists outside the minds of a few overimaginative reporters, I do not know of it. Probably the reporters who wrote of such a device had heard some mention of the stroboscopic tuning device. While it would not be possible to tune a piano if one were deaf, since the human ear is still very much involved in the subjective assessment of the tones and musical relationships of intervals played on pianos, it is true that much of the checking which must be required in pure aural tuning could be eliminated by a strobe unit. In fact, some tuners go so far as to assert that learning to tune a good temperament by ear is unnecessary if one owns and uses a strobe. I hesitate to agree in all details with such statements. But it certainly is true that one can set notes with great accuracy when using the Peterson Model 400 well.

The skills required for good piano tuning and craftsmanship are many and varied. They include setting not only a temperament, but also a whole lot more. Some of that "whole lot more" is knowing when something doesn't sound just right. For that reason, the human ear will always be necessary if one is to "hone to a fine finish" his tuning work on a piano.

A considerable number of experienced tuners who are devoted to the aural method of tuning have informed me that they do not agree with the beat rates they hear in temperaments tuned with a stroboscopic device. This could be the result of a less-than-careful setting of the pins on the part of the strobe tuner; it could also be the result of reading the disc of the strobe carelessly. But it also could be ignorance on the part of the man who uses the strobe unit in that he does not consider the compensations he must provide for spurious harmonics which are relayed to the disc from the sensitive microphone.

It is certain that a well-set string, with "firm" tuning included, set with the aid of a strobe unit, will make for a well-tuned piano. Many of the finest tuners in several areas of this country are using stroboscopic devices and satisfying the most critical artists, music teachers, and the general public as well. Their clients speak glowingly of their "precision instruments" and the good impression which these tuner-technicians make upon the public. Strobe tuning is here, and it is here to stay. It can be done well and will make a more careful and accurate workman of the person who will learn his instrument and, at the same time, learn his piano.

Suffice it to say, as our detailed description of working with this device will illustrate, that the piano tuner who uses a strobe is in a position to actually see the interaction of the coincident partials of piano tone as they overlap each other in the tuning process. Seeing them, he can accurately make the necessary compromises which will emphasize the tones he wishes to have brought out, and de-emphasize those harmonics he wishes were not present in the piano string. After all, the real problem lies not in the tuning device. It is supremely accurate. The problem lies in the fact that pianos do not emit pure tones from any one string. Allowing for this and utilizing it in all tuning decisions are what make piano tuning an art. Whether it is done with electronic aids or by the naked human ear makes no difference, so long as the harmonics and inharmonicities of piano string tone are satisfactorily handled by the tuner.

The designers of electronic instruments did not assume that the mere purchase of one would make a man a piano tuner. It is true that most of the pianos manufactured in America today, and some manufactured in foreign lands as well, are tuned at the factory by stroboscopic tuning. It is also true that much of the tuning done at factories is not up to the standards required by top-notch artists; or for that matter the standards required by top-notch tuners in this profession. However, the wedding of tuning skills with the intelligent use of a stroboscopic tuning device is constantly satisfying the most critical musicians.

This is not to imply that the strobe is a rough-tuning device. Far from it. All pianos must be rough-tuned when first made, and many are rough-tuned by production line employees at factories. But the strobe lends itself admirably to extreme fine tuning as well, especially when one is familiar with the meanings of its indications and equally familiar with piano tones.

It is extremely important that the reader thoroughly master the preceding chapters. These chapters deal with pin setting techniques as well as with the general reasons for compensation being used in piano tuning. In addition, I respectfully submit that while you may have bought this book in order to learn to tune with a strobe, you cannot master a piano by simply mastering a strobe tuning device. There are things involved in tuning which *must* be understood before you can do an acceptable job with any electronic device. These are described in earlier chapters, and each chapter builds upon the one that went before.

In their Model 400, Peterson has designed a stroboscopic tuning aid with the appearance of a fine laboratory instrument. The quality goes more than appearance-deep. Large, easy-to-read dials, a large scanning disc, and a special harmonic muting switch, make this unit a beauty. It performs as well as it looks in the hands of a careful craftsman.

### *Peterson Model 400 Tuning Procedure*

The best way to begin is to mute the center section of the piano, beginning at the unison just above the scale break, that is, the point at which the wrapped bass strings begin. Then go from this point upward into the treble, because as many outside strings should be muted as possible; and in the case of a grand piano, the complete treble section may be muted this way.

In some lines of smaller pianos, complete muting may be difficult, and it may be necessary to stop inserting the muting strip at the second or third octave above middle C (key No. 40). The strings bear down upon the bridge with 5 to 7 lbs. of pressure in most pianos, and it can be seen that muting the entire piano tenor and treble sections is more likely to give a stable tuning. All the center strings may be tuned completely up the piano, thereby applying one-third the total new pressure to the bridges and sound board evenly throughout the scale. Then, in completing the tuning of these unisons, the left-hand string may be made beatless with the center string previously set; the added one-third of additional tension is applied throughout the scale. Lastly, the right-hand strings may be made beatless to these two already tuned strings, and the total new pressure of tuning thus applied.

During this process, if there is to be any significant change in overall tonality due to the added pressure applied to the bridges, the change will show up in a manner that is easily noticed, and, in fact, will generally be negligible if the piano is nearly up to pitch to begin with. This method avoids sudden stresses on the various sections of the piano, and offers a more evenly distributed pressure to be applied to the total scale.

Where total strip muting is not possible, or too difficult, the treble strings not muted will generally be found to be located in a smaller "wing" of the plate casting, and over a less crowned area of the sound board. Thus, some tuners may find it no problem to mute these strings one by one, while proceeding upward to the top treble end of the piano.

While there are those who tune by muting the two outside strings with rubber wedges, and proceeding from note to note upward throughout the scale, this procedure seems to offer considerably more chance of building up uneven pressures upon the bridges and sound board while proceeding from note to note, and may cause unusual shifts in string pressure which could seriously mar the overall finished result in tuning. The complete muting is preferred; the complete center section muting is a second choice.

In the bass, since most pianos utilize only a two-string unison per note, and the bass bridge is in a different section of the sound board than the tenor and treble, individual muting may give as good a result as any other method.

## Location of Tuner

Any convenient location for the Model 400 may be used, preferably to the left of the technician, within a distance that permits him to handle the controls easily and to view the scanning disc with normal movements of his head and eyes. The microphone may be placed anywhere in or near the piano as long as it provides the tuner with a clear pattern on the disc for the series of notes he is tuning. Further, it is better to place the microphone the same distance from the tuner's ears as the distance from the sound board. Thus, the sound registered on the disc of the tuning instrument for the tuner will be the same as that registered by the piano for the performer.

## The Temperament Section

Having established the standard desired, such as A-440, A-435, etc., set the vernier control to provide it. For A-440, the control is set at zero. For A-435, a setting of 20 cents flat is required. This will assure that all notes registered thereafter will be compared to the original pitch set as a standard. During tuning operations the vernier dial may be moved as desired, but the operator must return to his basic setting when rechecking his temperament, and have it recorded as a basic setting when doing any stretching of the piano tone scale as a point of basic reference.

Beginning at middle C, key No. 40, set this string to register a stationary pattern on the scanning disc in Band 3. This band will be used from middle C to the B above. By observing the pattern in the next higher band, you can tell what amount of compensation will be required when you arrive at a note one octave above the one you are tuning. For example, if the pattern for middle C is set so that there is no movement in Band 3, and yet you discern a noticeable movement (which, if present, will be toward the sharp side) in Band 4, the amount of movement occuring in the band will be the amount of cents you will have to add to the C one octave above when it comes time to tune it.

A good idea at the outset is to set middle C, to observe the pattern in the next higher band, to turn the vernier control sharp enough to stop the pattern in that band, and then to set the C, key No. 52, which is one octave above middle C. One could proceed up the piano, setting all the C's in this way, increasing the cents control in accordance with the method just given and get the result of a perfect stretch from middle C to top C, No. 88.

However, since there is a possibility that tensions applied

may be uneven as regards the primary bridge pressure and sound board compression, it is probably better to tune gradually upward from middle C to the next note, which is C# and so forth. Naturally, the strobe vernier control is returned to the basic setting for each note being tuned from middle C to C52, which is 1 octave above. Switching the selector knob to the note desired, and observing the Band 3 indication, tune each note upward from middle C to C52, arranging the string so as to make the pattern in Band 3 stand still.

In the interest of good tempering, the next step is to begin to observe Band 2, and to tune the B next down from middle C, then the A#, and so on, until you run out of muted strings to tune heading into the bass. Not only will this be a useful procedure in that it applies pressure to the main curvature of the sound board throughout the center section of the piano (which often causes a shift of treble strings toward sharp) but it also provides a method for honing temperament before moving onward to tune the remainder of the piano.

## Honing the Temperament

This is an optional procedure. However, for optimum precision it is quite convenient. For those who do not desire to use it, the remainder of the piano is tuned by adjusting the cents control while basing all upward and downward intervals on the temperament as set, note by note, to the corresponding C40 to C52 range in Band 3.

Observing Band 3, play the F below middle C. Adjust this F so that the pattern in Band 3 stands still. Play the F above middle C. The pattern in Band 3 should stand still. Still watching Band 3, play F# below middle C, and adjust this note so that the pattern stands still in Band 3. Play F# above middle C. The pattern should stand still. Play G below middle C, while observing Band 3. Adjust this note so the pattern stands still in Band 3. Play the G above middle C. The pattern must stand still in Band 3. Play the G# below middle C, and adjust this tone so that the pattern stands still in Band 3. Test the G#

one octave up (the G# above middle C); the pattern in Band 3 should be standing still. Test the A below middle C, observing Band 3. The pattern should stand still. Test one octave up; the pattern should stand still in Band 3. Test the A# below middle C, observing Band 3. The pattern should stand still. Test one octave up to A#; the pattern in Band 3 should remain still. Test B next to middle C, observing Band 3. Adjust this tone, if necessary, so that the pattern stands still in Band 3. Check one octave up to B; the pattern should stand still in Band 3. Play middle C, observing Band 3. The pattern should stand still. Then play middle C, observe the pattern in Band 4, and adjust the C one octave above to make the pattern stand still in Band 4.

### Tuning Outward from the Temperament Octave

Moving the selector switch to the notes desired, proceed as follows: Play C# next to middle C, observing Band 4. The pattern, if moving, will be moving sharp. Tune the C# one octave up to stop the pattern in Band 4. Play D, key No. 42, observing Band 4. Tune the D one octave above to make this pattern stand still. Then D#, E, F, and so on up to the C64, which is two octaves above middle C.

Observing Band 5, play C#53. The pattern, if moving, will be moving sharp. Set C#65 so as to make the pattern remain stationary in Band 5. Play D54, observing Band 5, and set D66 so that the pattern remains still in Band 5. Play D#55, observing Band 5, and adjust D#67 so that the pattern stops in Band 5. Continue this way up to C76.

Play C64, observing the pattern in Band 6. Adjust C76 so that the pattern stands still in Band 6. Play C#65, observing Band 6. Adjust C#77 so that the pattern stands still in Band 6. Play D66, observing Band 6. Set D78 so that the pattern stands still in Band 6. Strike D#67, observing Band 6. Adjust D#79 so the pattern stands still in Band 6. Play E68, observing Band 6. Set E80 so the pattern stands still in Band 6.

From this point on, two methods are employed, either one

of which will do an acceptable job of tuning the last eight tones on the piano. You will have noticed, as you tuned up the treble, that the higher you go on a piano, the greater the stretch required to make the tones agree. With this in mind, the technician may select a method which adds 1 cent to 2 cents extra for each succeeding tone upward from note No. 80. To do this, play E80, and, observing the pattern in Band 7, set the vernier control sharp enough to stop the pattern in Band 7. Then, on F81, add .02 of a semitone (or 2 cents). For F#82, add an additional 2 cents, and continue adding for each note until finishing note C88. If, when playing a corresponding tone two octaves down from the top notes, one hears an objectionable beat, he may elect to raise the top note enough to stop the beat. Play the top and bottom double octave together and adjust to please the ear.

The second method is to continue upward by playing F69, and observing the pattern in Band 7. Adjust F81 tone so that the pattern stands still in Band 7. Continue in this way until you have completed C88.

## Points to Consider When Tuning the Tenor and Treble

Piano tones are compound tones made of harmonics which in most cases (especially in smaller pianos) are not even multiples of the fundamental frequency being played. Therefore, in all cases of tuning a piano, some stretching of the intervals is required. This is true because two piano tones played an exact octave apart in the treble will sound to the human ear as though the top tone were flat in relationship to the lower tone. The cause of this is the tendency of the upper partial harmonics of the lower tone to be sharp with respect to their fundamental. So the upper tone must be raised just enough to satisfy the human ear.

While no two pianos are exactly alike in this respect, nor in the amount of stretch required, it is possible, with the aid of the Model 400 strobe, to note exactly the amount of discrepancy existing between lower and upper tones. We then can adjust our tuning accordingly, as was exemplified in the preceding instructions. However, the ear must still be the final authority. That is to say that however meticulously one stretches the octaves according to the precise measurements of the scanning disc, the upper tone must in all cases be adjusted so that the fewest number of objectionable beats exist between upper and lower tones of the octave.

There will be some cases where complete cancellation of beats is impossible without having an upper tone sound flat with respect to the lower one. In such cases, the fewest beats possible which will still give a good musical interval must be the goal. A good check for this is to play notes two full octaves apart. Doing this up and down the piano will provide an excellent overall test of the gradual stretch of the tuning. Some adjustment may be required, but the combination of the Model 400 used as outlined and a perceptive ear will do a better job of tuning than either could do alone.

## Finishing the Bass Tuning

Once the Model 400 is set to its basic reference point, as at the beginning of the temperament octave, the bass can be tuned. While some tuners may prefer to tune the bass immediately after doing the temperament, and others prefer to tune the bass last, the decision is a personal one and has little if any bearing on the tenor and treble sections.

In the bass, the strongest tones are the upper partial tones of the bass notes. That is to say, the fundamental tones are mostly weaker in bass strings and what is heard is mostly upper partials. For that reason, these are the main tones with which the tuner deals in tuning the bass. In the bass, as well as in the treble, some stretching will probably be needed, depending on the individual piano. But the Model 400 will show accurately just how much is required.

Switch the image intensifier switch to LO position, which will in effect somewhat boost the fundamental image and remove many of the spurious upper partials which have no bearing on the tuning of the bass. Play F above middle C, or key No. 45, observing the pattern in Band 3. It should be stationary, or only slightly sharp. If it seems sharp, flip the image intensifier switch to HI. If the pattern still is sharp, your F has changed from its original setting.

Usually, the pattern will stabilize on HI on this note. If so, do not change the note, but switch the intensifier switch to LO and, observing Band 3, tune the F33 string to make the pattern stand still. Then play E44, watching Band 3, checking the same way as on the preceding note. With the switch on LO, tune E32 to make the pattern stationary in Band 3. Play D#43, observing Band 3, and tune D#31 to make the pattern stand still. Play D42, making sure the pattern stands still on Band 3 when the switch is in HI position, then switch to LO and tune D30 to make the pattern stand still in Band 3. Tune C#41 to make the pattern stand still on Band 3 on HI, then switch to LO and tune C#29 to make Band 3 stand still. Check middle C with switch in HI position, then switch to LO and tune C28 to make Band 3 stand still. From this point on, usually the switch may be left in LO position, but if a considerable amount of sharpness appears in Band 3 when you strike B39, continue to check the next few notes downward on HI until you are satisfied that the amount of sharpness is decreasing note by note as you go downward when viewed with the switch in the LO position.

Make B27 stand still in Band 3. Then, play A#38, observing Band 3, and tune A#26 to make the pattern stand still when it is played. Play A37, observing Band 3, then tune A25 to make the pattern stand still. Do the same with G#36, tuning G#24; G35, tuning G23; F#34, tuning F#22, and F33, tuning F21 to make the pattern stand still in Band 3 in each instance.

From this point onward into the bass, observe Band 2. Tune E32 to make the pattern stationary in Band 3 (this is a check of previous tuning, and can be left out, if desired).

Then tune E20 to make the pattern stand still in Band 2, continuing downward in this same manner, observing Band 2, until you reach E8.

To tune the notes downward from E8 to A1, it is possible to continue in the above fashion, while observing Band 1. But more often, it is easier to tune the remaining notes to Band 2, after checking each note an octave above the one being tuned so as to make sure it reveals a stationary pattern on the scanning disc.

Another method is to increase the amount of cents flat by 2 cents per note from this point onward into the bass. Remember, the ear alone is the final judge. The fundamentals are quite weak in the lowest bass tones, and therefore, we must work with the partial tones to get the most accurate-sounding bass we can in these lower areas. Generally, the lowest bass note on a piano of medium size will be about 24 to 26 cents flat when contrasted with the A, No. 49. Let this be your general guide, whichever method you use.

## Tuning the Unisons

While it is possible to tune each string alone to the Model 400, it is time consuming. Usually the simplest method is to tune the two side strings in the treble to the center string after setting it accurately by strobe. In the bass, the larger rubber wedges may be inserted to mute the second string of a two string unison, and then the second string may be immediately tuned to the primary string which is set by strobe. If done in this way, placing the mute wedge between the left-hand string of the note being tuned to the strobe and the right-hand side of the next lower unison, one can set the outside string of each of two unisons before withdrawing the mute and tuning the previously muted strings to beatless resonance with the primary ones. This way allows the mute to be moved only once for each two unisons being tuned, is convenient, and saves time for the tuner.

## *Tuning Electronic Instruments and Organs*

After calibrating the Model 400 to the standard desired (which may be done by turning the vernier control either to make the instrument match a tuning fork or to rely on the internal calibration), place the mike in a position to receive the best undistorted sound from the organ or other instrument to be tuned.

Being guided by any pertinent service manual instructions which may be available, proceed to use the Model 400 as a frequency standard for all the notes to be tuned. Do not attempt to stretch the octaves as in piano tuning. Organ tones are even multiples and organs will not sound well when tuned that way. Simply tune the oscillator cans for the notes of the organ, turning the selector knob on the Model 400 as you go along from note to note. In the case of the formant type organ with only 12 oscillators to be tuned, once the master oscillators are set the dividing networks provided in the organ circuits precisely tune all remaining octaves. Be careful in adjusting organ tuning slugs, since the circuits are delicate. The slugs need not be moved any great distance to make an appreciable change in frequency of tone.

## *Summary*

It is not possible or necessary to cover everything that a competent tuner should know about a piano in this instruction on the use of the Peterson Model 400, yet it is certain that both the novice tuner and the professional can benefit from the use of this precise instrument. The intervals of piano harmony, their fundamental tones and harmonics, their possible drifting while tuning takes place are easily observed while using the Model 400. In harmony with the practiced ear of the tuner, this instrument makes possible masterful tuning of all pianos. In addition, there is much to be understood about the sounds we hear, and we can gain understanding by observing the movements sharp and flat which occur during tuning. When a craftsman succeeds in the wedding of his feel for piano tone and the precision measurements possible while he tunes with this instrument, he may well be called a master tuner.

### *Additional Notes on Temperament Setting*

If he desires, the tuner may select the octave from C52 down to C40 for temperament setting, and even proceed downward below C40 to F33 by using the following settings for duplicating an aural temperament: Setting C52 on zero, proceed downward with this same setting to G#, setting all notes between C52 and G# at zero. Then, at G#48, set the strobe at -1. Continue setting each note going down at this setting. At D#43, change setting to -1.5; at D42 make the setting -2. Tune on down, one note at a time at this -2 setting until you reach G35, which is set at -2.5. F#34 is set at -2.5 also. F33 is then set at -3.

Charted, the temperament works out like this to duplicate aural tuning:

| | | | |
|---|---|---|---|
| C52 | 0 | D#43 | -.015 |
| B51 | 0 | D42 | -.02 |
| A#50 | 0 | C#41 | " |
| A49 | 0 | C40 | " |
| G#48 | -.01 of a semitone | B39 | " |
| G47 | " | A#38 | " |
| F#46 | " | A37 | " |
| F45 | " | G#36 | " |
| E44 | " | G35 | -.025 |
| F33 | -.03 of a semitone | | |

Using the table given, the fifths will beat as they should on most pianos, including spinets, and the fourths will have their proper spacing. Advancing thirds throughout the temperament are clearer in their best ratios than with most aural temperaments.

After some 18 months testing the electronic instruments available for tuning pianos, I became aware of the many advantages of the Peterson Model 400 Strobe Tuner. The case is fully covered with leatherette, eliminating the possibility of marring or scratching a piano during use. This is of greater importance than would appear at first glance, since the placement of the unit is less critical and there's no worry about damaging the customer's piano.

The Model 400 is well designed, with an overall impression of precision and beauty. This has a definite sales advantage for the tuner in the client's home, since he makes an excellent impression while using this device. The degree of accuracy is astounding.

The image clarifier makes bass tuning easier than with any other instrument I have ever used. The size of the unit is scaled so as to fit unobtrusively into a large tuning kit, or to make a compact unit when carried by itself. The arrangement for using the top cover as a stand for the instrument is ideal. In short, the Peterson 400 meets critical standards, and is superior in most of the requirements specified by a piano craftsman.

This instrument deserves careful consideration when one is considering purchasing an electronic tuning aid. In the long run it will do the job from the standpoint of accuracy, appearance, and dependability. Further, repair facilities are located in the Midwest. Judging from consultation with other tuners who have used the Peterson 400, I find that repairs are rarely needed. One of the finest piano men I know uses this device daily and has experienced no trouble with it. He finds it to be the best instrument he has ever used and would not be without it.

## Instructions
## Frequency to "Cents" Conversion Chart

*To Determine the Frequency of a Known Pitch:*

To use this chart to determine what frequency a certain note is, first turn to the page which lists the octave that you want. Next read across the top of the columns to the desired note name, i.e., C, D, E, etc. The numbers listed in the vertical center of this column (indicated by a triangle at either side of the page) are the exact frequencies of the notes based on an A of 440 cps.

If you would like to know the frequency of a note that is sharp or flat from the standard based on A-440 simply locate the amount of deviation in the left hand column and look across to the proper column (the minus prefix in the left hand column indicates flat).

In order to make certain that you understand how to use the chart try locating the frequency of the following notes:

| *Note* | *Octave* | *Deviation* | *Frequency* |
|---|---|---|---|
| G | 2 | 14 Cents Sharp | 197.589 |
| F | 4 | 3 Cents Flat | 697.247 |
| D | 3 | 0 | 293.665 |
| B | 6 | 23 Cents Sharp | 4003.908 |

*Determining the Note Name and Deviation of a Known Frequency*

In order to find the note name of a given frequency you must first find the page on which the frequency is located. If the exact frequency is not listed simply move up or down to the closest number. The note name will be found at the top of the column and the amount of deviation from the standard based on an A of 440 cycles per second is in the left-hand column.

# OCTAVE 0

| OCTAVE 0 | C | C# | D | D# | E | F | F# | G | G# | A | A# | B |
|---|---|---|---|---|---|---|---|---|---|---|---|---|
| -50 CENTS | 31.772 | 33.661 | 35.663 | 37.784 | 40.030 | 42.411 | 44.933 | 47.605 | 50.435 | 53.434 | 56.612 | 59.978 |
| -49 CENTS | 31.791 | 33.681 | 35.684 | 37.806 | 40.054 | 42.435 | 44.959 | 47.632 | 50.464 | 53.465 | 56.644 | 60.013 |
| -48 CENTS | 31.809 | 33.700 | 35.704 | 37.827 | 40.077 | 42.460 | 44.985 | 47.660 | 50.494 | 53.496 | 56.677 | 60.047 |
| -47 CENTS | 31.827 | 33.720 | 35.725 | 37.849 | 40.100 | 42.484 | 45.011 | 47.687 | 50.523 | 53.527 | 56.710 | 60.082 |
| -46 CENTS | 31.846 | 33.739 | 35.746 | 37.871 | 40.123 | 42.509 | 45.037 | 47.715 | 50.552 | 53.558 | 56.743 | 60.117 |
| -45 CENTS | 31.864 | 33.759 | 35.766 | 37.893 | 40.146 | 42.533 | 45.063 | 47.742 | 50.581 | 53.589 | 56.775 | 60.151 |
| -44 CENTS | 31.883 | 33.778 | 35.787 | 37.915 | 40.169 | 42.558 | 45.089 | 47.770 | 50.610 | 53.620 | 56.808 | 60.186 |
| -43 CENTS | 31.901 | 33.798 | 35.808 | 37.937 | 40.193 | 42.583 | 45.115 | 47.797 | 50.640 | 53.651 | 56.841 | 60.221 |
| -42 CENTS | 31.919 | 33.817 | 35.828 | 37.959 | 40.216 | 42.607 | 45.141 | 47.825 | 50.669 | 53.682 | 56.874 | 60.256 |
| -41 CENTS | 31.938 | 33.837 | 35.849 | 37.981 | 40.239 | 42.632 | 45.167 | 47.853 | 50.698 | 53.713 | 56.907 | 60.291 |
| -40 CENTS | 31.956 | 33.856 | 35.870 | 38.003 | 40.262 | 42.656 | 45.193 | 47.880 | 50.727 | 53.744 | 56.940 | 60.325 |
| -39 CENTS | 31.975 | 33.876 | 35.890 | 38.025 | 40.286 | 42.681 | 45.219 | 47.908 | 50.757 | 53.775 | 56.972 | 60.360 |
| -38 CENTS | 31.993 | 33.896 | 35.911 | 38.047 | 40.309 | 42.706 | 45.245 | 47.936 | 50.786 | 53.806 | 57.005 | 60.395 |
| -37 CENTS | 32.012 | 33.915 | 35.932 | 38.069 | 40.332 | 42.730 | 45.271 | 47.963 | 50.815 | 53.837 | 57.038 | 60.430 |
| -36 CENTS | 32.030 | 33.935 | 35.953 | 38.091 | 40.355 | 42.755 | 45.298 | 47.991 | 50.845 | 53.868 | 57.071 | 60.465 |
| -35 CENTS | 32.049 | 33.954 | 35.973 | 38.113 | 40.379 | 42.780 | 45.324 | 48.019 | 50.874 | 53.899 | 57.104 | 60.500 |
| -34 CENTS | 32.067 | 33.974 | 35.994 | 38.135 | 40.402 | 42.805 | 45.350 | 48.047 | 50.904 | 53.930 | 57.137 | 60.535 |
| -33 CENTS | 32.086 | 33.994 | 36.015 | 38.157 | 40.425 | 42.829 | 45.376 | 48.074 | 50.933 | 53.962 | 57.170 | 60.570 |
| -32 CENTS | 32.104 | 34.013 | 36.036 | 38.179 | 40.449 | 42.854 | 45.402 | 48.102 | 50.962 | 53.993 | 57.203 | 60.605 |
| -31 CENTS | 32.123 | 34.033 | 36.057 | 38.201 | 40.472 | 42.879 | 45.429 | 48.130 | 50.992 | 54.024 | 57.236 | 60.640 |
| -30 CENTS | 32.141 | 34.053 | 36.077 | 38.223 | 40.496 | 42.904 | 45.455 | 48.158 | 51.021 | 54.055 | 57.269 | 60.675 |
| -29 CENTS | 32.160 | 34.072 | 36.098 | 38.245 | 40.519 | 42.928 | 45.481 | 48.185 | 51.051 | 54.086 | 57.303 | 60.710 |
| -28 CENTS | 32.179 | 34.092 | 36.119 | 38.267 | 40.542 | 42.953 | 45.507 | 48.213 | 51.080 | 54.118 | 57.336 | 60.745 |
| -27 CENTS | 32.197 | 34.112 | 36.140 | 38.289 | 40.566 | 42.978 | 45.534 | 48.241 | 51.110 | 54.149 | 57.369 | 60.780 |
| -26 CENTS | 32.216 | 34.131 | 36.161 | 38.311 | 40.589 | 43.003 | 45.560 | 48.269 | 51.139 | 54.180 | 57.402 | 60.815 |
| -25 CENTS | 32.234 | 34.151 | 36.182 | 38.333 | 40.613 | 43.028 | 45.586 | 48.297 | 51.169 | 54.211 | 57.435 | 60.850 |
| -24 CENTS | 32.253 | 34.171 | 36.203 | 38.355 | 40.636 | 43.053 | 45.613 | 48.325 | 51.198 | 54.243 | 57.468 | 60.885 |
| -23 CENTS | 32.272 | 34.191 | 36.224 | 38.378 | 40.660 | 43.077 | 45.639 | 48.353 | 51.228 | 54.274 | 57.501 | 60.921 |
| -22 CENTS | 32.290 | 34.210 | 36.245 | 38.400 | 40.683 | 43.102 | 45.665 | 48.381 | 51.258 | 54.305 | 57.535 | 60.956 |
| -21 CENTS | 32.309 | 34.230 | 36.266 | 38.422 | 40.707 | 43.127 | 45.692 | 48.409 | 51.287 | 54.337 | 57.568 | 60.991 |
| -20 CENTS | 32.328 | 34.250 | 36.286 | 38.444 | 40.730 | 43.152 | 45.718 | 48.437 | 51.317 | 54.368 | 57.601 | 61.026 |
| -19 CENTS | 32.346 | 34.270 | 36.307 | 38.466 | 40.754 | 43.177 | 45.744 | 48.465 | 51.346 | 54.400 | 57.634 | 61.062 |
| -18 CENTS | 32.365 | 34.289 | 36.328 | 38.489 | 40.777 | 43.202 | 45.771 | 48.493 | 51.376 | 54.431 | 57.668 | 61.097 |
| -17 CENTS | 32.384 | 34.309 | 36.349 | 38.511 | 40.801 | 43.227 | 45.797 | 48.521 | 51.406 | 54.463 | 57.701 | 61.132 |
| -16 CENTS | 32.402 | 34.329 | 36.370 | 38.533 | 40.824 | 43.252 | 45.824 | 48.549 | 51.436 | 54.494 | 57.734 | 61.167 |
| -15 CENTS | 32.421 | 34.349 | 36.391 | 38.555 | 40.848 | 43.277 | 45.850 | 48.577 | 51.465 | 54.526 | 57.768 | 61.203 |
| -14 CENTS | 32.440 | 34.369 | 36.412 | 38.578 | 40.872 | 43.302 | 45.877 | 48.605 | 51.495 | 54.557 | 57.801 | 61.238 |
| -13 CENTS | 32.459 | 34.389 | 36.433 | 38.600 | 40.895 | 43.327 | 45.903 | 48.633 | 51.525 | 54.589 | 57.835 | 61.274 |
| -12 CENTS | 32.477 | 34.408 | 36.455 | 38.622 | 40.919 | 43.352 | 45.930 | 48.661 | 51.554 | 54.620 | 57.868 | 61.309 |
| -11 CENTS | 32.496 | 34.428 | 36.476 | 38.645 | 40.942 | 43.377 | 45.956 | 48.689 | 51.584 | 54.652 | 57.901 | 61.344 |
| -10 CENTS | 32.515 | 34.448 | 36.497 | 38.667 | 40.966 | 43.402 | 45.983 | 48.717 | 51.614 | 54.683 | 57.935 | 61.380 |
| -9 CENTS | 32.534 | 34.468 | 36.518 | 38.689 | 40.990 | 43.427 | 46.009 | 48.745 | 51.644 | 54.715 | 57.968 | 61.415 |
| -8 CENTS | 32.552 | 34.488 | 36.539 | 38.712 | 41.013 | 43.452 | 46.036 | 48.774 | 51.674 | 54.746 | 58.002 | 61.451 |
| -7 CENTS | 32.571 | 34.508 | 36.560 | 38.734 | 41.037 | 43.477 | 46.063 | 48.802 | 51.704 | 54.778 | 58.035 | 61.486 |
| -6 CENTS | 32.590 | 34.528 | 36.581 | 38.756 | 41.061 | 43.502 | 46.089 | 48.830 | 51.733 | 54.810 | 58.069 | 61.522 |
| -5 CENTS | 32.609 | 34.548 | 36.602 | 38.779 | 41.085 | 43.528 | 46.116 | 48.858 | 51.763 | 54.841 | 58.102 | 61.557 |
| -4 CENTS | 32.628 | 34.568 | 36.623 | 38.801 | 41.108 | 43.553 | 46.143 | 48.886 | 51.793 | 54.873 | 58.136 | 61.593 |
| -3 CENTS | 32.647 | 34.588 | 36.645 | 38.824 | 41.132 | 43.578 | 46.169 | 48.915 | 51.823 | 54.905 | 58.170 | 61.629 |

FLAT

A=440 ——— SHARP

| | | | | | | | | | | | | |
|---|---|---|---|---|---|---|---|---|---|---|---|---|
| -2 CENTS | 32.665 | 34.608 | 36.666 | 38.846 | 41.156 | 43.603 | 46.196 | 48.943 | 51.853 | 54.936 | 58.203 | 61.664 |
| -1 CENTS | 32.684 | 34.628 | 36.687 | 38.868 | 41.180 | 43.628 | 46.223 | 48.971 | 51.883 | 54.968 | 58.237 | 61.700 |
| 0 CENTS | 32.703 | 34.648 | 36.708 | 38.891 | 41.203 | 43.654 | 46.249 | 48.999 | 51.913 | 55.000 | 58.270 | 61.735 |
| 1 CENTS | 32.722 | 34.668 | 36.729 | 38.913 | 41.227 | 43.679 | 46.276 | 49.028 | 51.943 | 55.032 | 58.304 | 61.771 |
| 2 CENTS | 32.741 | 34.688 | 36.751 | 38.936 | 41.251 | 43.704 | 46.303 | 49.056 | 51.973 | 55.064 | 58.338 | 61.807 |
| 3 CENTS | 32.760 | 34.708 | 36.772 | 38.958 | 41.275 | 43.729 | 46.330 | 49.084 | 52.003 | 55.095 | 58.372 | 61.842 |
| 4 CENTS | 32.779 | 34.728 | 36.793 | 38.981 | 41.299 | 43.755 | 46.356 | 49.113 | 52.033 | 55.127 | 58.405 | 61.878 |
| 5 CENTS | 32.798 | 34.748 | 36.814 | 39.003 | 41.323 | 43.780 | 46.383 | 49.141 | 52.063 | 55.159 | 58.439 | 61.914 |
| 6 CENTS | 32.817 | 34.768 | 36.836 | 39.026 | 41.346 | 43.805 | 46.410 | 49.170 | 52.093 | 55.191 | 58.473 | 61.950 |
| 7 CENTS | 32.836 | 34.788 | 36.857 | 39.048 | 41.370 | 43.830 | 46.437 | 49.198 | 52.123 | 55.223 | 58.507 | 61.986 |
| 8 CENTS | 32.855 | 34.808 | 36.878 | 39.071 | 41.394 | 43.856 | 46.464 | 49.226 | 52.154 | 55.255 | 58.540 | 62.021 |
| 9 CENTS | 32.874 | 34.828 | 36.899 | 39.094 | 41.418 | 43.881 | 46.490 | 49.255 | 52.184 | 55.287 | 58.574 | 62.057 |
| 10 CENTS | 32.893 | 34.849 | 36.921 | 39.116 | 41.442 | 43.906 | 46.517 | 49.283 | 52.214 | 55.319 | 58.608 | 62.093 |
| 11 CENTS | 32.912 | 34.869 | 36.942 | 39.139 | 41.466 | 43.932 | 46.544 | 49.312 | 52.244 | 55.351 | 58.642 | 62.129 |
| 12 CENTS | 32.931 | 34.889 | 36.963 | 39.161 | 41.490 | 43.957 | 46.571 | 49.340 | 52.274 | 55.383 | 58.676 | 62.165 |
| 13 CENTS | 32.950 | 34.909 | 36.985 | 39.184 | 41.514 | 43.983 | 46.598 | 49.369 | 52.304 | 55.415 | 58.710 | 62.201 |
| 14 CENTS | 32.969 | 34.929 | 37.006 | 39.207 | 41.538 | 44.008 | 46.625 | 49.397 | 52.335 | 55.447 | 58.744 | 62.237 |
| 15 CENTS | 32.988 | 34.949 | 37.028 | 39.229 | 41.562 | 44.033 | 46.652 | 49.426 | 52.365 | 55.479 | 58.778 | 62.273 |
| 16 CENTS | 33.007 | 34.970 | 37.049 | 39.252 | 41.586 | 44.059 | 46.679 | 49.454 | 52.395 | 55.511 | 58.811 | 62.309 |
| 17 CENTS | 33.026 | 34.990 | 37.070 | 39.275 | 41.610 | 44.084 | 46.706 | 49.483 | 52.425 | 55.543 | 58.845 | 62.345 |
| 18 CENTS | 33.045 | 35.010 | 37.092 | 39.297 | 41.634 | 44.110 | 46.733 | 49.512 | 52.456 | 55.575 | 58.879 | 62.381 |
| 19 CENTS | 33.064 | 35.030 | 37.113 | 39.320 | 41.658 | 44.135 | 46.760 | 49.540 | 52.486 | 55.607 | 58.914 | 62.417 |
| 20 CENTS | 33.083 | 35.050 | 37.135 | 39.343 | 41.682 | 44.161 | 46.787 | 49.569 | 52.516 | 55.639 | 58.948 | 62.453 |
| 21 CENTS | 33.102 | 35.071 | 37.156 | 39.365 | 41.706 | 44.186 | 46.814 | 49.597 | 52.547 | 55.671 | 58.982 | 62.489 |
| 22 CENTS | 33.121 | 35.091 | 37.178 | 39.388 | 41.730 | 44.212 | 46.841 | 49.626 | 52.577 | 55.703 | 59.016 | 62.525 |
| 23 CENTS | 33.141 | 35.111 | 37.199 | 39.411 | 41.754 | 44.237 | 46.868 | 49.655 | 52.607 | 55.736 | 59.050 | 62.561 |
| 24 CENTS | 33.160 | 35.131 | 37.221 | 39.434 | 41.779 | 44.263 | 46.895 | 49.683 | 52.638 | 55.768 | 59.084 | 62.597 |
| 25 CENTS | 33.179 | 35.152 | 37.242 | 39.457 | 41.803 | 44.288 | 46.922 | 49.712 | 52.668 | 55.800 | 59.118 | 62.633 |
| 26 CENTS | 33.198 | 35.172 | 37.264 | 39.479 | 41.827 | 44.314 | 46.949 | 49.741 | 52.699 | 55.832 | 59.152 | 62.670 |
| 27 CENTS | 33.217 | 35.192 | 37.285 | 39.502 | 41.851 | 44.340 | 46.976 | 49.770 | 52.729 | 55.864 | 59.186 | 62.706 |
| 28 CENTS | 33.236 | 35.213 | 37.307 | 39.525 | 41.875 | 44.365 | 47.003 | 49.798 | 52.760 | 55.897 | 59.221 | 62.742 |
| 29 CENTS | 33.256 | 35.233 | 37.328 | 39.548 | 41.899 | 44.391 | 47.031 | 49.827 | 52.790 | 55.929 | 59.255 | 62.778 |
| 30 CENTS | 33.275 | 35.253 | 37.350 | 39.571 | 41.924 | 44.417 | 47.058 | 49.856 | 52.821 | 55.961 | 59.289 | 62.815 |
| 31 CENTS | 33.294 | 35.274 | 37.371 | 39.594 | 41.948 | 44.442 | 47.085 | 49.885 | 52.851 | 55.994 | 59.323 | 62.851 |
| 32 CENTS | 33.313 | 35.294 | 37.393 | 39.616 | 41.972 | 44.468 | 47.112 | 49.914 | 52.882 | 56.026 | 59.358 | 62.887 |
| 33 CENTS | 33.333 | 35.315 | 37.415 | 39.639 | 41.996 | 44.494 | 47.139 | 49.942 | 52.912 | 56.058 | 59.392 | 62.923 |
| 34 CENTS | 33.352 | 35.335 | 37.436 | 39.662 | 42.021 | 44.519 | 47.167 | 49.971 | 52.943 | 56.091 | 59.426 | 62.960 |
| 35 CENTS | 33.371 | 35.355 | 37.458 | 39.685 | 42.045 | 44.545 | 47.194 | 50.000 | 52.973 | 56.123 | 59.461 | 62.996 |
| 36 CENTS | 33.390 | 35.376 | 37.479 | 39.708 | 42.069 | 44.571 | 47.221 | 50.029 | 53.004 | 56.156 | 59.495 | 63.033 |
| 37 CENTS | 33.410 | 35.396 | 37.501 | 39.731 | 42.094 | 44.597 | 47.248 | 50.058 | 53.035 | 56.188 | 59.529 | 63.069 |
| 38 CENTS | 33.429 | 35.417 | 37.523 | 39.754 | 42.118 | 44.622 | 47.276 | 50.087 | 53.065 | 56.221 | 59.564 | 63.105 |
| 39 CENTS | 33.448 | 35.437 | 37.544 | 39.777 | 42.142 | 44.648 | 47.303 | 50.116 | 53.096 | 56.253 | 59.598 | 63.142 |
| 40 CENTS | 33.468 | 35.458 | 37.566 | 39.800 | 42.167 | 44.674 | 47.330 | 50.145 | 53.126 | 56.286 | 59.632 | 63.178 |
| 41 CENTS | 33.487 | 35.478 | 37.588 | 39.823 | 42.191 | 44.700 | 47.358 | 50.174 | 53.157 | 56.318 | 59.667 | 63.215 |
| 42 CENTS | 33.506 | 35.499 | 37.610 | 39.846 | 42.215 | 44.726 | 47.385 | 50.203 | 53.188 | 56.351 | 59.701 | 63.251 |
| 43 CENTS | 33.526 | 35.519 | 37.631 | 39.869 | 42.240 | 44.751 | 47.412 | 50.232 | 53.219 | 56.383 | 59.736 | 63.288 |
| 44 CENTS | 33.545 | 35.540 | 37.653 | 39.892 | 42.264 | 44.777 | 47.440 | 50.261 | 53.249 | 56.416 | 59.770 | 63.325 |
| 45 CENTS | 33.564 | 35.560 | 37.675 | 39.915 | 42.288 | 44.803 | 47.467 | 50.290 | 53.280 | 56.448 | 59.805 | 63.361 |
| 46 CENTS | 33.584 | 35.581 | 37.697 | 39.938 | 42.313 | 44.829 | 47.495 | 50.319 | 53.311 | 56.481 | 59.840 | 63.398 |
| 47 CENTS | 33.603 | 35.601 | 37.718 | 39.961 | 42.337 | 44.855 | 47.522 | 50.348 | 53.342 | 56.514 | 59.874 | 63.434 |
| 48 CENTS | 33.623 | 35.622 | 37.740 | 39.984 | 42.362 | 44.881 | 47.550 | 50.377 | 53.373 | 56.546 | 59.909 | 63.471 |
| 49 CENTS | 33.642 | 35.642 | 37.762 | 40.007 | 42.386 | 44.907 | 47.577 | 50.406 | 53.403 | 56.579 | 59.943 | 63.508 |
| 50 CENTS | 33.661 | 35.663 | 37.784 | 40.030 | 42.411 | 44.933 | 47.605 | 50.435 | 53.434 | 56.612 | 59.978 | 63.544 |

# OCTAVE I

| OCTAVE 1 | C | C# | D | D# | E | F | F# | G | G# | A | A# | B |
|---|---|---|---|---|---|---|---|---|---|---|---|---|
| -50 CENTS | 63.544 | 67.323 | 71.326 | 75.567 | 80.061 | 84.822 | 89.865 | 95.209 | 100.870 | 106.869 | 113.223 | 119.956 |
| -49 CENTS | 63.581 | 67.362 | 71.367 | 75.611 | 80.107 | 84.871 | 89.917 | 95.264 | 100.929 | 106.930 | 113.289 | 120.025 |
| -48 CENTS | 63.618 | 67.401 | 71.409 | 75.655 | 80.153 | 84.920 | 89.969 | 95.319 | 100.987 | 106.992 | 113.354 | 120.095 |
| -47 CENTS | 63.655 | 67.440 | 71.450 | 75.699 | 80.200 | 84.969 | 90.021 | 95.374 | 101.045 | 107.054 | 113.420 | 120.164 |
| -46 CENTS | 63.691 | 67.479 | 71.491 | 75.742 | 80.246 | 85.018 | 90.073 | 95.429 | 101.104 | 107.116 | 113.485 | 120.233 |
| -45 CENTS | 63.728 | 67.518 | 71.532 | 75.786 | 80.292 | 85.067 | 90.125 | 95.484 | 101.162 | 107.178 | 113.551 | 120.303 |
| -44 CENTS | 63.765 | 67.557 | 71.574 | 75.830 | 80.339 | 85.116 | 90.177 | 95.540 | 101.221 | 107.240 | 113.616 | 120.372 |
| -43 CENTS | 63.802 | 67.596 | 71.615 | 75.874 | 80.385 | 85.165 | 90.229 | 95.595 | 101.279 | 107.301 | 113.682 | 120.442 |
| -42 CENTS | 63.839 | 67.635 | 71.657 | 75.917 | 80.432 | 85.214 | 90.282 | 95.650 | 101.338 | 107.363 | 113.748 | 120.511 |
| -41 CENTS | 63.876 | 67.674 | 71.698 | 75.961 | 80.478 | 85.264 | 90.334 | 95.705 | 101.396 | 107.426 | 113.813 | 120.581 |
| -40 CENTS | 63.913 | 67.713 | 71.739 | 76.005 | 80.525 | 85.313 | 90.386 | 95.761 | 101.455 | 107.488 | 113.879 | 120.651 |
| -39 CENTS | 63.949 | 67.752 | 71.781 | 76.049 | 80.571 | 85.362 | 90.438 | 95.816 | 101.513 | 107.550 | 113.945 | 120.720 |
| -38 CENTS | 63.986 | 67.791 | 71.822 | 76.093 | 80.618 | 85.412 | 90.490 | 95.871 | 101.572 | 107.612 | 114.011 | 120.790 |
| -37 CENTS | 64.023 | 67.830 | 71.864 | 76.137 | 80.664 | 85.461 | 90.543 | 95.927 | 101.631 | 107.674 | 114.077 | 120.860 |
| -36 CENTS | 64.060 | 67.870 | 71.905 | 76.181 | 80.711 | 85.510 | 90.595 | 95.982 | 101.689 | 107.736 | 114.143 | 120.930 |
| -35 CENTS | 64.097 | 67.909 | 71.947 | 76.225 | 80.758 | 85.560 | 90.647 | 96.038 | 101.748 | 107.798 | 114.209 | 121.000 |
| -34 CENTS | 64.134 | 67.948 | 71.988 | 76.269 | 80.804 | 85.609 | 90.700 | 96.093 | 101.807 | 107.861 | 114.275 | 121.070 |
| -33 CENTS | 64.171 | 67.987 | 72.030 | 76.313 | 80.851 | 85.659 | 90.752 | 96.149 | 101.866 | 107.923 | 114.341 | 121.140 |
| -32 CENTS | 64.209 | 68.027 | 72.072 | 76.357 | 80.898 | 85.708 | 90.805 | 96.204 | 101.925 | 107.985 | 114.407 | 121.210 |
| -31 CENTS | 64.246 | 68.066 | 72.113 | 76.401 | 80.944 | 85.758 | 90.857 | 96.260 | 101.984 | 108.048 | 114.473 | 121.280 |
| -30 CENTS | 64.283 | 68.105 | 72.155 | 76.446 | 80.991 | 85.807 | 90.910 | 96.315 | 102.043 | 108.110 | 114.539 | 121.350 |
| -29 CENTS | 64.320 | 68.145 | 72.197 | 76.490 | 81.038 | 85.857 | 90.962 | 96.371 | 102.101 | 108.173 | 114.605 | 121.420 |
| -28 CENTS | 64.357 | 68.184 | 72.238 | 76.534 | 81.085 | 85.906 | 91.015 | 96.427 | 102.160 | 108.235 | 114.671 | 121.490 |
| -27 CENTS | 64.394 | 68.223 | 72.280 | 76.579 | 81.132 | 85.956 | 91.067 | 96.482 | 102.219 | 108.298 | 114.737 | 121.560 |
| -26 CENTS | 64.431 | 68.263 | 72.322 | 76.622 | 81.179 | 86.006 | 91.120 | 96.538 | 102.279 | 108.360 | 114.804 | 121.630 |
| -25 CENTS | 64.469 | 68.302 | 72.364 | 76.667 | 81.225 | 86.055 | 91.172 | 96.594 | 102.338 | 108.423 | 114.870 | 121.701 |
| -24 CENTS | 64.506 | 68.342 | 72.405 | 76.711 | 81.272 | 86.105 | 91.225 | 96.650 | 102.397 | 108.486 | 114.936 | 121.771 |
| -23 CENTS | 64.543 | 68.381 | 72.447 | 76.755 | 81.319 | 86.155 | 91.278 | 96.706 | 102.456 | 108.548 | 115.003 | 121.841 |
| -22 CENTS | 64.580 | 68.421 | 72.489 | 76.800 | 81.366 | 86.205 | 91.331 | 96.761 | 102.515 | 108.611 | 115.069 | 121.912 |
| -21 CENTS | 64.618 | 68.460 | 72.531 | 76.844 | 81.413 | 86.254 | 91.383 | 96.817 | 102.574 | 108.674 | 115.136 | 121.982 |
| -20 CENTS | 64.655 | 68.500 | 72.573 | 76.888 | 81.460 | 86.304 | 91.436 | 96.873 | 102.634 | 108.737 | 115.202 | 122.053 |
| -19 CENTS | 64.692 | 68.539 | 72.615 | 76.933 | 81.507 | 86.354 | 91.489 | 96.929 | 102.693 | 108.799 | 115.269 | 122.123 |
| -18 CENTS | 64.730 | 68.579 | 72.657 | 76.977 | 81.555 | 86.404 | 91.542 | 96.985 | 102.752 | 108.862 | 115.336 | 122.194 |
| -17 CENTS | 64.767 | 68.619 | 72.699 | 77.022 | 81.602 | 86.454 | 91.595 | 97.041 | 102.812 | 108.925 | 115.402 | 122.264 |
| -16 CENTS | 64.805 | 68.658 | 72.741 | 77.066 | 81.649 | 86.504 | 91.648 | 97.097 | 102.871 | 108.989 | 115.469 | 122.335 |
| -15 CENTS | 64.842 | 68.698 | 72.783 | 77.111 | 81.696 | 86.554 | 91.701 | 97.153 | 102.930 | 109.051 | 115.536 | 122.406 |
| -14 CENTS | 64.880 | 68.738 | 72.825 | 77.155 | 81.743 | 86.604 | 91.754 | 97.210 | 102.990 | 109.114 | 115.602 | 122.476 |
| -13 CENTS | 64.917 | 68.777 | 72.867 | 77.200 | 81.790 | 86.654 | 91.807 | 97.266 | 103.049 | 109.177 | 115.669 | 122.547 |
| -12 CENTS | 64.955 | 68.817 | 72.909 | 77.244 | 81.838 | 86.704 | 91.860 | 97.322 | 103.109 | 109.240 | 115.736 | 122.618 |
| -11 CENTS | 64.992 | 68.857 | 72.951 | 77.289 | 81.885 | 86.754 | 91.913 | 97.378 | 103.169 | 109.303 | 115.803 | 122.689 |
| -10 CENTS | 65.030 | 68.897 | 72.993 | 77.334 | 81.932 | 86.804 | 91.966 | 97.434 | 103.228 | 109.366 | 115.870 | 122.760 |
| -9 CENTS | 65.067 | 68.936 | 73.036 | 77.378 | 81.980 | 86.854 | 92.019 | 97.491 | 103.288 | 109.430 | 115.937 | 122.831 |
| -8 CENTS | 65.105 | 68.976 | 73.078 | 77.423 | 82.027 | 86.905 | 92.072 | 97.547 | 103.348 | 109.493 | 116.004 | 122.902 |
| -7 CENTS | 65.142 | 69.016 | 73.120 | 77.468 | 82.074 | 86.955 | 92.125 | 97.603 | 103.407 | 109.556 | 116.071 | 122.973 |
| -6 CENTS | 65.180 | 69.056 | 73.162 | 77.513 | 82.122 | 87.005 | 92.179 | 97.660 | 103.467 | 109.619 | 116.138 | 123.044 |
| -5 CENTS | 65.218 | 69.096 | 73.204 | 77.557 | 82.169 | 87.055 | 92.232 | 97.716 | 103.527 | 109.683 | 116.205 | 123.115 |
| -4 CENTS | 65.255 | 69.136 | 73.247 | 77.602 | 82.217 | 87.106 | 92.285 | 97.773 | 103.587 | 109.746 | 116.272 | 123.186 |
| -3 CENTS | 65.293 | 69.176 | 73.289 | 77.647 | 82.264 | 87.156 | 92.338 | 97.829 | 103.646 | 109.810 | 116.339 | 123.257 |

FLAT

SHARP — A=440

| | | | | | | | | | | | | |
|---|---|---|---|---|---|---|---|---|---|---|---|---|
| -2 CENTS | 65.331 | 69.216 | 73.331 | 77.692 | 82.312 | 87.206 | 92.392 | 97.886 | 103.706 | 109.873 | 116.406 | 123.328 |
| -1 CENTS | 65.369 | 69.256 | 73.374 | 77.737 | 82.359 | 87.257 | 92.445 | 97.942 | 103.766 | 109.936 | 116.474 | 123.400 |
| ▶ 0 CENTS | 65.406 | 69.296 | 73.416 | 77.782 | 82.407 | 87.307 | 92.499 | 97.999 | 103.826 | 110.000 | 116.541 | 123.471 ◀ |
| 1 CENTS | 65.444 | 69.336 | 73.459 | 77.827 | 82.455 | 87.358 | 92.552 | 98.055 | 103.886 | 110.064 | 116.608 | 123.542 |
| 2 CENTS | 65.482 | 69.376 | 73.501 | 77.872 | 82.502 | 87.408 | 92.606 | 98.112 | 103.946 | 110.127 | 116.676 | 123.614 |
| 3 CENTS | 65.520 | 69.416 | 73.544 | 77.917 | 82.550 | 87.458 | 92.659 | 98.169 | 104.006 | 110.191 | 116.743 | 123.685 |
| 4 CENTS | 65.558 | 69.456 | 73.586 | 77.962 | 82.598 | 87.509 | 92.713 | 98.226 | 104.066 | 110.254 | 116.811 | 123.756 |
| 5 CENTS | 65.596 | 69.496 | 73.629 | 78.007 | 82.645 | 87.560 | 92.766 | 98.282 | 104.126 | 110.318 | 116.878 | 123.828 |
| 6 CENTS | 65.633 | 69.536 | 73.671 | 78.052 | 82.693 | 87.610 | 92.820 | 98.339 | 104.187 | 110.382 | 116.946 | 123.899 |
| 7 CENTS | 65.671 | 69.576 | 73.714 | 78.097 | 82.741 | 87.661 | 92.873 | 98.396 | 104.247 | 110.446 | 117.013 | 123.971 |
| 8 CENTS | 65.709 | 69.617 | 73.756 | 78.142 | 82.789 | 87.711 | 92.927 | 98.453 | 104.307 | 110.509 | 117.081 | 124.043 |
| 9 CENTS | 65.747 | 69.657 | 73.799 | 78.187 | 82.836 | 87.762 | 92.981 | 98.510 | 104.367 | 110.573 | 117.148 | 124.114 |
| 10 CENTS | 65.785 | 69.697 | 73.841 | 78.232 | 82.884 | 87.813 | 93.034 | 98.567 | 104.428 | 110.637 | 117.216 | 124.186 |
| 11 CENTS | 65.823 | 69.737 | 73.884 | 78.278 | 82.932 | 87.864 | 93.088 | 98.624 | 104.488 | 110.701 | 117.284 | 124.258 |
| 12 CENTS | 65.861 | 69.778 | 73.927 | 78.323 | 82.980 | 87.914 | 93.142 | 98.680 | 104.548 | 110.765 | 117.352 | 124.330 |
| 13 CENTS | 65.899 | 69.818 | 73.970 | 78.368 | 83.028 | 87.965 | 93.196 | 98.738 | 104.609 | 110.829 | 117.419 | 124.401 |
| 14 CENTS | 65.937 | 69.858 | 74.012 | 78.413 | 83.076 | 88.016 | 93.250 | 98.795 | 104.669 | 110.893 | 117.487 | 124.473 |
| 15 CENTS | 65.976 | 69.899 | 74.055 | 78.459 | 83.124 | 88.067 | 93.304 | 98.852 | 104.730 | 110.957 | 117.555 | 124.545 |
| 16 CENTS | 66.014 | 69.939 | 74.098 | 78.504 | 83.172 | 88.118 | 93.357 | 98.909 | 104.790 | 111.021 | 117.623 | 124.617 |
| 17 CENTS | 66.052 | 69.979 | 74.141 | 78.549 | 83.220 | 88.169 | 93.411 | 98.966 | 104.851 | 111.085 | 117.691 | 124.689 |
| 18 CENTS | 66.090 | 70.020 | 74.183 | 78.595 | 83.268 | 88.220 | 93.465 | 99.023 | 104.911 | 111.150 | 117.759 | 124.761 |
| 19 CENTS | 66.128 | 70.060 | 74.226 | 78.640 | 83.316 | 88.271 | 93.519 | 99.080 | 104.972 | 111.214 | 117.827 | 124.833 |
| 20 CENTS | 66.166 | 70.101 | 74.269 | 78.686 | 83.364 | 88.322 | 93.573 | 99.138 | 105.033 | 111.278 | 117.895 | 124.905 |
| 21 CENTS | 66.205 | 70.141 | 74.312 | 78.731 | 83.413 | 88.373 | 93.627 | 99.195 | 105.093 | 111.342 | 117.963 | 124.978 |
| 22 CENTS | 66.243 | 70.182 | 74.355 | 78.776 | 83.461 | 88.424 | 93.682 | 99.252 | 105.154 | 111.407 | 118.031 | 125.050 |
| 23 CENTS | 66.281 | 70.222 | 74.398 | 78.822 | 83.509 | 88.475 | 93.736 | 99.309 | 105.215 | 111.471 | 118.100 | 125.122 |
| 24 CENTS | 66.319 | 70.263 | 74.441 | 78.868 | 83.557 | 88.526 | 93.790 | 99.367 | 105.276 | 111.536 | 118.168 | 125.194 |
| 25 CENTS | 66.358 | 70.304 | 74.484 | 78.913 | 83.606 | 88.577 | 93.844 | 99.424 | 105.336 | 111.600 | 118.236 | 125.267 |
| 26 CENTS | 66.396 | 70.344 | 74.527 | 78.959 | 83.654 | 88.628 | 93.898 | 99.482 | 105.397 | 111.664 | 118.304 | 125.339 |
| 27 CENTS | 66.434 | 70.385 | 74.570 | 79.004 | 83.702 | 88.679 | 93.953 | 99.539 | 105.458 | 111.729 | 118.373 | 125.412 |
| 28 CENTS | 66.473 | 70.426 | 74.613 | 79.050 | 83.751 | 88.731 | 94.007 | 99.597 | 105.519 | 111.794 | 118.441 | 125.484 |
| 29 CENTS | 66.511 | 70.466 | 74.656 | 79.096 | 83.799 | 88.782 | 94.061 | 99.654 | 105.580 | 111.858 | 118.510 | 125.557 |
| 30 CENTS | 66.550 | 70.507 | 74.699 | 79.141 | 83.847 | 88.833 | 94.115 | 99.712 | 105.641 | 111.923 | 118.578 | 125.629 |
| 31 CENTS | 66.588 | 70.548 | 74.743 | 79.187 | 83.896 | 88.884 | 94.170 | 99.769 | 105.702 | 111.987 | 118.647 | 125.702 |
| 32 CENTS | 66.627 | 70.588 | 74.786 | 79.233 | 83.944 | 88.936 | 94.224 | 99.827 | 105.763 | 112.052 | 118.715 | 125.774 |
| 33 CENTS | 66.665 | 70.629 | 74.829 | 79.279 | 83.993 | 88.987 | 94.279 | 99.885 | 105.824 | 112.117 | 118.784 | 125.847 |
| 34 CENTS | 66.704 | 70.670 | 74.872 | 79.324 | 84.041 | 89.039 | 94.333 | 99.942 | 105.885 | 112.182 | 118.852 | 125.920 |
| 35 CENTS | 66.742 | 70.711 | 74.916 | 79.370 | 84.090 | 89.090 | 94.388 | 100.000 | 105.947 | 112.246 | 118.921 | 125.992 |
| 36 CENTS | 66.781 | 70.752 | 74.959 | 79.416 | 84.138 | 89.142 | 94.442 | 100.058 | 106.008 | 112.311 | 118.990 | 126.065 |
| 37 CENTS | 66.819 | 70.793 | 75.002 | 79.462 | 84.187 | 89.193 | 94.497 | 100.116 | 106.069 | 112.376 | 119.058 | 126.138 |
| 38 CENTS | 66.858 | 70.833 | 75.045 | 79.508 | 84.236 | 89.245 | 94.551 | 100.174 | 106.130 | 112.441 | 119.127 | 126.211 |
| 39 CENTS | 66.897 | 70.874 | 75.089 | 79.554 | 84.284 | 89.296 | 94.606 | 100.232 | 106.192 | 112.506 | 119.196 | 126.284 |
| 40 CENTS | 66.935 | 70.915 | 75.132 | 79.600 | 84.333 | 89.348 | 94.661 | 100.289 | 106.253 | 112.571 | 119.265 | 126.357 |
| 41 CENTS | 66.974 | 70.956 | 75.176 | 79.646 | 84.382 | 89.399 | 94.715 | 100.347 | 106.314 | 112.636 | 119.334 | 126.430 |
| 42 CENTS | 67.013 | 70.997 | 75.219 | 79.692 | 84.431 | 89.451 | 94.770 | 100.405 | 106.376 | 112.701 | 119.403 | 126.503 |
| 43 CENTS | 67.051 | 71.038 | 75.263 | 79.738 | 84.479 | 89.503 | 94.825 | 100.463 | 106.437 | 112.766 | 119.472 | 126.576 |
| 44 CENTS | 67.090 | 71.079 | 75.306 | 79.784 | 84.528 | 89.554 | 94.880 | 100.521 | 106.499 | 112.832 | 119.541 | 126.649 |
| 45 CENTS | 67.129 | 71.120 | 75.350 | 79.830 | 84.577 | 89.606 | 94.934 | 100.580 | 106.560 | 112.897 | 119.610 | 126.722 |
| 46 CENTS | 67.168 | 71.162 | 75.393 | 79.876 | 84.626 | 89.658 | 94.989 | 100.638 | 106.622 | 112.962 | 119.679 | 126.795 |
| 47 CENTS | 67.206 | 71.203 | 75.437 | 79.922 | 84.675 | 89.710 | 95.044 | 100.696 | 106.683 | 113.027 | 119.748 | 126.869 |
| 48 CENTS | 67.245 | 71.244 | 75.480 | 79.968 | 84.724 | 89.762 | 95.099 | 100.754 | 106.745 | 113.093 | 119.817 | 126.942 |
| 49 CENTS | 67.284 | 71.285 | 75.524 | 80.015 | 84.773 | 89.813 | 95.154 | 100.812 | 106.807 | 113.158 | 119.887 | 127.015 |
| 50 CENTS | 67.323 | 71.326 | 75.567 | 80.061 | 84.822 | 89.865 | 95.209 | 100.870 | 106.869 | 113.223 | 119.956 | 127.089 |

## OCTAVE 2

FLAT

| OCTAVE 2 | C | C# | D | D# | E | F | F# | G | G# | A | A# | B |
|---|---|---|---|---|---|---|---|---|---|---|---|---|
| -50 CENTS | 127.089 | 134.646 | 142.652 | 151.135 | 160.122 | 169.643 | 179.731 | 190.418 | 201.741 | 213.737 | 226.446 | 239.912 |
| -49 CENTS | 127.162 | 134.724 | 142.735 | 151.222 | 160.214 | 169.741 | 179.835 | 190.528 | 201.857 | 213.861 | 226.577 | 240.050 |
| -48 CENTS | 127.236 | 134.802 | 142.817 | 151.310 | 160.307 | 169.839 | 179.938 | 190.638 | 201.974 | 213.984 | 226.708 | 240.189 |
| -47 CENTS | 127.309 | 134.879 | 142.900 | 151.397 | 160.400 | 169.937 | 180.042 | 190.748 | 202.091 | 214.108 | 226.839 | 240.328 |
| -46 CENTS | 127.383 | 134.957 | 142.982 | 151.485 | 160.492 | 170.036 | 180.146 | 190.859 | 202.208 | 214.231 | 226.970 | 240.467 |
| -45 CENTS | 127.456 | 135.035 | 143.065 | 151.572 | 160.585 | 170.134 | 180.251 | 190.969 | 202.324 | 214.355 | 227.101 | 240.606 |
| -44 CENTS | 127.530 | 135.113 | 143.148 | 151.660 | 160.678 | 170.232 | 180.355 | 191.079 | 202.441 | 214.479 | 227.233 | 240.745 |
| -43 CENTS | 127.604 | 135.191 | 143.230 | 151.747 | 160.771 | 170.331 | 180.459 | 191.190 | 202.558 | 214.603 | 227.364 | 240.884 |
| -42 CENTS | 127.677 | 135.270 | 143.313 | 151.835 | 160.863 | 170.429 | 180.563 | 191.300 | 202.675 | 214.727 | 227.495 | 241.023 |
| -41 CENTS | 127.751 | 135.348 | 143.396 | 151.923 | 160.956 | 170.527 | 180.667 | 191.411 | 202.792 | 214.851 | 227.627 | 241.162 |
| -40 CENTS | 127.825 | 135.426 | 143.479 | 152.010 | 161.049 | 170.626 | 180.772 | 191.521 | 202.910 | 214.975 | 227.758 | 241.301 |
| -39 CENTS | 127.899 | 135.504 | 143.562 | 152.098 | 161.142 | 170.725 | 180.876 | 191.632 | 203.027 | 215.099 | 227.890 | 241.441 |
| -38 CENTS | 127.973 | 135.582 | 143.645 | 152.186 | 161.236 | 170.823 | 180.981 | 191.743 | 203.144 | 215.224 | 228.022 | 241.580 |
| -37 CENTS | 128.047 | 135.661 | 143.728 | 152.274 | 161.329 | 170.922 | 181.085 | 191.853 | 203.261 | 215.348 | 228.153 | 241.720 |
| -36 CENTS | 128.121 | 135.739 | 143.811 | 152.362 | 161.422 | 171.021 | 181.190 | 191.964 | 203.379 | 215.472 | 228.285 | 241.860 |
| -35 CENTS | 128.195 | 135.818 | 143.894 | 152.450 | 161.515 | 171.119 | 181.295 | 192.075 | 203.496 | 215.597 | 228.417 | 241.999 |
| -34 CENTS | 128.269 | 135.896 | 143.977 | 152.538 | 161.609 | 171.218 | 181.399 | 192.186 | 203.614 | 215.722 | 228.549 | 242.139 |
| -33 CENTS | 128.343 | 135.975 | 144.060 | 152.626 | 161.702 | 171.317 | 181.504 | 192.297 | 203.732 | 215.846 | 228.681 | 242.279 |
| -32 CENTS | 128.417 | 136.053 | 144.143 | 152.714 | 161.795 | 171.416 | 181.609 | 192.408 | 203.849 | 215.971 | 228.813 | 242.419 |
| -31 CENTS | 128.491 | 136.132 | 144.227 | 152.803 | 161.889 | 171.515 | 181.714 | 192.519 | 203.967 | 216.096 | 228.945 | 242.559 |
| -30 CENTS | 128.565 | 136.210 | 144.310 | 152.891 | 161.982 | 171.614 | 181.819 | 192.631 | 204.085 | 216.221 | 229.078 | 242.699 |
| -29 CENTS | 128.640 | 136.289 | 144.393 | 152.979 | 162.076 | 171.714 | 181.924 | 192.742 | 204.203 | 216.345 | 229.210 | 242.840 |
| -28 CENTS | 128.714 | 136.368 | 144.477 | 153.068 | 162.170 | 171.813 | 182.029 | 192.853 | 204.321 | 216.470 | 229.342 | 242.980 |
| -27 CENTS | 128.788 | 136.447 | 144.560 | 153.156 | 162.263 | 171.912 | 182.134 | 192.965 | 204.439 | 216.596 | 229.475 | 243.120 |
| -26 CENTS | 128.862 | 136.525 | 144.644 | 153.245 | 162.357 | 172.011 | 182.240 | 193.076 | 204.557 | 216.721 | 229.608 | 243.261 |
| -25 CENTS | 128.937 | 136.604 | 144.727 | 153.333 | 162.451 | 172.111 | 182.345 | 193.188 | 204.675 | 216.846 | 229.740 | 243.401 |
| -24 CENTS | 129.012 | 136.683 | 144.811 | 153.422 | 162.545 | 172.210 | 182.450 | 193.299 | 204.794 | 216.971 | 229.873 | 243.542 |
| -23 CENTS | 129.086 | 136.762 | 144.895 | 153.510 | 162.639 | 172.310 | 182.556 | 193.411 | 204.912 | 217.097 | 230.006 | 243.683 |
| -22 CENTS | 129.161 | 136.841 | 144.978 | 153.599 | 162.733 | 172.409 | 182.661 | 193.523 | 205.030 | 217.222 | 230.139 | 243.823 |
| -21 CENTS | 129.236 | 136.920 | 145.062 | 153.688 | 162.827 | 172.509 | 182.767 | 193.635 | 205.149 | 217.348 | 230.272 | 243.964 |
| -20 CENTS | 129.310 | 136.999 | 145.146 | 153.777 | 162.921 | 172.609 | 182.872 | 193.746 | 205.267 | 217.473 | 230.405 | 244.105 |
| -19 CENTS | 129.385 | 137.079 | 145.230 | 153.866 | 163.015 | 172.708 | 182.978 | 193.858 | 205.386 | 217.599 | 230.538 | 244.246 |
| -18 CENTS | 129.460 | 137.158 | 145.314 | 153.954 | 163.109 | 172.808 | 183.084 | 193.970 | 205.505 | 217.724 | 230.671 | 244.387 |
| -17 CENTS | 129.535 | 137.237 | 145.398 | 154.043 | 163.203 | 172.908 | 183.190 | 194.083 | 205.623 | 217.850 | 230.804 | 244.529 |
| -16 CENTS | 129.609 | 137.316 | 145.482 | 154.132 | 163.298 | 173.008 | 183.295 | 194.195 | 205.742 | 217.976 | 230.938 | 244.670 |
| -15 CENTS | 129.684 | 137.396 | 145.566 | 154.221 | 163.392 | 173.108 | 183.401 | 194.307 | 205.861 | 218.102 | 231.071 | 244.811 |
| -14 CENTS | 129.759 | 137.475 | 145.650 | 154.311 | 163.486 | 173.208 | 183.507 | 194.419 | 205.980 | 218.228 | 231.205 | 244.953 |
| -13 CENTS | 129.834 | 137.555 | 145.734 | 154.400 | 163.581 | 173.308 | 183.613 | 194.531 | 206.099 | 218.354 | 231.338 | 245.094 |
| -12 CENTS | 129.909 | 137.634 | 145.818 | 154.489 | 163.675 | 173.408 | 183.719 | 194.644 | 206.218 | 218.480 | 231.472 | 245.236 |
| -11 CENTS | 129.984 | 137.714 | 145.902 | 154.578 | 163.770 | 173.508 | 183.825 | 194.756 | 206.337 | 218.607 | 231.606 | 245.378 |
| -10 CENTS | 130.059 | 137.793 | 145.987 | 154.668 | 163.865 | 173.608 | 183.932 | 194.869 | 206.456 | 218.733 | 231.739 | 245.519 |
| -9 CENTS | 130.135 | 137.873 | 146.071 | 154.757 | 163.959 | 173.709 | 184.038 | 194.981 | 206.576 | 218.859 | 231.873 | 245.661 |
| -8 CENTS | 130.210 | 137.952 | 146.155 | 154.846 | 164.054 | 173.809 | 184.144 | 195.094 | 206.695 | 218.986 | 232.007 | 245.803 |
| -7 CENTS | 130.285 | 138.032 | 146.240 | 154.935 | 164.149 | 173.910 | 184.251 | 195.207 | 206.814 | 219.112 | 232.141 | 245.945 |
| -6 CENTS | 130.360 | 138.112 | 146.324 | 155.025 | 164.244 | 174.010 | 184.357 | 195.320 | 206.934 | 219.239 | 232.275 | 246.087 |
| -5 CENTS | 130.436 | 138.192 | 146.409 | 155.115 | 164.338 | 174.111 | 184.464 | 195.432 | 207.053 | 219.366 | 232.410 | 246.229 |
| -4 CENTS | 130.511 | 138.271 | 146.494 | 155.204 | 164.433 | 174.211 | 184.570 | 195.545 | 207.173 | 219.492 | 232.544 | 246.372 |
| -3 CENTS | 130.586 | 138.351 | 146.578 | 155.294 | 164.529 | 174.312 | 184.677 | 195.658 | 207.293 | 219.619 | 232.678 | 246.514 |

SHARP — A=440

| | | | | | | | | | | | | |
|---|---|---|---|---|---|---|---|---|---|---|---|---|
| -2 CENTS | 130.662 | 138.431 | 146.663 | 155.384 | 164.623 | 174.413 | 184.784 | 195.771 | 207.413 | 219.746 | 232.813 | 246.657 |
| -1 CENTS | 130.737 | 138.511 | 146.748 | 155.474 | 164.719 | 174.513 | 184.890 | 195.885 | 207.532 | 219.873 | 232.947 | 246.799 |
| 0 CENTS | 130.813 | 138.591 | 146.832 | 155.563 | 164.814 | 174.614 | 184.997 | 195.998 | 207.652 | 220.000 | 233.082 | 246.942 |
| 1 CENTS | 130.888 | 138.671 | 146.917 | 155.653 | 164.909 | 174.715 | 185.104 | 196.111 | 207.772 | 220.127 | 233.217 | 247.084 |
| 2 CENTS | 130.964 | 138.752 | 147.002 | 155.743 | 165.004 | 174.816 | 185.211 | 196.224 | 207.892 | 220.254 | 233.351 | 247.227 |
| 3 CENTS | 131.040 | 138.832 | 147.087 | 155.833 | 165.100 | 174.917 | 185.318 | 196.338 | 208.012 | 220.382 | 233.486 | 247.370 |
| 4 CENTS | 131.115 | 138.912 | 147.172 | 155.923 | 165.195 | 175.018 | 185.425 | 196.451 | 208.133 | 220.509 | 233.621 | 247.513 |
| 5 CENTS | 131.191 | 138.992 | 147.257 | 156.013 | 165.290 | 175.119 | 185.532 | 196.565 | 208.253 | 220.636 | 233.756 | 247.656 |
| 6 CENTS | 131.267 | 139.072 | 147.342 | 156.104 | 165.386 | 175.220 | 185.639 | 196.678 | 208.373 | 220.764 | 233.891 | 247.799 |
| 7 CENTS | 131.343 | 139.153 | 147.427 | 156.194 | 165.482 | 175.322 | 185.747 | 196.792 | 208.494 | 220.891 | 234.026 | 247.942 |
| 8 CENTS | 131.419 | 139.233 | 147.512 | 156.284 | 165.577 | 175.423 | 185.854 | 196.906 | 208.614 | 221.019 | 234.161 | 248.085 |
| 9 CENTS | 131.495 | 139.314 | 147.598 | 156.374 | 165.673 | 175.524 | 185.961 | 197.019 | 208.735 | 221.147 | 234.297 | 248.229 |
| 10 CENTS | 131.571 | 139.394 | 147.683 | 156.465 | 165.769 | 175.626 | 186.069 | 197.133 | 208.855 | 221.274 | 234.432 | 248.372 |
| 11 CENTS | 131.647 | 139.475 | 147.768 | 156.555 | 165.864 | 175.727 | 186.176 | 197.247 | 208.976 | 221.402 | 234.568 | 248.516 |
| 12 CENTS | 131.723 | 139.555 | 147.854 | 156.646 | 165.960 | 175.829 | 186.284 | 197.361 | 209.097 | 221.530 | 234.703 | 248.659 |
| 13 CENTS | 131.799 | 139.636 | 147.939 | 156.736 | 166.056 | 175.930 | 186.392 | 197.475 | 209.217 | 221.658 | 234.839 | 248.803 |
| 14 CENTS | 131.875 | 139.717 | 148.025 | 156.827 | 166.152 | 176.032 | 186.499 | 197.589 | 209.338 | 221.786 | 234.974 | 248.947 |
| 15 CENTS | 131.951 | 139.797 | 148.110 | 156.917 | 166.248 | 176.134 | 186.607 | 197.703 | 209.459 | 221.914 | 235.110 | 249.091 |
| 16 CENTS | 132.027 | 139.878 | 148.196 | 157.008 | 166.344 | 176.235 | 186.715 | 197.818 | 209.580 | 222.043 | 235.246 | 249.234 |
| 17 CENTS | 132.104 | 139.959 | 148.281 | 157.099 | 166.440 | 176.337 | 186.823 | 197.932 | 209.701 | 222.171 | 235.382 | 249.378 |
| 18 CENTS | 132.180 | 140.040 | 148.367 | 157.189 | 166.536 | 176.439 | 186.931 | 198.046 | 209.823 | 222.299 | 235.518 | 249.523 |
| 19 CENTS | 132.256 | 140.121 | 148.453 | 157.280 | 166.633 | 176.541 | 187.039 | 198.161 | 209.944 | 222.428 | 235.654 | 249.667 |
| 20 CENTS | 132.333 | 140.202 | 148.538 | 157.371 | 166.729 | 176.643 | 187.147 | 198.275 | 210.065 | 222.556 | 235.790 | 249.811 |
| 21 CENTS | 132.409 | 140.283 | 148.624 | 157.462 | 166.825 | 176.745 | 187.255 | 198.390 | 210.187 | 222.685 | 235.926 | 249.955 |
| 22 CENTS | 132.486 | 140.364 | 148.710 | 157.553 | 166.922 | 176.847 | 187.363 | 198.504 | 210.308 | 222.814 | 236.063 | 250.100 |
| 23 CENTS | 132.562 | 140.445 | 148.796 | 157.644 | 167.018 | 176.949 | 187.471 | 198.619 | 210.429 | 222.942 | 236.199 | 250.244 |
| 24 CENTS | 132.639 | 140.526 | 148.882 | 157.735 | 167.114 | 177.052 | 187.580 | 198.734 | 210.551 | 223.071 | 236.336 | 250.389 |
| 25 CENTS | 132.715 | 140.607 | 148.968 | 157.826 | 167.211 | 177.154 | 187.688 | 198.849 | 210.673 | 223.200 | 236.472 | 250.533 |
| 26 CENTS | 132.792 | 140.688 | 149.054 | 157.917 | 167.308 | 177.256 | 187.797 | 198.963 | 210.794 | 223.329 | 236.609 | 250.678 |
| 27 CENTS | 132.869 | 140.770 | 149.140 | 158.009 | 167.404 | 177.359 | 187.905 | 199.078 | 210.916 | 223.458 | 236.745 | 250.823 |
| 28 CENTS | 132.946 | 140.851 | 149.226 | 158.100 | 167.501 | 177.461 | 188.014 | 199.193 | 211.038 | 223.587 | 236.882 | 250.968 |
| 29 CENTS | 133.022 | 140.932 | 149.313 | 158.191 | 167.598 | 177.564 | 188.122 | 199.309 | 211.160 | 223.716 | 237.019 | 251.113 |
| 30 CENTS | 133.099 | 141.014 | 149.399 | 158.283 | 167.695 | 177.666 | 188.231 | 199.424 | 211.282 | 223.846 | 237.156 | 251.258 |
| 31 CENTS | 133.176 | 141.095 | 149.485 | 158.374 | 167.792 | 177.769 | 188.340 | 199.539 | 211.404 | 223.975 | 237.293 | 251.403 |
| 32 CENTS | 133.253 | 141.177 | 149.572 | 158.466 | 167.889 | 177.872 | 188.448 | 199.654 | 211.526 | 224.104 | 237.430 | 251.549 |
| 33 CENTS | 133.330 | 141.258 | 149.658 | 158.557 | 167.986 | 177.974 | 188.557 | 199.770 | 211.648 | 224.234 | 237.567 | 251.694 |
| 34 CENTS | 133.407 | 141.340 | 149.745 | 158.649 | 168.083 | 178.077 | 188.666 | 199.885 | 211.771 | 224.363 | 237.705 | 251.839 |
| 35 CENTS | 133.484 | 141.422 | 149.831 | 158.740 | 168.180 | 178.180 | 188.775 | 200.000 | 211.893 | 224.493 | 237.842 | 251.985 |
| 36 CENTS | 133.561 | 141.503 | 149.918 | 158.832 | 168.277 | 178.283 | 188.884 | 200.116 | 212.016 | 224.623 | 237.979 | 252.130 |
| 37 CENTS | 133.639 | 141.585 | 150.004 | 158.924 | 168.374 | 178.386 | 188.994 | 200.232 | 212.138 | 224.752 | 238.117 | 252.276 |
| 38 CENTS | 133.716 | 141.667 | 150.091 | 159.016 | 168.471 | 178.489 | 189.103 | 200.347 | 212.261 | 224.882 | 238.255 | 252.422 |
| 39 CENTS | 133.793 | 141.749 | 150.178 | 159.108 | 168.569 | 178.592 | 189.212 | 200.463 | 212.383 | 225.012 | 238.392 | 252.568 |
| 40 CENTS | 133.870 | 141.831 | 150.264 | 159.200 | 168.666 | 178.696 | 189.321 | 200.579 | 212.506 | 225.142 | 238.530 | 252.714 |
| 41 CENTS | 133.948 | 141.913 | 150.351 | 159.292 | 168.764 | 178.799 | 189.431 | 200.695 | 212.629 | 225.272 | 238.668 | 252.860 |
| 42 CENTS | 134.025 | 141.995 | 150.438 | 159.384 | 168.861 | 178.902 | 189.540 | 200.811 | 212.752 | 225.403 | 238.806 | 253.006 |
| 43 CENTS | 134.103 | 142.077 | 150.525 | 159.476 | 168.959 | 179.005 | 189.650 | 200.927 | 212.875 | 225.533 | 238.944 | 253.152 |
| 44 CENTS | 134.180 | 142.159 | 150.612 | 159.568 | 169.056 | 179.109 | 189.759 | 201.043 | 212.998 | 225.663 | 239.082 | 253.298 |
| 45 CENTS | 134.258 | 142.241 | 150.699 | 159.660 | 169.154 | 179.212 | 189.869 | 201.159 | 213.121 | 225.793 | 239.220 | 253.445 |
| 46 CENTS | 134.335 | 142.323 | 150.786 | 159.752 | 169.252 | 179.316 | 189.979 | 201.275 | 213.244 | 225.924 | 239.358 | 253.591 |
| 47 CENTS | 134.413 | 142.405 | 150.873 | 159.845 | 169.349 | 179.420 | 190.089 | 201.392 | 213.367 | 226.054 | 239.496 | 253.738 |
| 48 CENTS | 134.490 | 142.488 | 150.960 | 159.937 | 169.447 | 179.523 | 190.198 | 201.508 | 213.490 | 226.185 | 239.635 | 253.884 |
| 49 CENTS | 134.568 | 142.570 | 151.048 | 160.029 | 169.545 | 179.627 | 190.308 | 201.624 | 213.614 | 226.316 | 239.773 | 254.031 |
| 50 CENTS | 134.646 | 142.652 | 151.135 | 160.122 | 169.643 | 179.731 | 190.418 | 201.741 | 213.737 | 226.446 | 239.912 | 254.178 |

# OCTAVE 3

| OCTAVE 3 | C | C# | D | D# | E | F | F# | G | G# | A | A# | B |
|---|---|---|---|---|---|---|---|---|---|---|---|---|
| -50 CENTS | 254.178 | 269.292 | 285.305 | 302.270 | 320.244 | 339.286 | 359.461 | 380.836 | 403.482 | 427.474 | 452.893 | 479.823 |
| -49 CENTS | 254.324 | 269.447 | 285.470 | 302.444 | 320.429 | 339.482 | 359.669 | 381.056 | 403.715 | 427.721 | 453.155 | 480.101 |
| -48 CENTS | 254.471 | 269.603 | 285.634 | 302.619 | 320.614 | 339.679 | 359.877 | 381.276 | 403.948 | 427.968 | 453.416 | 480.378 |
| -47 CENTS | 254.618 | 269.759 | 285.800 | 302.794 | 320.799 | 339.875 | 360.085 | 381.497 | 404.182 | 428.215 | 453.678 | 480.656 |
| -46 CENTS | 254.766 | 269.915 | 285.965 | 302.969 | 320.984 | 340.071 | 360.293 | 381.717 | 404.415 | 428.463 | 453.941 | 480.933 |
| -45 CENTS | 254.913 | 270.071 | 286.130 | 303.144 | 321.170 | 340.268 | 360.501 | 381.938 | 404.649 | 428.710 | 454.203 | 481.211 |
| -44 CENTS | 255.060 | 270.227 | 286.295 | 303.319 | 321.356 | 340.464 | 360.709 | 382.158 | 404.883 | 428.958 | 454.465 | 481.489 |
| -43 CENTS | 255.207 | 270.383 | 286.461 | 303.494 | 321.541 | 340.661 | 360.918 | 382.379 | 405.117 | 429.206 | 454.728 | 481.767 |
| -42 CENTS | 255.355 | 270.539 | 286.626 | 303.670 | 321.727 | 340.858 | 361.126 | 382.600 | 405.351 | 429.454 | 454.991 | 482.046 |
| -41 CENTS | 255.502 | 270.695 | 286.792 | 303.845 | 321.913 | 341.055 | 361.335 | 382.821 | 405.585 | 429.702 | 455.254 | 482.324 |
| -40 CENTS | 255.650 | 270.852 | 286.957 | 304.021 | 322.099 | 341.252 | 361.544 | 383.042 | 405.819 | 429.950 | 455.517 | 482.603 |
| -39 CENTS | 255.798 | 271.008 | 287.123 | 304.196 | 322.285 | 341.449 | 361.753 | 383.264 | 406.054 | 430.199 | 455.780 | 482.882 |
| -38 CENTS | 255.946 | 271.165 | 287.289 | 304.372 | 322.471 | 341.646 | 361.962 | 383.485 | 406.288 | 430.447 | 456.043 | 483.161 |
| -37 CENTS | 256.093 | 271.322 | 287.455 | 304.548 | 322.657 | 341.844 | 362.171 | 383.707 | 406.523 | 430.696 | 456.307 | 483.440 |
| -36 CENTS | 256.241 | 271.478 | 287.621 | 304.724 | 322.844 | 342.041 | 362.380 | 383.928 | 406.758 | 430.945 | 456.570 | 483.719 |
| -35 CENTS | 256.389 | 271.635 | 287.787 | 304.900 | 323.030 | 342.239 | 362.589 | 384.150 | 406.993 | 431.194 | 456.834 | 483.999 |
| -34 CENTS | 256.538 | 271.792 | 287.954 | 305.076 | 323.217 | 342.437 | 362.799 | 384.372 | 407.228 | 431.443 | 457.098 | 484.278 |
| -33 CENTS | 256.686 | 271.949 | 288.120 | 305.253 | 323.404 | 342.634 | 363.009 | 384.594 | 407.463 | 431.692 | 457.362 | 484.558 |
| -32 CENTS | 256.834 | 272.106 | 288.287 | 305.429 | 323.591 | 342.832 | 363.218 | 384.816 | 407.699 | 431.942 | 457.626 | 484.838 |
| -31 CENTS | 256.983 | 272.263 | 288.453 | 305.605 | 323.778 | 343.031 | 363.428 | 385.039 | 407.934 | 432.191 | 457.891 | 485.118 |
| -30 CENTS | 257.131 | 272.421 | 288.620 | 305.782 | 323.965 | 343.229 | 363.638 | 385.261 | 408.170 | 432.441 | 458.155 | 485.399 |
| -29 CENTS | 257.280 | 272.578 | 288.787 | 305.959 | 324.152 | 343.427 | 363.848 | 385.484 | 408.406 | 432.691 | 458.420 | 485.679 |
| -28 CENTS | 257.428 | 272.736 | 288.953 | 306.135 | 324.339 | 343.625 | 364.058 | 385.707 | 408.642 | 432.941 | 458.685 | 485.960 |
| -27 CENTS | 257.577 | 272.893 | 289.120 | 306.312 | 324.527 | 343.824 | 364.269 | 385.929 | 408.878 | 433.191 | 458.950 | 486.241 |
| -26 CENTS | 257.726 | 273.051 | 289.287 | 306.489 | 324.714 | 344.023 | 364.479 | 386.152 | 409.114 | 433.441 | 459.215 | 486.521 |
| -25 CENTS | 257.875 | 273.209 | 289.455 | 306.666 | 324.902 | 344.221 | 364.690 | 386.375 | 409.351 | 433.692 | 459.480 | 486.803 |
| -24 CENTS | 258.024 | 273.367 | 289.622 | 306.844 | 325.089 | 344.420 | 364.901 | 386.599 | 409.587 | 433.942 | 459.746 | 487.084 |
| -23 CENTS | 258.173 | 273.525 | 289.789 | 307.021 | 325.277 | 344.619 | 365.111 | 386.822 | 409.824 | 434.193 | 460.012 | 487.365 |
| -22 CENTS | 258.322 | 273.683 | 289.957 | 307.198 | 325.465 | 344.818 | 365.322 | 387.046 | 410.061 | 434.444 | 460.277 | 487.647 |
| -21 CENTS | 258.471 | 273.841 | 290.124 | 307.376 | 325.653 | 345.018 | 365.533 | 387.269 | 410.297 | 434.695 | 460.543 | 487.929 |
| -20 CENTS | 258.621 | 273.999 | 290.292 | 307.553 | 325.841 | 345.217 | 365.745 | 387.493 | 410.535 | 434.946 | 460.809 | 488.211 |
| -19 CENTS | 258.770 | 274.157 | 290.459 | 307.731 | 326.030 | 345.416 | 365.956 | 387.717 | 410.772 | 435.197 | 461.076 | 488.493 |
| -18 CENTS | 258.919 | 274.316 | 290.627 | 307.909 | 326.218 | 345.616 | 366.167 | 387.941 | 411.009 | 435.449 | 461.342 | 488.775 |
| -17 CENTS | 259.069 | 274.474 | 290.795 | 308.087 | 326.407 | 345.816 | 366.379 | 388.165 | 411.247 | 435.701 | 461.609 | 489.057 |
| -16 CENTS | 259.219 | 274.633 | 290.963 | 308.265 | 326.595 | 346.016 | 366.591 | 388.389 | 411.484 | 435.952 | 461.875 | 489.340 |
| -15 CENTS | 259.369 | 274.791 | 291.131 | 308.443 | 326.784 | 346.215 | 366.803 | 388.614 | 411.722 | 436.204 | 462.142 | 489.623 |
| -14 CENTS | 259.518 | 274.950 | 291.300 | 308.621 | 326.973 | 346.416 | 367.014 | 388.838 | 411.960 | 436.456 | 462.409 | 489.906 |
| -13 CENTS | 259.668 | 275.109 | 291.468 | 308.799 | 327.162 | 346.616 | 367.227 | 389.063 | 412.198 | 436.708 | 462.676 | 490.189 |
| -12 CENTS | 259.818 | 275.268 | 291.636 | 308.978 | 327.351 | 346.816 | 367.439 | 389.288 | 412.436 | 436.961 | 462.944 | 490.472 |
| -11 CENTS | 259.969 | 275.427 | 291.805 | 309.156 | 327.540 | 347.016 | 367.651 | 389.513 | 412.674 | 437.213 | 463.211 | 490.755 |
| -10 CENTS | 260.119 | 275.586 | 291.973 | 309.335 | 327.729 | 347.217 | 367.863 | 389.738 | 412.913 | 437.466 | 463.479 | 491.039 |
| -9 CENTS | 260.269 | 275.745 | 292.142 | 309.514 | 327.918 | 347.417 | 368.076 | 389.963 | 413.151 | 437.719 | 463.747 | 491.322 |
| -8 CENTS | 260.419 | 275.905 | 292.311 | 309.693 | 328.108 | 347.618 | 368.289 | 390.188 | 413.390 | 437.971 | 464.015 | 491.606 |
| -7 CENTS | 260.570 | 276.064 | 292.480 | 309.872 | 328.297 | 347.819 | 368.501 | 390.414 | 413.629 | 438.225 | 464.283 | 491.890 |
| -6 CENTS | 260.720 | 276.224 | 292.649 | 310.051 | 328.487 | 348.020 | 368.714 | 390.639 | 413.868 | 438.478 | 464.551 | 492.175 |
| -5 CENTS | 260.871 | 276.383 | 292.818 | 310.230 | 328.677 | 348.221 | 368.927 | 390.865 | 414.107 | 438.731 | 464.819 | 492.459 |
| -4 CENTS | 261.022 | 276.543 | 292.987 | 310.409 | 328.867 | 348.422 | 369.141 | 391.091 | 414.346 | 438.985 | 465.088 | 492.744 |
| -3 CENTS | 261.173 | 276.703 | 293.156 | 310.588 | 329.057 | 348.624 | 369.354 | 391.317 | 414.586 | 439.238 | 465.357 | 493.028 |

FLAT

SHARP — A=440

| | | | | | | | | | | | | |
|---|---|---|---|---|---|---|---|---|---|---|---|---|
| -2 CENTS | 261.323 | 276.863 | 293.326 | 310.768 | 329.247 | 348.825 | 369.567 | 391.543 | 414.825 | 439.492 | 465.626 | 493.313 |
| -1 CENTS | 261.474 | 277.023 | 293.495 | 310.947 | 329.437 | 349.027 | 369.781 | 391.769 | 415.065 | 439.746 | 465.895 | 493.598 |
| 0 CENTS | 261.626 | 277.183 | 293.665 | 311.127 | 329.628 | 349.228 | 369.994 | 391.995 | 415.305 | 440.000 | 466.164 | 493.883 |
| 1 CENTS | 261.777 | 277.343 | 293.834 | 311.307 | 329.818 | 349.430 | 370.208 | 392.222 | 415.545 | 440.254 | 466.433 | 494.169 |
| 2 CENTS | 261.928 | 277.503 | 294.004 | 311.487 | 330.009 | 349.632 | 370.422 | 392.449 | 415.785 | 440.509 | 466.703 | 494.454 |
| 3 CENTS | 262.079 | 277.663 | 294.174 | 311.667 | 330.199 | 349.834 | 370.636 | 392.675 | 416.025 | 440.763 | 466.972 | 494.740 |
| 4 CENTS | 262.231 | 277.824 | 294.344 | 311.847 | 330.390 | 350.036 | 370.850 | 392.902 | 416.265 | 441.018 | 467.242 | 495.026 |
| 5 CENTS | 262.382 | 277.984 | 294.514 | 312.027 | 330.581 | 350.238 | 371.065 | 393.129 | 416.506 | 441.273 | 467.512 | 495.312 |
| 6 CENTS | 262.534 | 278.145 | 294.684 | 312.207 | 330.772 | 350.441 | 371.279 | 393.356 | 416.747 | 441.528 | 467.782 | 495.598 |
| 7 CENTS | 262.686 | 278.306 | 294.855 | 312.388 | 330.963 | 350.643 | 371.493 | 393.584 | 416.987 | 441.783 | 468.052 | 495.884 |
| 8 CENTS | 262.837 | 278.466 | 295.025 | 312.568 | 331.154 | 350.846 | 371.708 | 393.811 | 417.228 | 442.038 | 468.323 | 496.171 |
| 9 CENTS | 262.989 | 278.627 | 295.195 | 312.749 | 331.346 | 351.048 | 371.923 | 394.039 | 417.469 | 442.293 | 468.593 | 496.457 |
| 10 CENTS | 263.141 | 278.788 | 295.366 | 312.929 | 331.537 | 351.251 | 372.138 | 394.266 | 417.711 | 442.549 | 468.864 | 496.744 |
| 11 CENTS | 263.293 | 278.949 | 295.537 | 313.110 | 331.729 | 351.454 | 372.353 | 394.494 | 417.952 | 442.805 | 469.135 | 497.031 |
| 12 CENTS | 263.445 | 279.111 | 295.707 | 313.291 | 331.920 | 351.657 | 372.568 | 394.722 | 418.193 | 443.060 | 469.406 | 497.319 |
| 13 CENTS | 263.598 | 279.272 | 295.878 | 313.472 | 332.112 | 351.860 | 372.783 | 394.950 | 418.435 | 443.316 | 469.677 | 497.606 |
| 14 CENTS | 263.750 | 279.433 | 296.049 | 313.653 | 332.304 | 352.064 | 372.999 | 395.178 | 418.677 | 443.573 | 469.949 | 497.893 |
| 15 CENTS | 263.902 | 279.595 | 296.220 | 313.834 | 332.496 | 352.267 | 373.214 | 395.407 | 418.919 | 443.829 | 470.220 | 498.181 |
| 16 CENTS | 264.055 | 279.756 | 296.391 | 314.016 | 332.688 | 352.471 | 373.430 | 395.635 | 419.161 | 444.085 | 470.492 | 498.469 |
| 17 CENTS | 264.207 | 279.918 | 296.563 | 314.197 | 332.880 | 352.674 | 373.646 | 395.864 | 419.403 | 444.342 | 470.764 | 498.757 |
| 18 CENTS | 264.360 | 280.080 | 296.734 | 314.379 | 333.073 | 352.878 | 373.861 | 396.092 | 419.645 | 444.599 | 471.036 | 499.045 |
| 19 CENTS | 264.513 | 280.241 | 296.905 | 314.560 | 333.265 | 353.082 | 374.077 | 396.321 | 419.888 | 444.856 | 471.308 | 499.333 |
| 20 CENTS | 264.666 | 280.403 | 297.077 | 314.742 | 333.458 | 353.286 | 374.294 | 396.550 | 420.130 | 445.113 | 471.580 | 499.622 |
| 21 CENTS | 264.818 | 280.565 | 297.249 | 314.924 | 333.650 | 353.490 | 374.510 | 396.779 | 420.373 | 445.370 | 471.853 | 499.911 |
| 22 CENTS | 264.971 | 280.727 | 297.420 | 315.106 | 333.843 | 353.694 | 374.726 | 397.009 | 420.616 | 445.627 | 472.125 | 500.199 |
| 23 CENTS | 265.125 | 280.890 | 297.592 | 315.288 | 334.036 | 353.899 | 374.943 | 397.238 | 420.859 | 445.885 | 472.398 | 500.488 |
| 24 CENTS | 265.278 | 281.052 | 297.764 | 315.470 | 334.229 | 354.103 | 375.159 | 397.467 | 421.102 | 446.142 | 472.671 | 500.778 |
| 25 CENTS | 265.431 | 281.214 | 297.936 | 315.652 | 334.422 | 354.308 | 375.376 | 397.697 | 421.345 | 446.400 | 472.944 | 501.067 |
| 26 CENTS | 265.584 | 281.377 | 298.108 | 315.835 | 334.615 | 354.513 | 375.593 | 397.927 | 421.589 | 446.658 | 473.218 | 501.357 |
| 27 CENTS | 265.738 | 281.539 | 298.281 | 316.017 | 334.809 | 354.717 | 375.810 | 398.157 | 421.832 | 446.916 | 473.491 | 501.646 |
| 28 CENTS | 265.891 | 281.702 | 298.453 | 316.200 | 335.002 | 354.922 | 376.027 | 398.387 | 422.076 | 447.174 | 473.765 | 501.936 |
| 29 CENTS | 266.045 | 281.865 | 298.625 | 316.383 | 335.196 | 355.127 | 376.244 | 398.617 | 422.320 | 447.433 | 474.038 | 502.226 |
| 30 CENTS | 266.199 | 282.028 | 298.798 | 316.565 | 335.389 | 355.333 | 376.462 | 398.847 | 422.564 | 447.691 | 474.312 | 502.516 |
| 31 CENTS | 266.353 | 282.191 | 298.971 | 316.748 | 335.583 | 355.539 | 376.679 | 399.078 | 422.808 | 447.950 | 474.586 | 502.807 |
| 32 CENTS | 266.506 | 282.354 | 299.143 | 316.931 | 335.777 | 355.743 | 376.897 | 399.308 | 423.053 | 448.209 | 474.860 | 503.097 |
| 33 CENTS | 266.660 | 282.517 | 299.316 | 317.114 | 335.971 | 355.949 | 377.115 | 399.539 | 423.297 | 448.468 | 475.135 | 503.388 |
| 34 CENTS | 266.814 | 282.680 | 299.489 | 317.298 | 336.165 | 356.155 | 377.333 | 399.770 | 423.542 | 448.727 | 475.409 | 503.679 |
| 35 CENTS | 266.969 | 282.843 | 299.662 | 317.481 | 336.359 | 356.360 | 377.551 | 400.001 | 423.786 | 448.986 | 475.684 | 503.970 |
| 36 CENTS | 267.123 | 283.007 | 299.835 | 317.664 | 336.554 | 356.566 | 377.769 | 400.232 | 424.031 | 449.245 | 475.959 | 504.261 |
| 37 CENTS | 267.277 | 283.170 | 300.009 | 317.848 | 336.748 | 356.772 | 377.987 | 400.463 | 424.276 | 449.505 | 476.234 | 504.552 |
| 38 CENTS | 267.432 | 283.334 | 300.182 | 318.032 | 336.943 | 356.978 | 378.205 | 400.695 | 424.521 | 449.765 | 476.509 | 504.844 |
| 39 CENTS | 267.586 | 283.498 | 300.355 | 318.215 | 337.137 | 357.185 | 378.424 | 400.926 | 424.767 | 450.024 | 476.784 | 505.135 |
| 40 CENTS | 267.741 | 283.661 | 300.529 | 318.399 | 337.332 | 357.391 | 378.643 | 401.158 | 425.012 | 450.285 | 477.060 | 505.427 |
| 41 CENTS | 267.895 | 283.825 | 300.702 | 318.583 | 337.527 | 357.598 | 378.861 | 401.390 | 425.258 | 450.545 | 477.335 | 505.719 |
| 42 CENTS | 268.050 | 283.989 | 300.876 | 318.767 | 337.722 | 357.804 | 379.080 | 401.622 | 425.503 | 450.805 | 477.611 | 506.012 |
| 43 CENTS | 268.205 | 284.153 | 301.050 | 318.951 | 337.917 | 358.011 | 379.299 | 401.854 | 425.749 | 451.065 | 477.887 | 506.304 |
| 44 CENTS | 268.360 | 284.318 | 301.224 | 319.136 | 338.113 | 358.218 | 379.518 | 402.086 | 425.995 | 451.326 | 478.163 | 506.596 |
| 45 CENTS | 268.515 | 284.482 | 301.398 | 319.320 | 338.308 | 358.425 | 379.738 | 402.318 | 426.241 | 451.587 | 478.440 | 506.889 |
| 46 CENTS | 268.670 | 284.646 | 301.572 | 319.505 | 338.503 | 358.632 | 379.957 | 402.551 | 426.488 | 451.848 | 478.716 | 507.182 |
| 47 CENTS | 268.826 | 284.811 | 301.746 | 319.689 | 338.699 | 358.839 | 380.177 | 402.783 | 426.734 | 452.109 | 478.993 | 507.475 |
| 48 CENTS | 268.981 | 284.975 | 301.921 | 319.874 | 338.895 | 359.046 | 380.396 | 403.016 | 426.981 | 452.370 | 479.269 | 507.768 |
| 49 CENTS | 269.136 | 285.140 | 302.095 | 320.059 | 339.090 | 359.254 | 380.616 | 403.249 | 427.227 | 452.631 | 479.546 | 508.062 |
| 50 CENTS | 269.292 | 285.305 | 302.270 | 320.244 | 339.286 | 359.461 | 380.836 | 403.482 | 427.474 | 452.893 | 479.823 | 508.355 |

# OCTAVE 4

| OCTAVE 4 | C | C# | D | D# | E | F | F# | G | G# | A | A# | B |
|---|---|---|---|---|---|---|---|---|---|---|---|---|
| -50 CENTS | 508.355 | 538.584 | 570.609 | 604.540 | 640.487 | 678.573 | 718.923 | 761.672 | 806.964 | 854.948 | 905.786 | 959.647 |
| -49 CENTS | 508.649 | 538.895 | 570.939 | 604.889 | 640.857 | 678.965 | 719.338 | 762.112 | 807.430 | 855.442 | 906.309 | 960.201 |
| -48 CENTS | 508.943 | 539.206 | 571.269 | 605.239 | 641.228 | 679.357 | 719.754 | 762.553 | 807.896 | 855.936 | 906.833 | 960.756 |
| -47 CENTS | 509.237 | 539.518 | 571.599 | 605.588 | 641.598 | 679.750 | 720.170 | 762.993 | 808.363 | 856.431 | 907.357 | 961.311 |
| -46 CENTS | 509.531 | 539.829 | 571.929 | 605.938 | 641.969 | 680.142 | 720.586 | 763.434 | 808.830 | 856.926 | 907.881 | 961.867 |
| -45 CENTS | 509.825 | 540.141 | 572.260 | 606.288 | 642.340 | 680.535 | 721.002 | 763.875 | 809.298 | 857.421 | 908.406 | 962.422 |
| -44 CENTS | 510.120 | 540.453 | 572.590 | 606.638 | 642.711 | 680.929 | 721.419 | 764.317 | 809.765 | 857.916 | 908.931 | 962.978 |
| -43 CENTS | 510.415 | 540.766 | 572.921 | 606.989 | 643.082 | 681.322 | 721.836 | 764.758 | 810.233 | 858.412 | 909.456 | 963.535 |
| -42 CENTS | 510.710 | 541.078 | 573.252 | 607.340 | 643.454 | 681.716 | 722.253 | 765.200 | 810.701 | 858.908 | 909.981 | 964.092 |
| -41 CENTS | 511.005 | 541.391 | 573.584 | 607.691 | 643.826 | 682.110 | 722.670 | 765.642 | 811.170 | 859.404 | 910.507 | 964.649 |
| -40 CENTS | 511.300 | 541.704 | 573.915 | 608.042 | 644.198 | 682.504 | 723.087 | 766.084 | 811.638 | 859.901 | 911.033 | 965.206 |
| -39 CENTS | 511.595 | 542.017 | 574.247 | 608.393 | 644.570 | 682.898 | 723.505 | 766.527 | 812.107 | 860.398 | 911.560 | 965.764 |
| -38 CENTS | 511.891 | 542.330 | 574.578 | 608.745 | 644.942 | 683.293 | 723.923 | 766.970 | 812.576 | 860.895 | 912.086 | 966.322 |
| -37 CENTS | 512.187 | 542.643 | 574.910 | 609.096 | 645.315 | 683.687 | 724.342 | 767.413 | 813.046 | 861.392 | 912.613 | 966.880 |
| -36 CENTS | 512.483 | 542.957 | 575.242 | 609.448 | 645.688 | 684.082 | 724.760 | 767.857 | 813.516 | 861.890 | 913.141 | 967.439 |
| -35 CENTS | 512.779 | 543.270 | 575.575 | 609.800 | 646.061 | 684.478 | 725.179 | 768.300 | 813.986 | 862.388 | 913.668 | 967.998 |
| -34 CENTS | 513.075 | 543.584 | 575.907 | 610.153 | 646.434 | 684.873 | 725.598 | 768.744 | 814.456 | 862.886 | 914.196 | 968.557 |
| -33 CENTS | 513.372 | 543.898 | 576.240 | 610.505 | 646.808 | 685.269 | 726.017 | 769.188 | 814.927 | 863.385 | 914.724 | 969.117 |
| -32 CENTS | 513.668 | 544.213 | 576.573 | 610.858 | 647.181 | 685.665 | 726.437 | 769.633 | 815.397 | 863.884 | 915.253 | 969.677 |
| -31 CENTS | 513.965 | 544.527 | 576.906 | 611.211 | 647.555 | 686.061 | 726.856 | 770.077 | 815.869 | 864.383 | 915.782 | 970.237 |
| -30 CENTS | 514.262 | 544.842 | 577.240 | 611.564 | 647.930 | 686.457 | 727.276 | 770.522 | 816.340 | 864.882 | 916.311 | 970.797 |
| -29 CENTS | 514.559 | 545.156 | 577.573 | 611.917 | 648.304 | 686.854 | 727.696 | 770.968 | 816.812 | 865.382 | 916.840 | 971.358 |
| -28 CENTS | 514.856 | 545.471 | 577.907 | 612.271 | 648.678 | 687.251 | 728.117 | 771.413 | 817.284 | 865.882 | 917.370 | 971.920 |
| -27 CENTS | 515.154 | 545.787 | 578.241 | 612.625 | 649.053 | 687.648 | 728.538 | 771.859 | 817.756 | 866.382 | 917.900 | 972.481 |
| -26 CENTS | 515.452 | 546.102 | 578.575 | 612.979 | 649.428 | 688.045 | 728.959 | 772.305 | 818.228 | 866.883 | 918.430 | 973.043 |
| -25 CENTS | 515.749 | 546.417 | 578.909 | 613.333 | 649.804 | 688.443 | 729.380 | 772.751 | 818.701 | 867.384 | 918.961 | 973.605 |
| -24 CENTS | 516.047 | 546.733 | 579.244 | 613.687 | 650.179 | 688.841 | 729.801 | 773.197 | 819.174 | 867.885 | 919.492 | 974.168 |
| -23 CENTS | 516.346 | 547.049 | 579.578 | 614.042 | 650.555 | 689.239 | 730.223 | 773.644 | 819.647 | 868.386 | 920.023 | 974.731 |
| -22 CENTS | 516.644 | 547.365 | 579.913 | 614.397 | 650.931 | 689.637 | 730.645 | 774.091 | 820.121 | 868.888 | 920.555 | 975.294 |
| -21 CENTS | 516.942 | 547.681 | 580.248 | 614.752 | 651.307 | 690.035 | 731.067 | 774.538 | 820.595 | 869.390 | 921.087 | 975.857 |
| -20 CENTS | 517.241 | 547.998 | 580.583 | 615.107 | 651.683 | 690.434 | 731.489 | 774.986 | 821.069 | 869.892 | 921.619 | 976.421 |
| -19 CENTS | 517.540 | 548.314 | 580.919 | 615.462 | 652.059 | 690.833 | 731.912 | 775.434 | 821.543 | 870.395 | 922.151 | 976.985 |
| -18 CENTS | 517.839 | 548.631 | 581.255 | 615.818 | 652.436 | 691.232 | 732.335 | 775.882 | 822.018 | 870.898 | 922.684 | 977.550 |
| -17 CENTS | 518.138 | 548.948 | 581.590 | 616.174 | 652.813 | 691.631 | 732.758 | 776.330 | 822.493 | 871.401 | 923.217 | 978.115 |
| -16 CENTS | 518.438 | 549.265 | 581.926 | 616.530 | 653.190 | 692.031 | 733.181 | 776.779 | 822.968 | 871.905 | 923.751 | 978.680 |
| -15 CENTS | 518.737 | 549.583 | 582.263 | 616.886 | 653.568 | 692.431 | 733.605 | 777.227 | 823.444 | 872.408 | 924.284 | 979.245 |
| -14 CENTS | 519.037 | 549.900 | 582.599 | 617.242 | 653.945 | 692.831 | 734.029 | 777.677 | 823.920 | 872.912 | 924.818 | 979.811 |
| -13 CENTS | 519.337 | 550.218 | 582.936 | 617.599 | 654.323 | 693.231 | 734.453 | 778.126 | 824.396 | 873.417 | 925.353 | 980.377 |
| -12 CENTS | 519.637 | 550.536 | 583.273 | 617.956 | 654.701 | 693.632 | 734.877 | 778.575 | 824.872 | 873.921 | 925.887 | 980.944 |
| -11 CENTS | 519.937 | 550.854 | 583.610 | 618.313 | 655.080 | 694.033 | 735.302 | 779.025 | 825.349 | 874.426 | 926.422 | 981.510 |
| -10 CENTS | 520.237 | 551.172 | 583.947 | 618.670 | 655.458 | 694.434 | 735.727 | 779.475 | 825.825 | 874.932 | 926.958 | 982.077 |
| -9 CENTS | 520.538 | 551.491 | 584.284 | 619.028 | 655.837 | 694.835 | 736.152 | 779.926 | 826.303 | 875.437 | 927.493 | 982.645 |
| -8 CENTS | 520.839 | 551.809 | 584.622 | 619.385 | 656.216 | 695.236 | 736.577 | 780.376 | 826.780 | 875.943 | 928.029 | 983.213 |
| -7 CENTS | 521.140 | 552.128 | 584.960 | 619.743 | 656.595 | 695.638 | 737.003 | 780.827 | 827.258 | 876.449 | 928.565 | 983.781 |
| -6 CENTS | 521.441 | 552.447 | 585.298 | 620.101 | 656.974 | 696.040 | 737.429 | 781.278 | 827.736 | 876.955 | 929.102 | 984.349 |
| -5 CENTS | 521.742 | 552.767 | 585.636 | 620.459 | 657.354 | 696.442 | 737.855 | 781.730 | 828.214 | 877.462 | 929.639 | 984.918 |
| -4 CENTS | 522.044 | 553.086 | 585.974 | 620.818 | 657.734 | 696.845 | 738.281 | 782.182 | 828.692 | 877.965 | 930.176 | 985.487 |
| -3 CENTS | 522.345 | 553.405 | 586.313 | 621.177 | 658.114 | 697.247 | 738.708 | 782.633 | 829.171 | 878.476 | 930.713 | 986.056 |

FLAT

SHARP — A=440

| | | | | | | | | | | | | |
|---|---|---|---|---|---|---|---|---|---|---|---|---|
| -2 CENTS | 522.647 | 553.725 | 586.651 | 621.536 | 658.494 | 697.650 | 739.134 | 783.086 | 829.650 | 878.984 | 931.251 | 986.626 |
| -1 CENTS | 522.949 | 554.045 | 586.990 | 621.895 | 658.874 | 698.053 | 739.562 | 783.538 | 830.130 | 879.492 | 931.789 | 987.196 |
| 0 CENTS | 523.251 | 554.365 | 587.330 | 622.254 | 659.255 | 698.456 | 739.989 | 783.991 | 830.609 | 880.000 | 932.328 | 987.767 |
| 1 CENTS | 523.553 | 554.686 | 587.669 | 622.613 | 659.636 | 698.860 | 740.416 | 784.444 | 831.089 | 880.508 | 932.866 | 988.337 |
| 2 CENTS | 523.856 | 555.006 | 588.008 | 622.973 | 660.017 | 699.264 | 740.844 | 784.897 | 831.570 | 881.017 | 933.405 | 988.908 |
| 3 CENTS | 524.159 | 555.327 | 588.348 | 623.333 | 660.399 | 699.668 | 741.272 | 785.351 | 832.050 | 881.526 | 933.945 | 989.480 |
| 4 CENTS | 524.461 | 555.648 | 588.688 | 623.693 | 660.780 | 700.072 | 741.701 | 785.804 | 832.531 | 882.036 | 934.484 | 990.051 |
| 5 CENTS | 524.765 | 555.969 | 589.028 | 624.054 | 661.162 | 700.477 | 742.129 | 786.258 | 833.012 | 882.545 | 935.024 | 990.624 |
| 6 CENTS | 525.068 | 556.290 | 589.369 | 624.414 | 661.544 | 700.881 | 742.558 | 786.713 | 833.493 | 883.055 | 935.564 | 991.196 |
| 7 CENTS | 525.371 | 556.611 | 589.709 | 624.775 | 661.926 | 701.286 | 742.987 | 787.167 | 833.975 | 883.565 | 936.105 | 991.769 |
| 8 CENTS | 525.675 | 556.933 | 590.050 | 625.136 | 662.309 | 701.691 | 743.416 | 787.622 | 834.457 | 884.076 | 936.646 | 992.342 |
| 9 CENTS | 525.978 | 557.255 | 590.391 | 625.497 | 662.691 | 702.097 | 743.846 | 788.077 | 834.939 | 884.587 | 937.187 | 992.915 |
| 10 CENTS | 526.282 | 557.577 | 590.732 | 625.859 | 663.074 | 702.503 | 744.276 | 788.532 | 835.421 | 885.098 | 937.728 | 993.489 |
| 11 CENTS | 526.586 | 557.899 | 591.073 | 626.220 | 663.457 | 702.908 | 744.706 | 788.988 | 835.904 | 885.609 | 938.270 | 994.063 |
| 12 CENTS | 526.891 | 558.221 | 591.415 | 626.582 | 663.841 | 703.315 | 745.136 | 789.444 | 836.387 | 886.121 | 938.812 | 994.637 |
| 13 CENTS | 527.195 | 558.544 | 591.756 | 626.944 | 664.224 | 703.721 | 745.566 | 789.900 | 836.870 | 886.633 | 939.355 | 995.212 |
| 14 CENTS | 527.500 | 558.866 | 592.098 | 627.306 | 664.608 | 704.128 | 745.997 | 790.356 | 837.354 | 887.145 | 939.898 | 995.787 |
| 15 CENTS | 527.804 | 559.189 | 592.440 | 627.669 | 664.992 | 704.534 | 746.428 | 790.813 | 837.837 | 887.658 | 940.441 | 996.362 |
| 16 CENTS | 528.109 | 559.512 | 592.783 | 628.031 | 665.376 | 704.941 | 746.859 | 791.270 | 838.321 | 888.171 | 940.984 | 996.938 |
| 17 CENTS | 528.415 | 559.836 | 593.125 | 628.394 | 665.761 | 705.349 | 747.291 | 791.727 | 838.806 | 888.684 | 941.528 | 997.514 |
| 18 CENTS | 528.720 | 560.159 | 593.468 | 628.757 | 666.145 | 705.756 | 747.723 | 792.185 | 839.290 | 889.197 | 942.072 | 998.090 |
| 19 CENTS | 529.025 | 560.483 | 593.811 | 629.121 | 666.530 | 706.164 | 748.155 | 792.642 | 839.775 | 889.711 | 942.616 | 998.667 |
| 20 CENTS | 529.331 | 560.807 | 594.154 | 629.484 | 666.915 | 706.572 | 748.587 | 793.100 | 840.261 | 890.225 | 943.161 | 999.244 |
| 21 CENTS | 529.637 | 561.131 | 594.497 | 629.848 | 667.301 | 706.980 | 749.020 | 793.559 | 840.746 | 890.739 | 943.706 | 999.821 |
| 22 CENTS | 529.943 | 561.455 | 594.841 | 630.212 | 667.686 | 707.389 | 749.452 | 794.017 | 841.232 | 891.254 | 944.251 | 1000.399 |
| 23 CENTS | 530.249 | 561.779 | 595.184 | 630.576 | 668.072 | 707.798 | 749.885 | 794.476 | 841.718 | 891.769 | 944.796 | 1000.977 |
| 24 CENTS | 530.555 | 562.104 | 595.528 | 630.940 | 668.458 | 708.207 | 750.319 | 794.935 | 842.204 | 892.284 | 945.342 | 1001.555 |
| 25 CENTS | 530.862 | 562.429 | 595.872 | 631.305 | 668.844 | 708.616 | 750.752 | 795.394 | 842.691 | 892.800 | 945.889 | 1002.134 |
| 26 CENTS | 531.169 | 562.754 | 596.217 | 631.670 | 669.231 | 709.025 | 751.186 | 795.854 | 843.178 | 893.316 | 946.435 | 1002.713 |
| 27 CENTS | 531.476 | 563.079 | 596.561 | 632.035 | 669.617 | 709.435 | 751.620 | 796.314 | 843.665 | 893.832 | 946.982 | 1003.292 |
| 28 CENTS | 531.783 | 563.404 | 596.906 | 632.400 | 670.004 | 709.845 | 752.054 | 796.774 | 844.152 | 894.348 | 947.529 | 1003.872 |
| 29 CENTS | 532.090 | 563.730 | 597.251 | 632.765 | 670.391 | 710.255 | 752.489 | 797.234 | 844.640 | 894.865 | 948.077 | 1004.452 |
| 30 CENTS | 532.397 | 564.055 | 597.596 | 633.131 | 670.779 | 710.665 | 752.924 | 797.695 | 845.128 | 895.382 | 948.624 | 1005.032 |
| 31 CENTS | 532.705 | 564.381 | 597.941 | 633.497 | 671.166 | 711.076 | 753.359 | 798.156 | 845.616 | 895.899 | 949.172 | 1005.613 |
| 32 CENTS | 533.013 | 564.707 | 598.287 | 633.863 | 671.554 | 711.487 | 753.794 | 798.617 | 846.105 | 896.417 | 949.721 | 1006.194 |
| 33 CENTS | 533.321 | 565.034 | 598.632 | 634.229 | 671.942 | 711.898 | 754.229 | 799.078 | 846.594 | 896.935 | 950.270 | 1006.776 |
| 34 CENTS | 533.629 | 565.360 | 598.978 | 634.595 | 672.330 | 712.309 | 754.665 | 799.540 | 847.083 | 897.453 | 950.819 | 1007.357 |
| 35 CENTS | 533.937 | 565.687 | 599.324 | 634.962 | 672.719 | 712.721 | 755.101 | 800.002 | 847.573 | 897.972 | 951.368 | 1007.939 |
| 36 CENTS | 534.246 | 566.014 | 599.671 | 635.329 | 673.107 | 713.133 | 755.538 | 800.464 | 848.062 | 898.491 | 951.918 | 1008.522 |
| 37 CENTS | 534.554 | 566.341 | 600.017 | 635.696 | 673.496 | 713.545 | 755.974 | 800.927 | 848.552 | 899.010 | 952.468 | 1009.104 |
| 38 CENTS | 534.863 | 566.668 | 600.364 | 636.063 | 673.886 | 713.957 | 756.411 | 801.389 | 849.043 | 899.529 | 953.018 | 1009.687 |
| 39 CENTS | 535.172 | 566.995 | 600.711 | 636.431 | 674.275 | 714.369 | 756.848 | 801.852 | 849.533 | 900.049 | 953.569 | 1010.271 |
| 40 CENTS | 535.482 | 567.323 | 601.058 | 636.798 | 674.664 | 714.782 | 757.285 | 802.316 | 850.024 | 900.569 | 954.120 | 1010.855 |
| 41 CENTS | 535.791 | 567.651 | 601.405 | 637.166 | 675.054 | 715.195 | 757.723 | 802.779 | 850.515 | 901.089 | 954.671 | 1011.439 |
| 42 CENTS | 536.101 | 567.979 | 601.752 | 637.535 | 675.444 | 715.608 | 758.161 | 803.243 | 851.007 | 901.610 | 955.223 | 1012.023 |
| 43 CENTS | 536.410 | 568.307 | 602.100 | 637.903 | 675.835 | 716.022 | 758.599 | 803.707 | 851.498 | 902.131 | 955.774 | 1012.608 |
| 44 CENTS | 536.720 | 568.635 | 602.448 | 638.271 | 676.225 | 716.436 | 759.037 | 804.172 | 851.990 | 902.652 | 956.327 | 1013.193 |
| 45 CENTS | 537.030 | 568.964 | 602.796 | 638.640 | 676.616 | 716.849 | 759.476 | 804.636 | 852.482 | 903.174 | 956.879 | 1013.778 |
| 46 CENTS | 537.341 | 569.293 | 603.144 | 639.009 | 677.007 | 717.264 | 759.914 | 805.101 | 852.975 | 903.696 | 957.432 | 1014.364 |
| 47 CENTS | 537.651 | 569.621 | 603.493 | 639.378 | 677.398 | 717.678 | 760.353 | 805.566 | 853.468 | 904.218 | 957.985 | 1014.950 |
| 48 CENTS | 537.962 | 569.951 | 603.842 | 639.748 | 677.789 | 718.093 | 760.793 | 806.032 | 853.961 | 904.740 | 958.539 | 1015.537 |
| 49 CENTS | 538.273 | 570.280 | 604.191 | 640.118 | 678.181 | 718.508 | 761.232 | 806.498 | 854.454 | 905.263 | 959.093 | 1016.123 |
| 50 CENTS | 538.584 | 570.609 | 604.540 | 640.487 | 678.573 | 718.923 | 761.672 | 806.964 | 854.948 | 905.786 | 959.647 | 1016.710 |

# OCTAVE 5

FLAT

| OCTAVE 5 | C | C# | D | D# | E | F | F# | G | G# | A | A# | B |
|---|---|---|---|---|---|---|---|---|---|---|---|---|
| -50 CENTS | 1016.710 | 1077.167 | 1141.219 | 1209.079 | 1280.975 | 1357.146 | 1437.846 | 1523.344 | 1613.927 | 1709.896 | 1811.572 | 1919.294 |
| -49 CENTS | 1017.298 | 1077.789 | 1141.878 | 1209.778 | 1281.715 | 1357.930 | 1438.676 | 1524.225 | 1614.860 | 1710.884 | 1812.619 | 1920.403 |
| -48 CENTS | 1017.886 | 1078.412 | 1142.538 | 1210.477 | 1282.455 | 1358.714 | 1439.508 | 1525.105 | 1615.793 | 1711.873 | 1813.666 | 1921.512 |
| -47 CENTS | 1018.474 | 1079.035 | 1143.198 | 1211.176 | 1283.196 | 1359.499 | 1440.339 | 1525.986 | 1616.726 | 1712.862 | 1814.714 | 1922.622 |
| -46 CENTS | 1019.062 | 1079.659 | 1143.859 | 1211.876 | 1283.938 | 1360.285 | 1441.172 | 1526.868 | 1617.660 | 1713.851 | 1815.762 | 1923.733 |
| -45 CENTS | 1019.651 | 1080.283 | 1144.520 | 1212.576 | 1284.680 | 1361.071 | 1442.004 | 1527.750 | 1618.595 | 1714.842 | 1816.812 | 1924.845 |
| -44 CENTS | 1020.240 | 1080.907 | 1145.181 | 1213.277 | 1285.422 | 1361.857 | 1442.837 | 1528.633 | 1619.530 | 1715.833 | 1817.861 | 1925.957 |
| -43 CENTS | 1020.830 | 1081.531 | 1145.843 | 1213.978 | 1286.165 | 1362.644 | 1443.671 | 1529.516 | 1620.466 | 1716.824 | 1818.912 | 1927.070 |
| -42 CENTS | 1021.419 | 1082.156 | 1146.505 | 1214.679 | 1286.908 | 1363.431 | 1444.505 | 1530.400 | 1621.402 | 1717.816 | 1819.963 | 1928.183 |
| -41 CENTS | 1022.010 | 1082.781 | 1147.167 | 1215.381 | 1287.651 | 1364.219 | 1445.340 | 1531.284 | 1622.339 | 1718.808 | 1821.014 | 1929.297 |
| -40 CENTS | 1022.600 | 1083.407 | 1147.830 | 1216.083 | 1288.395 | 1365.007 | 1446.175 | 1532.169 | 1623.277 | 1719.802 | 1822.066 | 1930.412 |
| -39 CENTS | 1023.191 | 1084.033 | 1148.493 | 1216.786 | 1289.140 | 1365.796 | 1447.011 | 1533.054 | 1624.214 | 1720.795 | 1823.119 | 1931.527 |
| -38 CENTS | 1023.782 | 1084.659 | 1149.157 | 1217.489 | 1289.885 | 1366.585 | 1447.847 | 1533.940 | 1625.153 | 1721.789 | 1824.172 | 1932.643 |
| -37 CENTS | 1024.374 | 1085.286 | 1149.821 | 1218.192 | 1290.630 | 1367.375 | 1448.683 | 1534.826 | 1626.092 | 1722.784 | 1825.226 | 1933.760 |
| -36 CENTS | 1024.966 | 1085.913 | 1150.485 | 1218.896 | 1291.376 | 1368.165 | 1449.520 | 1535.713 | 1627.031 | 1723.780 | 1826.281 | 1934.877 |
| -35 CENTS | 1025.558 | 1086.541 | 1151.150 | 1219.601 | 1292.122 | 1368.955 | 1450.358 | 1536.600 | 1627.971 | 1724.776 | 1827.336 | 1935.995 |
| -34 CENTS | 1026.150 | 1087.168 | 1151.815 | 1220.305 | 1292.868 | 1369.746 | 1451.196 | 1537.488 | 1628.912 | 1725.772 | 1828.392 | 1937.114 |
| -33 CENTS | 1026.743 | 1087.797 | 1152.480 | 1221.010 | 1293.615 | 1370.538 | 1452.034 | 1538.377 | 1629.853 | 1726.769 | 1829.448 | 1938.233 |
| -32 CENTS | 1027.336 | 1088.425 | 1153.146 | 1221.716 | 1294.363 | 1371.330 | 1452.873 | 1539.265 | 1630.795 | 1727.767 | 1830.505 | 1939.353 |
| -31 CENTS | 1027.930 | 1089.054 | 1153.812 | 1222.422 | 1295.111 | 1372.122 | 1453.713 | 1540.155 | 1631.737 | 1728.765 | 1831.563 | 1940.474 |
| -30 CENTS | 1028.524 | 1089.683 | 1154.479 | 1223.128 | 1295.859 | 1372.915 | 1454.553 | 1541.045 | 1632.680 | 1729.764 | 1832.621 | 1941.595 |
| -29 CENTS | 1029.118 | 1090.313 | 1155.146 | 1223.835 | 1296.608 | 1373.708 | 1455.393 | 1541.935 | 1633.623 | 1730.764 | 1833.680 | 1942.717 |
| -28 CENTS | 1029.713 | 1090.943 | 1155.814 | 1224.542 | 1297.357 | 1374.502 | 1456.234 | 1542.826 | 1634.567 | 1731.764 | 1834.740 | 1943.839 |
| -27 CENTS | 1030.308 | 1091.573 | 1156.481 | 1225.249 | 1298.107 | 1375.296 | 1457.075 | 1543.717 | 1635.512 | 1732.764 | 1835.800 | 1944.962 |
| -26 CENTS | 1030.903 | 1092.204 | 1157.150 | 1225.957 | 1298.857 | 1376.091 | 1457.917 | 1544.609 | 1636.457 | 1733.765 | 1836.861 | 1946.086 |
| -25 CENTS | 1031.499 | 1092.835 | 1157.818 | 1226.666 | 1299.607 | 1376.886 | 1458.760 | 1545.502 | 1637.402 | 1734.767 | 1837.922 | 1947.210 |
| -24 CENTS | 1032.095 | 1093.466 | 1158.487 | 1227.374 | 1300.358 | 1377.681 | 1459.602 | 1546.395 | 1638.348 | 1735.770 | 1838.984 | 1948.335 |
| -23 CENTS | 1032.691 | 1094.098 | 1159.157 | 1228.084 | 1301.109 | 1378.477 | 1460.446 | 1547.288 | 1639.295 | 1736.772 | 1840.046 | 1949.461 |
| -22 CENTS | 1033.288 | 1094.730 | 1159.826 | 1228.793 | 1301.861 | 1379.274 | 1461.290 | 1548.182 | 1640.242 | 1737.776 | 1841.109 | 1950.588 |
| -21 CENTS | 1033.885 | 1095.363 | 1160.496 | 1229.503 | 1302.613 | 1380.071 | 1462.134 | 1549.077 | 1641.190 | 1738.780 | 1842.173 | 1951.715 |
| -20 CENTS | 1034.482 | 1095.996 | 1161.167 | 1230.214 | 1303.366 | 1380.868 | 1462.979 | 1549.972 | 1642.138 | 1739.785 | 1843.238 | 1952.842 |
| -19 CENTS | 1035.080 | 1096.629 | 1161.838 | 1230.924 | 1304.119 | 1381.666 | 1463.824 | 1550.867 | 1643.087 | 1740.790 | 1844.303 | 1953.971 |
| -18 CENTS | 1035.678 | 1097.263 | 1162.509 | 1231.636 | 1304.872 | 1382.464 | 1464.670 | 1551.764 | 1644.036 | 1741.796 | 1845.368 | 1955.100 |
| -17 CENTS | 1036.276 | 1097.897 | 1163.181 | 1232.347 | 1305.626 | 1383.263 | 1465.516 | 1552.660 | 1644.986 | 1742.802 | 1846.435 | 1956.229 |
| -16 CENTS | 1036.875 | 1098.531 | 1163.853 | 1233.059 | 1306.381 | 1384.062 | 1466.363 | 1553.557 | 1645.937 | 1743.809 | 1847.501 | 1957.360 |
| -15 CENTS | 1037.474 | 1099.166 | 1164.525 | 1233.772 | 1307.136 | 1384.862 | 1467.210 | 1554.455 | 1646.888 | 1744.817 | 1848.569 | 1958.490 |
| -14 CENTS | 1038.074 | 1099.801 | 1165.198 | 1234.485 | 1307.891 | 1385.662 | 1468.058 | 1555.353 | 1647.839 | 1745.825 | 1849.637 | 1959.622 |
| -13 CENTS | 1038.673 | 1100.436 | 1165.871 | 1235.193 | 1308.646 | 1386.463 | 1468.906 | 1556.252 | 1648.791 | 1746.833 | 1850.706 | 1960.754 |
| -12 CENTS | 1039.274 | 1101.072 | 1166.545 | 1235.911 | 1309.403 | 1387.264 | 1469.755 | 1557.151 | 1649.744 | 1747.843 | 1851.775 | 1961.887 |
| -11 CENTS | 1039.874 | 1101.708 | 1167.219 | 1236.626 | 1310.159 | 1388.065 | 1470.604 | 1558.051 | 1650.697 | 1748.853 | 1852.845 | 1963.021 |
| -10 CENTS | 1040.475 | 1102.345 | 1167.894 | 1237.340 | 1310.916 | 1388.867 | 1471.454 | 1558.951 | 1651.651 | 1749.863 | 1853.915 | 1964.155 |
| -9 CENTS | 1041.076 | 1102.982 | 1168.568 | 1238.055 | 1311.674 | 1389.670 | 1472.304 | 1559.852 | 1652.605 | 1750.874 | 1854.987 | 1965.290 |
| -8 CENTS | 1041.678 | 1103.619 | 1169.244 | 1238.770 | 1312.431 | 1390.473 | 1473.155 | 1560.753 | 1653.560 | 1751.886 | 1856.058 | 1966.425 |
| -7 CENTS | 1042.279 | 1104.257 | 1169.919 | 1239.486 | 1313.190 | 1391.276 | 1474.006 | 1561.655 | 1654.515 | 1752.898 | 1857.131 | 1967.562 |
| -6 CENTS | 1042.882 | 1104.895 | 1170.595 | 1240.202 | 1313.949 | 1392.080 | 1474.857 | 1562.557 | 1655.471 | 1753.911 | 1858.204 | 1968.698 |
| -5 CENTS | 1043.484 | 1105.533 | 1171.271 | 1240.919 | 1314.708 | 1392.884 | 1475.710 | 1563.460 | 1656.428 | 1754.924 | 1859.277 | 1969.836 |
| -4 CENTS | 1044.087 | 1106.172 | 1171.948 | 1241.635 | 1315.467 | 1393.689 | 1476.562 | 1564.363 | 1657.385 | 1755.938 | 1860.352 | 1970.974 |
| -3 CENTS | 1044.690 | 1106.811 | 1172.625 | 1242.353 | 1316.227 | 1394.494 | 1477.415 | 1565.267 | 1658.343 | 1756.953 | 1861.427 | 1972.113 |

SHARP — A=440

| | | | | | | | | | | | | |
|---|---|---|---|---|---|---|---|---|---|---|---|---|
| -2 CENTS | 1045.294 | 1107.450 | 1173.303 | 1243.071 | 1316.988 | 1395.300 | 1478.269 | 1566.171 | 1659.301 | 1757.968 | 1862.502 | 1973.252 |
| -1 CENTS | 1045.898 | 1108.090 | 1173.981 | 1243.789 | 1317.749 | 1396.106 | 1479.123 | 1567.076 | 1660.260 | 1758.984 | 1863.578 | 1974.392 |
| 0 CENTS | 1046.502 | 1108.731 | 1174.659 | 1244.508 | 1318.510 | 1396.913 | 1479.978 | 1567.982 | 1661.219 | 1760.000 | 1864.655 | 1975.533 |
| 1 CENTS | 1047.107 | 1109.371 | 1175.338 | 1245.227 | 1319.272 | 1397.720 | 1480.833 | 1568.888 | 1662.179 | 1761.017 | 1865.732 | 1976.675 |
| 2 CENTS | 1047.712 | 1110.012 | 1176.017 | 1245.946 | 1320.034 | 1398.528 | 1481.688 | 1569.794 | 1663.139 | 1762.034 | 1866.810 | 1977.817 |
| 3 CENTS | 1048.317 | 1110.653 | 1176.696 | 1246.666 | 1320.797 | 1399.336 | 1482.545 | 1570.701 | 1664.100 | 1763.052 | 1867.889 | 1978.960 |
| 4 CENTS | 1048.923 | 1111.295 | 1177.376 | 1247.387 | 1321.560 | 1400.144 | 1483.401 | 1571.609 | 1665.061 | 1764.071 | 1868.968 | 1980.103 |
| 5 CENTS | 1049.529 | 1111.937 | 1178.057 | 1248.107 | 1322.324 | 1400.953 | 1484.258 | 1572.517 | 1666.024 | 1765.090 | 1870.048 | 1981.247 |
| 6 CENTS | 1050.135 | 1112.580 | 1178.737 | 1248.829 | 1323.088 | 1401.763 | 1485.116 | 1573.425 | 1666.986 | 1766.110 | 1871.129 | 1982.392 |
| 7 CENTS | 1050.742 | 1113.223 | 1179.418 | 1249.550 | 1323.852 | 1402.573 | 1485.974 | 1574.334 | 1667.949 | 1767.131 | 1872.210 | 1983.537 |
| 8 CENTS | 1051.349 | 1113.866 | 1180.100 | 1250.272 | 1324.617 | 1403.383 | 1486.832 | 1575.244 | 1668.913 | 1768.152 | 1873.292 | 1984.683 |
| 9 CENTS | 1051.957 | 1114.509 | 1180.782 | 1250.994 | 1325.382 | 1404.194 | 1487.692 | 1576.154 | 1669.877 | 1769.173 | 1874.374 | 1985.830 |
| 10 CENTS | 1052.565 | 1115.153 | 1181.464 | 1251.717 | 1326.148 | 1405.005 | 1488.551 | 1577.065 | 1670.842 | 1770.196 | 1875.457 | 1986.977 |
| 11 CENTS | 1053.173 | 1115.798 | 1182.146 | 1252.441 | 1326.915 | 1405.817 | 1489.411 | 1577.976 | 1671.808 | 1771.218 | 1876.541 | 1988.125 |
| 12 CENTS | 1053.781 | 1116.442 | 1182.829 | 1253.164 | 1327.681 | 1406.629 | 1490.272 | 1578.888 | 1672.773 | 1772.242 | 1877.625 | 1989.274 |
| 13 CENTS | 1054.390 | 1117.087 | 1183.513 | 1253.888 | 1328.448 | 1407.442 | 1491.133 | 1579.800 | 1673.740 | 1773.266 | 1878.710 | 1990.424 |
| 14 CENTS | 1054.999 | 1117.733 | 1184.197 | 1254.613 | 1329.216 | 1408.255 | 1491.994 | 1580.713 | 1674.707 | 1774.290 | 1879.795 | 1991.574 |
| 15 CENTS | 1055.609 | 1118.379 | 1184.881 | 1255.339 | 1329.984 | 1409.069 | 1492.856 | 1581.626 | 1675.675 | 1775.315 | 1880.881 | 1992.724 |
| 16 CENTS | 1056.219 | 1119.025 | 1185.566 | 1256.063 | 1330.752 | 1409.883 | 1493.719 | 1582.540 | 1676.643 | 1776.341 | 1881.968 | 1993.876 |
| 17 CENTS | 1056.829 | 1119.671 | 1186.251 | 1256.789 | 1331.521 | 1410.698 | 1494.582 | 1583.455 | 1677.612 | 1777.368 | 1883.055 | 1995.028 |
| 18 CENTS | 1057.440 | 1120.318 | 1186.936 | 1257.515 | 1332.291 | 1411.513 | 1495.446 | 1584.369 | 1678.581 | 1778.395 | 1884.143 | 1996.180 |
| 19 CENTS | 1058.051 | 1120.966 | 1187.622 | 1258.241 | 1333.060 | 1412.328 | 1496.310 | 1585.285 | 1679.551 | 1779.422 | 1885.232 | 1997.334 |
| 20 CENTS | 1058.662 | 1121.613 | 1188.308 | 1258.968 | 1333.831 | 1413.144 | 1497.174 | 1586.201 | 1680.521 | 1780.450 | 1886.321 | 1998.488 |
| 21 CENTS | 1059.274 | 1122.261 | 1188.995 | 1259.696 | 1334.601 | 1413.961 | 1498.039 | 1587.117 | 1681.492 | 1781.479 | 1887.411 | 1999.643 |
| 22 CENTS | 1059.886 | 1122.910 | 1189.682 | 1260.424 | 1335.372 | 1414.778 | 1498.905 | 1588.034 | 1682.464 | 1782.508 | 1888.502 | 2000.798 |
| 23 CENTS | 1060.498 | 1123.559 | 1190.369 | 1261.152 | 1336.144 | 1415.595 | 1499.771 | 1588.952 | 1683.436 | 1783.538 | 1889.593 | 2001.954 |
| 24 CENTS | 1061.111 | 1124.208 | 1191.057 | 1261.881 | 1336.916 | 1416.413 | 1500.637 | 1589.870 | 1684.409 | 1784.569 | 1890.685 | 2003.111 |
| 25 CENTS | 1061.724 | 1124.857 | 1191.745 | 1262.610 | 1337.688 | 1417.231 | 1501.504 | 1590.789 | 1685.382 | 1785.600 | 1891.777 | 2004.268 |
| 26 CENTS | 1062.337 | 1125.507 | 1192.433 | 1263.339 | 1338.461 | 1418.050 | 1502.372 | 1591.708 | 1686.356 | 1786.631 | 1892.870 | 2005.426 |
| 27 CENTS | 1062.951 | 1126.158 | 1193.122 | 1264.069 | 1339.235 | 1418.870 | 1503.240 | 1592.627 | 1687.330 | 1787.664 | 1893.964 | 2006.585 |
| 28 CENTS | 1063.565 | 1126.808 | 1193.812 | 1264.800 | 1340.008 | 1419.689 | 1504.109 | 1593.548 | 1688.305 | 1788.697 | 1895.058 | 2007.744 |
| 29 CENTS | 1064.180 | 1127.459 | 1194.502 | 1265.530 | 1340.783 | 1420.510 | 1504.978 | 1594.468 | 1689.280 | 1789.730 | 1896.153 | 2008.904 |
| 30 CENTS | 1064.795 | 1128.111 | 1195.192 | 1266.262 | 1341.557 | 1421.331 | 1505.847 | 1595.390 | 1690.256 | 1790.764 | 1897.249 | 2010.065 |
| 31 CENTS | 1065.410 | 1128.763 | 1195.882 | 1266.993 | 1342.333 | 1422.152 | 1506.717 | 1596.311 | 1691.233 | 1791.799 | 1898.345 | 2011.226 |
| 32 CENTS | 1066.026 | 1129.415 | 1196.573 | 1267.725 | 1343.108 | 1422.973 | 1507.588 | 1597.234 | 1692.210 | 1792.834 | 1899.442 | 2012.388 |
| 33 CENTS | 1066.642 | 1130.067 | 1197.265 | 1268.458 | 1343.884 | 1423.796 | 1508.459 | 1598.157 | 1693.188 | 1793.870 | 1900.539 | 2013.551 |
| 34 CENTS | 1067.258 | 1130.720 | 1197.956 | 1269.191 | 1344.661 | 1424.618 | 1509.331 | 1599.080 | 1694.166 | 1794.907 | 1901.637 | 2014.715 |
| 35 CENTS | 1067.874 | 1131.374 | 1198.649 | 1269.924 | 1345.438 | 1425.441 | 1510.203 | 1600.004 | 1695.145 | 1795.944 | 1902.736 | 2015.879 |
| 36 CENTS | 1068.491 | 1132.027 | 1199.341 | 1270.658 | 1346.215 | 1426.265 | 1511.075 | 1600.928 | 1696.125 | 1796.981 | 1903.835 | 2017.043 |
| 37 CENTS | 1069.109 | 1132.681 | 1200.034 | 1271.392 | 1346.993 | 1427.089 | 1511.948 | 1601.853 | 1697.105 | 1798.020 | 1904.935 | 2018.209 |
| 38 CENTS | 1069.727 | 1133.336 | 1200.727 | 1272.126 | 1347.771 | 1427.914 | 1512.822 | 1602.779 | 1698.085 | 1799.058 | 1906.036 | 2019.375 |
| 39 CENTS | 1070.345 | 1133.991 | 1201.421 | 1272.861 | 1348.550 | 1428.739 | 1513.696 | 1603.705 | 1699.066 | 1800.098 | 1907.137 | 2020.542 |
| 40 CENTS | 1070.963 | 1134.646 | 1202.115 | 1273.597 | 1349.329 | 1429.564 | 1514.571 | 1604.632 | 1700.048 | 1801.138 | 1908.239 | 2021.709 |
| 41 CENTS | 1071.582 | 1135.301 | 1202.810 | 1274.333 | 1350.109 | 1430.390 | 1515.446 | 1605.559 | 1701.030 | 1802.179 | 1909.342 | 2022.877 |
| 42 CENTS | 1072.201 | 1135.957 | 1203.505 | 1275.069 | 1350.889 | 1431.217 | 1516.321 | 1606.486 | 1702.013 | 1803.220 | 1910.445 | 2024.046 |
| 43 CENTS | 1072.821 | 1136.614 | 1204.200 | 1275.806 | 1351.669 | 1432.044 | 1517.197 | 1607.415 | 1702.996 | 1804.262 | 1911.549 | 2025.215 |
| 44 CENTS | 1073.440 | 1137.270 | 1204.896 | 1276.543 | 1352.450 | 1432.871 | 1518.074 | 1608.343 | 1703.980 | 1805.304 | 1912.653 | 2026.386 |
| 45 CENTS | 1074.061 | 1137.928 | 1205.592 | 1277.281 | 1353.232 | 1433.699 | 1518.951 | 1609.273 | 1704.965 | 1806.347 | 1913.758 | 2027.556 |
| 46 CENTS | 1074.681 | 1138.585 | 1206.289 | 1278.019 | 1354.013 | 1434.527 | 1519.829 | 1610.202 | 1705.950 | 1807.391 | 1914.864 | 2028.728 |
| 47 CENTS | 1075.302 | 1139.243 | 1206.986 | 1278.757 | 1354.796 | 1435.356 | 1520.707 | 1611.133 | 1706.936 | 1808.435 | 1915.971 | 2029.900 |
| 48 CENTS | 1075.923 | 1139.901 | 1207.683 | 1279.496 | 1355.579 | 1436.185 | 1521.586 | 1612.064 | 1707.922 | 1809.480 | 1917.078 | 2031.073 |
| 49 CENTS | 1076.545 | 1140.560 | 1208.381 | 1280.235 | 1356.362 | 1437.015 | 1522.465 | 1612.995 | 1708.909 | 1810.526 | 1918.185 | 2032.247 |
| 50 CENTS | 1077.167 | 1141.219 | 1209.079 | 1280.975 | 1357.146 | 1437.846 | 1523.344 | 1613.927 | 1709.896 | 1811.572 | 1919.294 | 2033.421 |

# OCTAVE 6

FLAT

| OCTAVE 6 | C | C# | D | D# | E | F | F# | G | G# | A | A# | B |
|---|---|---|---|---|---|---|---|---|---|---|---|---|
| -50 CENTS | 2033.421 | 2154.334 | 2282.438 | 2418.158 | 2561.950 | 2714.291 | 2875.691 | 3046.689 | 3227.854 | 3419.792 | 3623.144 | 3838.587 |
| -49 CENTS | 2034.596 | 2155.579 | 2283.756 | 2419.556 | 2563.430 | 2715.859 | 2877.353 | 3048.449 | 3229.719 | 3421.768 | 3625.237 | 3840.805 |
| -48 CENTS | 2035.771 | 2156.824 | 2285.076 | 2420.954 | 2564.911 | 2717.429 | 2879.015 | 3050.210 | 3231.585 | 3423.745 | 3627.332 | 3843.024 |
| -47 CENTS | 2036.947 | 2158.071 | 2286.396 | 2422.352 | 2566.393 | 2718.999 | 2880.679 | 3051.973 | 3233.453 | 3425.724 | 3629.428 | 3845.245 |
| -46 CENTS | 2038.124 | 2159.318 | 2287.717 | 2423.752 | 2567.876 | 2720.570 | 2882.343 | 3053.736 | 3235.321 | 3427.703 | 3631.525 | 3847.466 |
| -45 CENTS | 2039.302 | 2160.565 | 2289.039 | 2425.152 | 2569.359 | 2722.142 | 2884.009 | 3055.501 | 3237.190 | 3429.683 | 3633.623 | 3849.690 |
| -44 CENTS | 2040.480 | 2161.814 | 2290.362 | 2426.554 | 2570.844 | 2723.714 | 2885.675 | 3057.266 | 3239.061 | 3431.665 | 3635.723 | 3851.914 |
| -43 CENTS | 2041.659 | 2163.063 | 2291.685 | 2427.956 | 2572.329 | 2725.288 | 2887.342 | 3059.032 | 3240.932 | 3433.648 | 3637.823 | 3854.139 |
| -42 CENTS | 2042.839 | 2164.312 | 2293.009 | 2429.359 | 2573.816 | 2726.863 | 2889.010 | 3060.800 | 3242.805 | 3435.632 | 3639.925 | 3856.366 |
| -41 CENTS | 2044.019 | 2165.563 | 2294.334 | 2430.762 | 2575.303 | 2728.438 | 2890.680 | 3062.568 | 3244.678 | 3437.617 | 3642.028 | 3858.594 |
| -40 CENTS | 2045.200 | 2166.814 | 2295.660 | 2432.167 | 2576.791 | 2730.015 | 2892.350 | 3064.338 | 3246.553 | 3439.603 | 3644.133 | 3860.824 |
| -39 CENTS | 2046.382 | 2168.066 | 2296.986 | 2433.572 | 2578.280 | 2731.592 | 2894.021 | 3066.109 | 3248.429 | 3441.590 | 3646.238 | 3863.055 |
| -38 CENTS | 2047.564 | 2169.319 | 2298.313 | 2434.978 | 2579.769 | 2733.170 | 2895.693 | 3067.880 | 3250.306 | 3443.579 | 3648.345 | 3865.287 |
| -37 CENTS | 2048.747 | 2170.572 | 2299.641 | 2436.385 | 2581.260 | 2734.750 | 2897.366 | 3069.653 | 3252.184 | 3445.569 | 3650.453 | 3867.520 |
| -36 CENTS | 2049.931 | 2171.826 | 2300.970 | 2437.793 | 2582.751 | 2736.330 | 2899.040 | 3071.426 | 3254.063 | 3447.559 | 3652.562 | 3869.755 |
| -35 CENTS | 2051.116 | 2173.081 | 2302.299 | 2439.201 | 2584.244 | 2737.911 | 2900.715 | 3073.201 | 3255.943 | 3449.551 | 3654.672 | 3871.991 |
| -34 CENTS | 2052.301 | 2174.337 | 2303.630 | 2440.611 | 2585.737 | 2739.493 | 2902.391 | 3074.977 | 3257.824 | 3451.545 | 3656.784 | 3874.228 |
| -33 CENTS | 2053.486 | 2175.593 | 2304.961 | 2442.021 | 2587.231 | 2741.076 | 2904.068 | 3076.753 | 3259.707 | 3453.539 | 3658.897 | 3876.466 |
| -32 CENTS | 2054.673 | 2176.850 | 2306.292 | 2443.432 | 2588.726 | 2742.659 | 2905.746 | 3078.531 | 3261.590 | 3455.534 | 3661.011 | 3878.706 |
| -31 CENTS | 2055.860 | 2178.108 | 2307.625 | 2444.843 | 2590.221 | 2744.244 | 2907.425 | 3080.310 | 3263.474 | 3457.531 | 3663.126 | 3880.947 |
| -30 CENTS | 2057.048 | 2179.366 | 2308.958 | 2446.256 | 2591.718 | 2745.830 | 2909.105 | 3082.090 | 3265.360 | 3459.529 | 3665.243 | 3883.189 |
| -29 CENTS | 2058.236 | 2180.626 | 2310.292 | 2447.669 | 2593.215 | 2747.416 | 2910.786 | 3083.870 | 3267.247 | 3461.527 | 3667.361 | 3885.433 |
| -28 CENTS | 2059.426 | 2181.886 | 2311.627 | 2449.084 | 2594.714 | 2749.004 | 2912.468 | 3085.652 | 3269.135 | 3463.527 | 3669.479 | 3887.678 |
| -27 CENTS | 2060.616 | 2183.146 | 2312.963 | 2450.499 | 2596.213 | 2750.592 | 2914.151 | 3087.435 | 3271.023 | 3465.529 | 3671.600 | 3889.924 |
| -26 CENTS | 2061.806 | 2184.408 | 2314.299 | 2451.915 | 2597.713 | 2752.181 | 2915.834 | 3089.219 | 3272.913 | 3467.531 | 3673.721 | 3892.172 |
| -25 CENTS | 2062.998 | 2185.670 | 2315.636 | 2453.331 | 2599.214 | 2753.771 | 2917.519 | 3091.004 | 3274.804 | 3469.534 | 3675.844 | 3894.421 |
| -24 CENTS | 2064.190 | 2186.933 | 2316.974 | 2454.749 | 2600.716 | 2755.362 | 2919.205 | 3092.790 | 3276.697 | 3471.539 | 3677.968 | 3896.671 |
| -23 CENTS | 2065.382 | 2188.196 | 2318.313 | 2456.167 | 2602.218 | 2756.954 | 2920.891 | 3094.577 | 3278.590 | 3473.545 | 3680.093 | 3898.922 |
| -22 CENTS | 2066.576 | 2189.461 | 2319.653 | 2457.586 | 2603.722 | 2758.547 | 2922.579 | 3096.365 | 3280.484 | 3475.552 | 3682.219 | 3901.175 |
| -21 CENTS | 2067.770 | 2190.726 | 2320.993 | 2459.006 | 2605.226 | 2760.141 | 2924.268 | 3098.154 | 3282.380 | 3477.560 | 3684.347 | 3903.429 |
| -20 CENTS | 2068.964 | 2191.991 | 2322.334 | 2460.427 | 2606.732 | 2761.736 | 2925.957 | 3099.944 | 3284.276 | 3479.569 | 3686.475 | 3905.685 |
| -19 CENTS | 2070.160 | 2193.258 | 2323.676 | 2461.849 | 2608.238 | 2763.332 | 2927.648 | 3101.735 | 3286.174 | 3481.580 | 3688.605 | 3907.941 |
| -18 CENTS | 2071.356 | 2194.525 | 2325.018 | 2463.271 | 2609.745 | 2764.928 | 2929.340 | 3103.527 | 3288.072 | 3483.591 | 3690.737 | 3910.199 |
| -17 CENTS | 2072.553 | 2195.793 | 2326.362 | 2464.694 | 2611.253 | 2766.526 | 2931.032 | 3105.320 | 3289.972 | 3485.604 | 3692.869 | 3912.458 |
| -16 CENTS | 2073.750 | 2197.062 | 2327.706 | 2466.118 | 2612.761 | 2768.124 | 2932.726 | 3107.115 | 3291.873 | 3487.618 | 3695.003 | 3914.719 |
| -15 CENTS | 2074.948 | 2198.331 | 2329.051 | 2467.543 | 2614.271 | 2769.724 | 2934.420 | 3108.910 | 3293.775 | 3489.633 | 3697.138 | 3916.981 |
| -14 CENTS | 2076.147 | 2199.601 | 2330.396 | 2468.969 | 2615.782 | 2771.324 | 2936.116 | 3110.706 | 3295.678 | 3491.650 | 3699.274 | 3919.244 |
| -13 CENTS | 2077.347 | 2200.872 | 2331.743 | 2470.396 | 2617.293 | 2772.925 | 2937.812 | 3112.503 | 3297.583 | 3493.667 | 3701.411 | 3921.509 |
| -12 CENTS | 2078.547 | 2202.144 | 2333.090 | 2471.823 | 2618.805 | 2774.527 | 2939.509 | 3114.302 | 3299.488 | 3495.686 | 3703.550 | 3923.774 |
| -11 CENTS | 2079.748 | 2203.416 | 2334.438 | 2473.251 | 2620.318 | 2776.131 | 2941.208 | 3116.101 | 3301.394 | 3497.705 | 3705.690 | 3926.042 |
| -10 CENTS | 2080.950 | 2204.689 | 2335.787 | 2474.680 | 2621.832 | 2777.735 | 2942.907 | 3117.902 | 3303.302 | 3499.726 | 3707.831 | 3928.310 |
| -9 CENTS | 2082.152 | 2205.963 | 2337.137 | 2476.110 | 2623.347 | 2779.340 | 2944.608 | 3119.703 | 3305.210 | 3501.748 | 3709.973 | 3930.580 |
| -8 CENTS | 2083.355 | 2207.238 | 2338.487 | 2477.541 | 2624.863 | 2780.945 | 2946.309 | 3121.506 | 3307.120 | 3503.772 | 3712.117 | 3932.851 |
| -7 CENTS | 2084.559 | 2208.513 | 2339.838 | 2478.972 | 2626.380 | 2782.552 | 2948.011 | 3123.309 | 3309.031 | 3505.796 | 3714.262 | 3935.123 |
| -6 CENTS | 2085.763 | 2209.789 | 2341.190 | 2480.405 | 2627.897 | 2784.160 | 2949.715 | 3125.114 | 3310.943 | 3507.822 | 3716.408 | 3937.397 |
| -5 CENTS | 2086.968 | 2211.066 | 2342.543 | 2481.838 | 2629.415 | 2785.769 | 2951.419 | 3126.920 | 3312.856 | 3509.849 | 3718.555 | 3939.672 |
| -4 CENTS | 2088.174 | 2212.344 | 2343.896 | 2483.272 | 2630.935 | 2787.378 | 2953.124 | 3128.726 | 3314.770 | 3511.876 | 3720.704 | 3941.948 |
| -3 CENTS | 2089.381 | 2213.622 | 2345.251 | 2484.706 | 2632.455 | 2788.989 | 2954.831 | 3130.534 | 3316.685 | 3513.906 | 3722.853 | 3944.226 |

SHARP — A=440

| | | | | | | | | | | | | |
|---|---|---|---|---|---|---|---|---|---|---|---|---|
| -2 CENTS | 2090.588 | 2214.991 | 2346.606 | 2486.142 | 2633.976 | 2790.600 | 2956.538 | 3132.343 | 3318.602 | 3515.936 | 3725.004 | 3946.505 |
| -1 CENTS | 2091.796 | 2216.181 | 2347.962 | 2487.579 | 2635.498 | 2792.213 | 2958.246 | 3134.153 | 3320.519 | 3517.967 | 3727.157 | 3948.785 |
| ▶ 0 CENTS | 2093.005 | 2217.461 | 2349.318 | 2489.016 | 2637.020 | 2793.826 | 2959.955 | 3135.963 | 3322.438 | 3520.000 | 3729.310 | 3951.066 ◀ |
| 1 CENTS | 2094.214 | 2218.742 | 2350.676 | 2490.454 | 2638.544 | 2795.440 | 2961.666 | 3137.775 | 3324.357 | 3522.034 | 3731.465 | 3953.349 |
| 2 CENTS | 2095.424 | 2220.024 | 2352.034 | 2491.893 | 2640.069 | 2797.055 | 2963.377 | 3139.588 | 3326.278 | 3524.069 | 3733.621 | 3955.633 |
| 3 CENTS | 2096.635 | 2221.307 | 2353.393 | 2493.333 | 2641.594 | 2798.671 | 2965.089 | 3141.402 | 3328.200 | 3526.105 | 3735.779 | 3957.919 |
| 4 CENTS | 2097.846 | 2222.590 | 2354.752 | 2494.773 | 2643.120 | 2800.288 | 2966.802 | 3143.217 | 3330.123 | 3528.142 | 3737.937 | 3960.206 |
| 5 CENTS | 2099.058 | 2223.875 | 2356.113 | 2496.215 | 2644.647 | 2801.906 | 2968.516 | 3145.034 | 3332.047 | 3530.181 | 3740.096 | 3962.494 |
| 6 CENTS | 2100.271 | 2225.160 | 2357.474 | 2497.657 | 2646.176 | 2803.525 | 2970.232 | 3146.851 | 3333.972 | 3532.221 | 3742.257 | 3964.784 |
| 7 CENTS | 2101.484 | 2226.445 | 2358.837 | 2499.100 | 2647.704 | 2805.145 | 2971.948 | 3148.669 | 3335.899 | 3534.261 | 3744.420 | 3967.074 |
| 8 CENTS | 2102.699 | 2227.732 | 2360.199 | 2500.544 | 2649.234 | 2806.766 | 2973.665 | 3150.488 | 3337.826 | 3536.303 | 3746.583 | 3969.366 |
| 9 CENTS | 2103.914 | 2229.019 | 2361.563 | 2501.989 | 2650.765 | 2808.388 | 2975.383 | 3152.309 | 3339.755 | 3538.347 | 3748.748 | 3971.660 |
| 10 CENTS | 2105.129 | 2230.307 | 2362.928 | 2503.435 | 2652.297 | 2810.010 | 2977.102 | 3154.130 | 3341.684 | 3540.391 | 3750.914 | 3973.955 |
| 11 CENTS | 2106.345 | 2231.595 | 2364.293 | 2504.881 | 2653.829 | 2811.634 | 2978.822 | 3155.952 | 3343.615 | 3542.437 | 3753.081 | 3976.251 |
| 12 CENTS | 2107.563 | 2232.885 | 2365.659 | 2506.328 | 2655.362 | 2813.258 | 2980.543 | 3157.776 | 3345.547 | 3544.484 | 3755.249 | 3978.548 |
| 13 CENTS | 2108.780 | 2234.175 | 2367.026 | 2507.776 | 2656.897 | 2814.884 | 2982.266 | 3159.600 | 3347.480 | 3546.532 | 3757.419 | 3980.847 |
| 14 CENTS | 2109.999 | 2235.466 | 2368.393 | 2509.225 | 2658.432 | 2816.510 | 2983.989 | 3161.426 | 3349.414 | 3548.581 | 3759.590 | 3983.147 |
| 15 CENTS | 2111.218 | 2236.757 | 2369.762 | 2510.675 | 2659.968 | 2818.138 | 2985.713 | 3163.253 | 3351.349 | 3550.631 | 3761.762 | 3985.449 |
| 16 CENTS | 2112.438 | 2238.050 | 2371.131 | 2512.126 | 2661.505 | 2819.766 | 2987.438 | 3165.080 | 3353.286 | 3552.683 | 3763.936 | 3987.751 |
| 17 CENTS | 2113.658 | 2239.343 | 2372.501 | 2513.577 | 2663.042 | 2821.395 | 2989.164 | 3166.909 | 3355.223 | 3554.735 | 3766.111 | 3990.055 |
| 18 CENTS | 2114.879 | 2240.637 | 2373.872 | 2515.030 | 2664.581 | 2823.025 | 2990.891 | 3168.739 | 3357.162 | 3556.789 | 3768.287 | 3992.361 |
| 19 CENTS | 2116.101 | 2241.931 | 2375.244 | 2516.483 | 2666.121 | 2824.656 | 2992.619 | 3170.570 | 3359.102 | 3558.844 | 3770.464 | 3994.668 |
| 20 CENTS | 2117.324 | 2243.227 | 2376.616 | 2517.937 | 2667.661 | 2826.289 | 2994.348 | 3172.402 | 3361.042 | 3560.900 | 3772.643 | 3996.976 |
| 21 CENTS | 2118.547 | 2244.523 | 2377.989 | 2519.392 | 2669.203 | 2827.922 | 2996.079 | 3174.235 | 3362.984 | 3562.958 | 3774.822 | 3999.285 |
| 22 CENTS | 2119.772 | 2245.820 | 2379.363 | 2520.847 | 2670.745 | 2829.555 | 2997.810 | 3176.069 | 3364.928 | 3565.017 | 3777.003 | 4001.596 |
| 23 CENTS | 2120.996 | 2247.117 | 2380.738 | 2522.304 | 2672.288 | 2831.190 | 2999.542 | 3177.904 | 3366.872 | 3567.076 | 3779.186 | 4003.908 |
| 24 CENTS | 2122.222 | 2248.416 | 2382.113 | 2523.761 | 2673.832 | 2832.826 | 3001.275 | 3179.740 | 3368.817 | 3569.137 | 3781.369 | 4006.221 |
| 25 CENTS | 2123.448 | 2249.715 | 2383.490 | 2525.219 | 2675.377 | 2834.463 | 3003.009 | 3181.577 | 3370.764 | 3571.200 | 3783.554 | 4008.536 |
| 26 CENTS | 2124.675 | 2251.015 | 2384.867 | 2526.678 | 2676.923 | 2836.101 | 3004.744 | 3183.415 | 3372.711 | 3573.263 | 3785.740 | 4010.852 |
| 27 CENTS | 2125.902 | 2252.315 | 2386.245 | 2528.138 | 2678.469 | 2837.739 | 3006.480 | 3185.255 | 3374.660 | 3575.328 | 3787.928 | 4013.170 |
| 28 CENTS | 2127.131 | 2253.617 | 2387.624 | 2529.599 | 2680.017 | 2839.379 | 3008.217 | 3187.095 | 3376.610 | 3577.393 | 3790.116 | 4015.488 |
| 29 CENTS | 2128.360 | 2254.919 | 2389.003 | 2531.061 | 2681.565 | 2841.020 | 3009.955 | 3188.937 | 3378.561 | 3579.460 | 3792.306 | 4017.808 |
| 30 CENTS | 2129.590 | 2256.222 | 2390.384 | 2532.523 | 2683.115 | 2842.661 | 3011.694 | 3190.779 | 3380.513 | 3581.529 | 3794.497 | 4020.130 |
| 31 CENTS | 2130.820 | 2257.525 | 2391.765 | 2533.986 | 2684.665 | 2844.304 | 3013.435 | 3192.623 | 3382.466 | 3583.598 | 3796.690 | 4022.453 |
| 32 CENTS | 2132.051 | 2258.830 | 2393.147 | 2535.450 | 2686.216 | 2845.947 | 3015.176 | 3194.467 | 3384.420 | 3585.668 | 3798.883 | 4024.777 |
| 33 CENTS | 2133.283 | 2260.135 | 2394.529 | 2536.915 | 2687.768 | 2847.591 | 3016.918 | 3196.313 | 3386.376 | 3587.740 | 3801.078 | 4027.102 |
| 34 CENTS | 2134.516 | 2261.441 | 2395.913 | 2538.381 | 2689.321 | 2849.237 | 3018.661 | 3198.160 | 3388.332 | 3589.813 | 3803.275 | 4029.429 |
| 35 CENTS | 2135.749 | 2262.747 | 2397.297 | 2539.848 | 2690.875 | 2850.883 | 3020.405 | 3200.008 | 3390.290 | 3591.887 | 3805.472 | 4031.757 |
| 36 CENTS | 2136.983 | 2264.055 | 2398.682 | 2541.315 | 2692.430 | 2852.530 | 3022.150 | 3201.857 | 3392.249 | 3593.963 | 3807.671 | 4034.087 |
| 37 CENTS | 2138.218 | 2265.363 | 2400.068 | 2542.784 | 2693.986 | 2854.178 | 3023.897 | 3203.707 | 3394.209 | 3596.039 | 3809.871 | 4036.418 |
| 38 CENTS | 2139.453 | 2266.672 | 2401.455 | 2544.253 | 2695.542 | 2855.827 | 3025.644 | 3205.558 | 3396.170 | 3598.117 | 3812.072 | 4038.750 |
| 39 CENTS | 2140.689 | 2267.981 | 2402.843 | 2545.723 | 2697.100 | 2857.477 | 3027.392 | 3207.410 | 3398.132 | 3600.196 | 3814.275 | 4041.083 |
| 40 CENTS | 2141.926 | 2269.292 | 2404.231 | 2547.194 | 2698.658 | 2859.128 | 3029.141 | 3209.263 | 3400.096 | 3602.276 | 3816.479 | 4043.418 |
| 41 CENTS | 2143.164 | 2270.603 | 2405.620 | 2548.666 | 2700.217 | 2860.780 | 3030.891 | 3211.117 | 3402.060 | 3604.357 | 3818.684 | 4045.754 |
| 42 CENTS | 2144.402 | 2271.915 | 2407.010 | 2550.138 | 2701.777 | 2862.433 | 3032.642 | 3212.973 | 3404.026 | 3606.440 | 3820.890 | 4048.092 |
| 43 CENTS | 2145.641 | 2273.228 | 2408.401 | 2551.612 | 2703.338 | 2864.087 | 3034.395 | 3214.829 | 3405.993 | 3608.524 | 3823.098 | 4050.431 |
| 44 CENTS | 2146.881 | 2274.541 | 2409.792 | 2553.086 | 2704.900 | 2865.742 | 3036.148 | 3216.687 | 3407.961 | 3610.609 | 3825.307 | 4052.771 |
| 45 CENTS | 2148.121 | 2275.855 | 2411.185 | 2554.561 | 2706.463 | 2867.398 | 3037.902 | 3218.545 | 3409.930 | 3612.695 | 3827.517 | 4055.113 |
| 46 CENTS | 2149.362 | 2277.170 | 2412.578 | 2556.037 | 2708.027 | 2869.055 | 3039.657 | 3220.405 | 3411.900 | 3614.782 | 3829.728 | 4057.456 |
| 47 CENTS | 2150.604 | 2278.486 | 2413.972 | 2557.514 | 2709.592 | 2870.712 | 3041.414 | 3222.266 | 3413.872 | 3616.871 | 3831.941 | 4059.800 |
| 48 CENTS | 2151.847 | 2279.802 | 2415.366 | 2558.992 | 2711.157 | 2872.371 | 3043.171 | 3224.127 | 3415.844 | 3618.961 | 3834.155 | 4062.146 |
| 49 CENTS | 2153.090 | 2281.120 | 2416.762 | 2560.470 | 2712.724 | 2874.031 | 3044.929 | 3225.990 | 3417.818 | 3621.052 | 3836.371 | 4064.493 |
| 50 CENTS | 2154.334 | 2282.438 | 2418.158 | 2561.950 | 2714.291 | 2875.691 | 3046.689 | 3227.854 | 3419.792 | 3623.144 | 3838.587 | 4066.841 |

# OCTAVE 7

FLAT

| OCTAVE 7 | C | C# | D | D# | E | F | F# | G | G# | A | A# | B |
|---|---|---|---|---|---|---|---|---|---|---|---|---|
| -50 CENTS | 4066.841 | 4308.668 | 4564.875 | 4836.317 | 5123.899 | 5428.582 | 5751.382 | 6093.377 | 6455.708 | 6839.585 | 7246.288 | 7677.174 |
| -49 CENTS | 4069.191 | 4311.158 | 4567.513 | 4839.111 | 5126.860 | 5431.719 | 5754.705 | 6096.898 | 6459.439 | 6843.537 | 7250.475 | 7681.610 |
| -48 CENTS | 4071.542 | 4313.649 | 4570.152 | 4841.907 | 5129.822 | 5434.857 | 5758.030 | 6100.421 | 6463.171 | 6847.451 | 7254.664 | 7686.049 |
| -47 CENTS | 4073.895 | 4316.141 | 4572.792 | 4844.705 | 5132.786 | 5437.997 | 5761.357 | 6103.946 | 6466.905 | 6851.447 | 7258.855 | 7690.490 |
| -46 CENTS | 4076.249 | 4318.635 | 4575.435 | 4847.504 | 5135.752 | 5441.139 | 5764.686 | 6107.472 | 6470.642 | 6855.406 | 7263.050 | 7694.933 |
| -45 CENTS | 4078.604 | 4321.130 | 4578.078 | 4850.305 | 5138.719 | 5444.283 | 5768.017 | 6111.001 | 6474.380 | 6859.367 | 7267.246 | 7699.379 |
| -44 CENTS | 4080.961 | 4323.627 | 4580.723 | 4853.107 | 5141.688 | 5447.429 | 5771.350 | 6114.532 | 6478.121 | 6863.330 | 7271.445 | 7703.828 |
| -43 CENTS | 4083.318 | 4326.125 | 4583.370 | 4855.911 | 5144.659 | 5450.576 | 5774.684 | 6118.065 | 6481.864 | 6867.296 | 7275.646 | 7708.279 |
| -42 CENTS | 4085.678 | 4328.625 | 4586.018 | 4858.717 | 5147.631 | 5453.726 | 5778.021 | 6121.600 | 6485.609 | 6871.264 | 7279.850 | 7712.733 |
| -41 CENTS | 4088.038 | 4331.126 | 4588.668 | 4861.524 | 5150.606 | 5456.877 | 5781.359 | 6125.137 | 6489.357 | 6875.234 | 7284.056 | 7717.189 |
| -40 CENTS | 4090.400 | 4333.628 | 4591.319 | 4864.333 | 5153.582 | 5460.030 | 5784.700 | 6128.676 | 6493.106 | 6879.206 | 7288.265 | 7721.648 |
| -39 CENTS | 4092.764 | 4336.132 | 4593.972 | 4867.144 | 5156.559 | 5463.184 | 5788.042 | 6132.217 | 6496.858 | 6883.181 | 7292.476 | 7726.109 |
| -38 CENTS | 4095.129 | 4338.638 | 4596.626 | 4869.956 | 5159.539 | 5466.341 | 5791.386 | 6135.760 | 6500.611 | 6887.158 | 7296.690 | 7730.573 |
| -37 CENTS | 4097.495 | 4341.144 | 4599.282 | 4872.770 | 5162.520 | 5469.499 | 5794.733 | 6139.305 | 6504.367 | 6891.137 | 7300.906 | 7735.040 |
| -36 CENTS | 4099.862 | 4343.653 | 4601.940 | 4875.585 | 5165.503 | 5472.659 | 5798.081 | 6142.853 | 6508.126 | 6895.119 | 7305.124 | 7739.509 |
| -35 CENTS | 4102.231 | 4346.162 | 4604.599 | 4878.402 | 5168.487 | 5475.822 | 5801.431 | 6146.402 | 6511.886 | 6899.103 | 7309.345 | 7743.981 |
| -34 CENTS | 4104.601 | 4348.674 | 4607.259 | 4881.221 | 5171.474 | 5478.985 | 5804.783 | 6149.953 | 6515.648 | 6903.089 | 7313.568 | 7748.455 |
| -33 CENTS | 4106.973 | 4351.186 | 4609.921 | 4884.041 | 5174.462 | 5482.151 | 5808.137 | 6153.507 | 6519.413 | 6907.078 | 7317.794 | 7752.932 |
| -32 CENTS | 4109.346 | 4353.700 | 4612.585 | 4886.863 | 5177.451 | 5485.319 | 5811.493 | 6157.062 | 6523.180 | 6911.068 | 7322.022 | 7757.412 |
| -31 CENTS | 4111.720 | 4356.216 | 4615.250 | 4889.687 | 5180.443 | 5488.488 | 5814.850 | 6160.619 | 6526.949 | 6915.062 | 7326.253 | 7761.894 |
| -30 CENTS | 4114.096 | 4358.733 | 4617.917 | 4892.512 | 5183.436 | 5491.659 | 5818.210 | 6164.179 | 6530.720 | 6919.057 | 7330.486 | 7766.379 |
| -29 CENTS | 4116.473 | 4361.251 | 4620.585 | 4895.339 | 5186.431 | 5494.832 | 5821.572 | 6167.741 | 6534.494 | 6923.055 | 7334.721 | 7770.866 |
| -28 CENTS | 4118.851 | 4363.771 | 4623.254 | 4898.167 | 5189.428 | 5498.007 | 5824.936 | 6171.304 | 6538.269 | 6927.055 | 7338.959 | 7775.356 |
| -27 CENTS | 4121.231 | 4366.292 | 4625.926 | 4900.998 | 5192.426 | 5501.184 | 5828.301 | 6174.870 | 6542.047 | 6931.057 | 7343.199 | 7779.849 |
| -26 CENTS | 4123.612 | 4368.815 | 4628.599 | 4903.829 | 5195.426 | 5504.362 | 5831.669 | 6178.438 | 6545.827 | 6935.062 | 7347.442 | 7784.344 |
| -25 CENTS | 4125.995 | 4371.339 | 4631.273 | 4906.663 | 5198.428 | 5507.543 | 5835.038 | 6182.008 | 6549.609 | 6939.069 | 7351.687 | 7788.842 |
| -24 CENTS | 4128.379 | 4373.865 | 4633.949 | 4909.498 | 5201.432 | 5510.725 | 5838.410 | 6185.580 | 6553.393 | 6943.078 | 7355.935 | 7793.342 |
| -23 CENTS | 4130.764 | 4376.392 | 4636.626 | 4912.334 | 5204.437 | 5513.909 | 5841.783 | 6189.153 | 6557.180 | 6947.090 | 7360.185 | 7797.845 |
| -22 CENTS | 4133.151 | 4378.921 | 4639.305 | 4915.173 | 5207.444 | 5517.095 | 5845.158 | 6192.729 | 6560.968 | 6951.104 | 7364.438 | 7802.350 |
| -21 CENTS | 4135.539 | 4381.451 | 4641.986 | 4918.013 | 5210.453 | 5520.282 | 5848.536 | 6196.308 | 6564.759 | 6955.120 | 7368.693 | 7806.858 |
| -20 CENTS | 4137.929 | 4383.983 | 4644.668 | 4920.854 | 5213.463 | 5523.472 | 5851.915 | 6199.888 | 6568.552 | 6959.139 | 7372.951 | 7811.369 |
| -19 CENTS | 4140.319 | 4386.516 | 4647.351 | 4923.697 | 5216.476 | 5526.663 | 5855.296 | 6203.470 | 6572.348 | 6963.160 | 7377.211 | 7815.882 |
| -18 CENTS | 4142.712 | 4389.050 | 4650.037 | 4926.542 | 5219.490 | 5529.857 | 5858.679 | 6207.054 | 6576.145 | 6967.183 | 7381.473 | 7820.398 |
| -17 CENTS | 4145.105 | 4391.586 | 4652.723 | 4929.389 | 5222.505 | 5533.052 | 5862.064 | 6210.641 | 6579.945 | 6971.208 | 7385.738 | 7824.917 |
| -16 CENTS | 4147.500 | 4394.124 | 4655.412 | 4932.237 | 5225.523 | 5536.249 | 5865.451 | 6214.229 | 6583.746 | 6975.236 | 7390.005 | 7829.438 |
| -15 CENTS | 4149.897 | 4396.662 | 4658.102 | 4935.087 | 5228.542 | 5539.448 | 5868.840 | 6217.820 | 6587.550 | 6979.267 | 7394.275 | 7833.962 |
| -14 CENTS | 4152.294 | 4399.203 | 4660.793 | 4937.938 | 5231.563 | 5542.648 | 5872.231 | 6221.412 | 6591.357 | 6983.299 | 7398.548 | 7838.488 |
| -13 CENTS | 4154.694 | 4401.745 | 4663.486 | 4940.791 | 5234.586 | 5545.851 | 5875.624 | 6225.007 | 6595.165 | 6987.334 | 7402.822 | 7843.017 |
| -12 CENTS | 4157.094 | 4404.288 | 4666.180 | 4943.646 | 5237.610 | 5549.055 | 5879.019 | 6228.604 | 6598.976 | 6991.371 | 7407.100 | 7847.549 |
| -11 CENTS | 4159.496 | 4406.833 | 4668.877 | 4946.502 | 5240.637 | 5552.261 | 5882.416 | 6232.202 | 6602.788 | 6995.411 | 7411.379 | 7852.083 |
| -10 CENTS | 4161.899 | 4409.379 | 4671.574 | 4949.360 | 5243.665 | 5555.469 | 5885.815 | 6235.803 | 6606.603 | 6999.453 | 7415.662 | 7856.620 |
| -9 CENTS | 4164.304 | 4411.927 | 4674.273 | 4952.220 | 5246.694 | 5558.679 | 5889.215 | 6239.406 | 6610.421 | 7003.497 | 7419.946 | 7861.159 |
| -8 CENTS | 4166.710 | 4414.476 | 4676.974 | 4955.081 | 5249.726 | 5561.891 | 5892.618 | 6243.011 | 6614.240 | 7007.543 | 7424.234 | 7865.701 |
| -7 CENTS | 4169.118 | 4417.026 | 4679.676 | 4957.944 | 5252.759 | 5565.104 | 5896.023 | 6246.619 | 6618.062 | 7011.592 | 7428.523 | 7870.246 |
| -6 CENTS | 4171.527 | 4419.578 | 4682.380 | 4960.809 | 5255.794 | 5568.320 | 5899.429 | 6250.228 | 6621.886 | 7015.643 | 7432.815 | 7874.794 |
| -5 CENTS | 4173.937 | 4422.132 | 4685.086 | 4963.675 | 5258.831 | 5571.537 | 5902.838 | 6253.839 | 6625.712 | 7019.697 | 7437.110 | 7879.343 |
| -4 CENTS | 4176.348 | 4424.687 | 4687.793 | 4966.543 | 5261.869 | 5574.756 | 5906.249 | 6257.452 | 6629.540 | 7023.753 | 7441.407 | 7883.896 |
| -3 CENTS | 4178.762 | 4427.244 | 4690.501 | 4969.413 | 5264.910 | 5577.977 | 5909.661 | 6261.068 | 6633.370 | 7027.811 | 7445.707 | 7888.451 |

| | | | | | | | | | | | | |
|---|---|---|---|---|---|---|---|---|---|---|---|---|
| -2 CENTS | 4181.176 | 4429.802 | 4693.211 | 4972.284 | 5267.952 | 5581.200 | 5913.076 | 6264.686 | 6637.203 | 7031.872 | 7450.009 | 7893.009 |
| -1 CENTS | 4183.592 | 4432.361 | 4695.923 | 4975.157 | 5270.995 | 5584.425 | 5916.492 | 6268.305 | 6641.038 | 7035.935 | 7454.313 | 7897.570 |
| 0 CENTS | 4186.009 | 4434.922 | 4698.636 | 4978.032 | 5274.041 | 5587.652 | 5919.911 | 6271.927 | 6644.875 | 7040.000 | 7458.620 | 7902.133 |
| 1 CENTS | 4188.428 | 4437.485 | 4701.351 | 4980.908 | 5277.088 | 5590.880 | 5923.331 | 6275.551 | 6648.715 | 7044.068 | 7462.930 | 7906.699 |
| 2 CENTS | 4190.848 | 4440.048 | 4704.068 | 4983.786 | 5280.137 | 5594.111 | 5926.754 | 6279.177 | 6652.556 | 7048.138 | 7467.242 | 7911.267 |
| 3 CENTS | 4193.269 | 4442.614 | 4706.785 | 4986.665 | 5283.188 | 5597.343 | 5930.178 | 6282.805 | 6656.400 | 7052.210 | 7471.556 | 7915.838 |
| 4 CENTS | 4195.692 | 4445.181 | 4709.505 | 4989.547 | 5286.241 | 5600.577 | 5933.604 | 6286.435 | 6660.246 | 7056.285 | 7475.873 | 7920.412 |
| 5 CENTS | 4198.116 | 4447.749 | 4712.226 | 4992.430 | 5289.295 | 5603.813 | 5937.033 | 6290.067 | 6664.094 | 7060.362 | 7480.193 | 7924.988 |
| 6 CENTS | 4200.542 | 4450.319 | 4714.949 | 4995.314 | 5292.351 | 5607.051 | 5940.463 | 6293.702 | 6667.944 | 7064.441 | 7484.515 | 7929.567 |
| 7 CENTS | 4202.969 | 4452.890 | 4717.673 | 4998.200 | 5295.409 | 5610.290 | 5943.896 | 6297.338 | 6671.797 | 7068.523 | 7488.839 | 7934.149 |
| 8 CENTS | 4205.397 | 4455.463 | 4720.399 | 5001.088 | 5298.469 | 5613.532 | 5947.330 | 6300.976 | 6675.652 | 7072.607 | 7493.166 | 7938.733 |
| 9 CENTS | 4207.827 | 4458.038 | 4723.126 | 5003.978 | 5301.530 | 5616.775 | 5950.766 | 6304.617 | 6679.509 | 7076.693 | 7497.496 | 7943.320 |
| 10 CENTS | 4210.258 | 4460.613 | 4725.855 | 5006.869 | 5304.593 | 5620.021 | 5954.204 | 6308.260 | 6683.369 | 7080.782 | 7501.828 | 7947.909 |
| 11 CENTS | 4212.691 | 4463.191 | 4728.586 | 5009.762 | 5307.658 | 5623.268 | 5957.645 | 6311.905 | 6687.230 | 7084.874 | 7506.162 | 7952.502 |
| 12 CENTS | 4215.125 | 4465.769 | 4731.318 | 5012.657 | 5310.725 | 5626.517 | 5961.087 | 6315.552 | 6691.094 | 7088.967 | 7510.499 | 7957.097 |
| 13 CENTS | 4217.560 | 4468.350 | 4734.052 | 5015.553 | 5313.793 | 5629.768 | 5964.531 | 6319.201 | 6694.960 | 7093.063 | 7514.838 | 7961.694 |
| 14 CENTS | 4219.997 | 4470.931 | 4736.787 | 5018.451 | 5316.864 | 5633.021 | 5967.977 | 6322.852 | 6698.828 | 7097.161 | 7519.180 | 7966.294 |
| 15 CENTS | 4222.436 | 4473.515 | 4739.524 | 5021.350 | 5319.936 | 5636.275 | 5971.426 | 6326.505 | 6702.699 | 7101.262 | 7523.525 | 7970.897 |
| 16 CENTS | 4224.875 | 4476.099 | 4742.262 | 5024.252 | 5323.009 | 5639.532 | 5974.876 | 6330.161 | 6706.572 | 7105.365 | 7527.872 | 7975.503 |
| 17 CENTS | 4227.316 | 4478.686 | 4745.002 | 5027.155 | 5326.085 | 5642.790 | 5978.328 | 6333.818 | 6710.446 | 7109.470 | 7532.222 | 7980.111 |
| 18 CENTS | 4229.759 | 4481.273 | 4747.744 | 5030.059 | 5329.162 | 5646.051 | 5981.782 | 6337.478 | 6714.324 | 7113.578 | 7536.574 | 7984.722 |
| 19 CENTS | 4232.203 | 4483.863 | 4750.487 | 5032.966 | 5332.241 | 5649.313 | 5985.239 | 6341.139 | 6718.203 | 7117.688 | 7540.928 | 7989.335 |
| 20 CENTS | 4234.648 | 4486.453 | 4753.232 | 5035.874 | 5335.322 | 5652.577 | 5988.697 | 6344.803 | 6722.085 | 7121.801 | 7545.285 | 7993.951 |
| 21 CENTS | 4237.095 | 4489.046 | 4755.978 | 5038.783 | 5338.405 | 5655.843 | 5992.157 | 6348.469 | 6725.969 | 7125.916 | 7549.645 | 7998.570 |
| 22 CENTS | 4239.543 | 4491.639 | 4758.726 | 5041.695 | 5341.489 | 5659.111 | 5995.619 | 6352.137 | 6729.855 | 7130.033 | 7554.007 | 8003.191 |
| 23 CENTS | 4241.993 | 4494.235 | 4761.476 | 5044.608 | 5344.576 | 5662.381 | 5999.083 | 6355.807 | 6733.743 | 7134.153 | 7558.371 | 8007.816 |
| 24 CENTS | 4244.444 | 4496.831 | 4764.227 | 5047.522 | 5347.664 | 5665.652 | 6002.550 | 6359.480 | 6737.634 | 7138.275 | 7562.739 | 8012.442 |
| 25 CENTS | 4246.896 | 4499.430 | 4766.980 | 5050.439 | 5350.754 | 5668.926 | 6006.018 | 6363.154 | 6741.527 | 7142.399 | 7567.108 | 8017.072 |
| 26 CENTS | 4249.350 | 4502.029 | 4769.734 | 5053.357 | 5353.845 | 5672.201 | 6009.488 | 6366.831 | 6745.422 | 7146.526 | 7571.481 | 8021.704 |
| 27 CENTS | 4251.805 | 4504.630 | 4772.490 | 5056.277 | 5356.939 | 5675.479 | 6012.960 | 6370.510 | 6749.320 | 7150.655 | 7575.855 | 8026.339 |
| 28 CENTS | 4254.262 | 4507.233 | 4775.247 | 5059.198 | 5360.034 | 5678.758 | 6016.435 | 6374.190 | 6753.219 | 7154.787 | 7580.232 | 8030.977 |
| 29 CENTS | 4256.720 | 4509.837 | 4778.006 | 5062.121 | 5363.131 | 5682.039 | 6019.911 | 6377.873 | 6757.121 | 7158.921 | 7584.612 | 8035.617 |
| 30 CENTS | 4259.179 | 4512.443 | 4780.767 | 5065.046 | 5366.230 | 5685.322 | 6023.389 | 6381.558 | 6761.026 | 7163.057 | 7588.995 | 8040.260 |
| 31 CENTS | 4261.640 | 4515.050 | 4783.529 | 5067.973 | 5369.330 | 5688.607 | 6026.869 | 6385.246 | 6764.932 | 7167.196 | 7593.379 | 8044.905 |
| 32 CENTS | 4264.102 | 4517.659 | 4786.293 | 5070.901 | 5372.432 | 5691.894 | 6030.351 | 6388.935 | 6768.841 | 7171.337 | 7597.767 | 8049.554 |
| 33 CENTS | 4266.566 | 4520.269 | 4789.059 | 5073.831 | 5375.537 | 5695.183 | 6033.836 | 6392.626 | 6772.752 | 7175.480 | 7602.157 | 8054.204 |
| 34 CENTS | 4269.031 | 4522.881 | 4791.826 | 5076.762 | 5378.642 | 5698.473 | 6037.322 | 6396.320 | 6776.665 | 7179.626 | 7606.549 | 8058.858 |
| 35 CENTS | 4271.498 | 4525.494 | 4794.594 | 5079.696 | 5381.750 | 5701.766 | 6040.810 | 6400.016 | 6780.580 | 7183.775 | 7610.944 | 8063.514 |
| 36 CENTS | 4273.966 | 4528.109 | 4797.365 | 5082.631 | 5384.860 | 5705.060 | 6044.301 | 6403.713 | 6784.498 | 7187.925 | 7615.342 | 8068.173 |
| 37 CENTS | 4276.435 | 4530.726 | 4800.136 | 5085.567 | 5387.971 | 5708.356 | 6047.793 | 6407.413 | 6788.418 | 7192.078 | 7619.742 | 8072.835 |
| 38 CENTS | 4278.906 | 4533.343 | 4802.910 | 5088.506 | 5391.084 | 5711.655 | 6051.287 | 6411.116 | 6792.340 | 7196.234 | 7624.144 | 8077.500 |
| 39 CENTS | 4281.379 | 4535.963 | 4805.685 | 5091.446 | 5394.199 | 5714.955 | 6054.784 | 6414.820 | 6796.265 | 7200.392 | 7628.549 | 8082.167 |
| 40 CENTS | 4283.852 | 4538.583 | 4808.462 | 5094.388 | 5397.316 | 5718.257 | 6058.282 | 6418.526 | 6800.192 | 7204.552 | 7632.957 | 8086.836 |
| 41 CENTS | 4286.328 | 4541.206 | 4811.240 | 5097.331 | 5400.434 | 5721.561 | 6061.783 | 6422.235 | 6804.121 | 7208.715 | 7637.367 | 8091.509 |
| 42 CENTS | 4288.804 | 4543.830 | 4814.020 | 5100.276 | 5403.555 | 5724.867 | 6065.285 | 6425.946 | 6808.052 | 7212.880 | 7641.780 | 8096.184 |
| 43 CENTS | 4291.282 | 4546.455 | 4816.801 | 5103.223 | 5406.677 | 5728.174 | 6068.789 | 6429.658 | 6811.986 | 7217.048 | 7646.196 | 8100.862 |
| 44 CENTS | 4293.762 | 4549.082 | 4819.584 | 5106.172 | 5409.801 | 5731.484 | 6072.296 | 6433.373 | 6815.922 | 7221.217 | 7650.613 | 8105.543 |
| 45 CENTS | 4296.243 | 4551.710 | 4822.369 | 5109.122 | 5412.926 | 5734.796 | 6075.804 | 6437.091 | 6819.860 | 7225.390 | 7655.034 | 8110.226 |
| 46 CENTS | 4298.725 | 4554.340 | 4825.155 | 5112.074 | 5416.054 | 5738.109 | 6079.315 | 6440.810 | 6823.800 | 7229.565 | 7659.457 | 8114.912 |
| 47 CENTS | 4301.209 | 4556.972 | 4827.943 | 5115.028 | 5419.183 | 5741.425 | 6082.828 | 6444.531 | 6827.743 | 7233.742 | 7663.882 | 8119.601 |
| 48 CENTS | 4303.694 | 4559.605 | 4830.733 | 5117.983 | 5422.314 | 5744.742 | 6086.342 | 6448.255 | 6831.688 | 7237.921 | 7668.311 | 8124.292 |
| 49 CENTS | 4306.180 | 4562.239 | 4833.524 | 5120.940 | 5425.447 | 5748.061 | 6089.859 | 6451.981 | 6835.635 | 7242.103 | 7672.741 | 8128.986 |
| 50 CENTS | 4308.668 | 4564.875 | 4836.317 | 5123.899 | 5428.582 | 5751.382 | 6093.377 | 6455.708 | 6839.585 | 7246.288 | 7677.174 | 8133.683 |

SHARP

A=440

# 5
# Using the Conn Strobotuner Model ST-6

***Setting Up***

Plug the power cord into a power outlet supplying 105 to 120 volts of 60 cycle alternating current. Insert the microphone plug into the signal input receptacle if a microphone is to be used, and turn on the power switch by sliding it upward as far as it will go. The pilot lamp will light when the power is on.

Soon after the Strobotuner power is turned on, an internal motor will start turning the scanning disc and a red lamp behind the disc will glow. While it is possible to begin using the Strobotuner as soon as the disc is turning and illuminated from behind, the instrument should be allowed to warm up for approximately 10 minutes to insure accuracy.

Do not obstruct the ventilating grill on the back of the Strobotuner while it is in use. Air must be allowed to circulate through this grill to protect the instrument from overheating and possible damage.

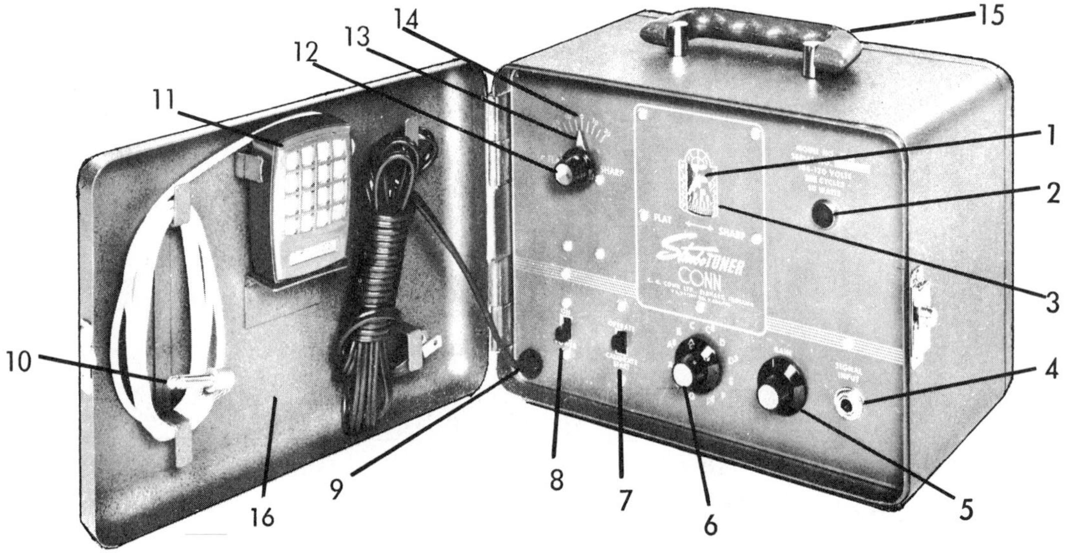


*Figure 5.1* **The Conn Strobotuner**

The Conn Strobotuner with controls numbered and identified. More elaborate instruments are also available.

1 scanning disc
2 pilot light
3 octave band numbers
4 signal input
5 gain control
6 tone selector knob
7 operate-calibrate
8 power switch
9 power cord
10 microphone plug
11 microphone
12 tuning knob
13 tuning pointer
14 tuning scale
15 carrying handle
16 cover

### *Calibration*

It is necessary that the Strobotuner be calibrated with a standard frequency in order to establish a standard internal pitch. The frequency standard for calibration can be the power line frequency of 60 cycles per second or it can be the tone from a tuning fork, a piano string, or any other steady tone within the seven octave range of the instrument.

A handy reference frequency, which generally is sufficiently accurate, is the frequency of the power line supplying the Strobotuner. It establishes an A-440 cps in the Strobotuner if used. The procedure for calibrating the instrument to the power line frequency after allowing a warm-up time is as follows:

1. Slide the operate-calibrate switch downward as far as it will go.

2. Turn the tuning knob to the right or to the left to cause the Stroboscopic pattern in the No. 1 Band of the scanning disc to become stationary. The No. 1 Band is closest to the center of the disc. If the stroboscopic pattern is rotating toward the left (flat), turn the tuning knob so its pointer moves to the left until the pattern becomes stationary. If the stroboscopic pattern on the disc is moving to the right (sharp), turn the tuning knob so its pointer moves to the right until the pattern becomes stationary.

3. Hold the tuning knob stationary with one hand while moving the metal pointer with the other hand until it is in the zero position for the pointer.

4. Slide the operate-calibrate switch upward as far as it will go to the operate position, and when the calibration procedure using the power line frequency as a reference standard is completed, the instrument is ready for use. The standard frequency level in the Strobotuner is A-440 as long as the tuning knob remains as positioned in the second step.

At any time during the use of the Strobotuner it is possible to quickly recheck the calibration with respect to the 60 cps power line frequency by merely sliding the operate-calibrate switch down again to calibrate the position and noting that the stroboscopic pattern on the inner band on the scanning disc is still stationary. If it is drifting in either direction when the pointer is at the zero position, the above calibration procedure is repeated. The operate-calibrate switch must be returned to the operate position after checking the calibration.

The procedure for calibrating the Strobotuner to any tone or signal other than the 60 cps power line frequency after allowing it to warm is as follows:

1. Connect the tone or signal to be used as the calibrating standard into the signal input receptacle. If the tone from a tuning fork or other tone source is used, it is fed into the microphone which is plugged into the signal input receptacle. If the signal from an oscillator, radio, or other electrical device is used as the calibration standard, its signal can be fed directly into the signal input receptacle. One millivolt (.001 volt) is sufficient to produce a stroboscopic pattern (an excess of 1 volt is not recommended) though more than 1 volt may be applied if the gain control is turned down (counterclockwise).

2. The operate-calibrate switch is not used when calibrating the Strobotuner to an external signal. It should remain in its uppermost (operate) position.

3. Set the tone selector knob to the appropriate setting for the tone or signal that is being used to calibrate, using the C on the knob as the indicator. For example, if an A tuning fork or bar is being used as the calibrating standard, set the C on the knob opposite the A on the panel.

4. Turn the tuning knob to the right or to the left to cause the stroboscopic pattern on the appropriate band of the scanning disc to become stationary. For example, if a 440 cps tuning fork or bar is being used as the calibrating standard, the stroboscopic pattern will appear in the fourth band from the center of the scanning disc.

5. Hold the tuning knob stationary with one hand while moving the metal pointer with the other hand until the pointer

is in the zero position. This completes the calibration procedure with an external standard, and the instrument is ready for use. If a 440 cps external standard was used, the Strobotuner is standardized at A-440 when the pointer is in the zero position. If a 435 cps fork was used, the Strobotuner is standardized at A-435 when the pointer is in the zero position.

The Strobotuner can be operated from a power line having an alternating current frequency between 50 and 60 cycles per second; however, if the power line frequency is used as the standardizing frequency in calibrating the Strobotuner, it should be known to be 60 cps if an A-440 standard is desired. In most power systems the frequency is held quite close to 60 cps.

### *How to Use*

After the calibration has been completed, the Strobotuner is ready to use.

An airborne microphone is standard equipment with the Strobotuner and it is usually used to pick up tones and to supply an electrical signal to the input signal receptacle. A contact microphone, or vibration pickup, can be used instead of the airborne microphone if desired. In some applications, such as tuning electronic organs, an electrical signal can be supplied to the input signal receptacle directly without the use of a microphone. The voltage of the signal supplied should be between 1 millivolt (.001 volt) and 1 volt.

Set the tone selector knob for the tone to be checked. If concert pitch is being used (such as piano or other instrument in C), the C on the knob is used as the indicator. The tone selector knob can be used as a transposing device also for instruments in the keys of B♭, E♭, or F. For example, when playing the note C (as written) on a B♭ instrument, the B♭ on the tone selector knob can be set opposite C on the panel and the Strobotuner will be set for measuring the C (as written) which is A# (B♭) concert. Since keyboard instruments, such as pianos, harpsichords, and organs, are in the key of C, no transposition is involved between the written note and the tone sounded. Therefore the C on the tone selector knob is used as the indicator to line up with the appropriate letter on the panel.

After the tone selector knob has been properly set for the tone to be tested, and the tone signal has been properly fed into the input signal receptacle, a stroboscopic pattern should appear on the scanning disc. If the tone being tested is between $C_1$ (32.703 cps) and $B_1$ (61.735 cps), the pattern will be on the band nearest the center of the disc (Band No. 1).

| Band Number | Frequency Range |
|---|---|
| 1 | $C_1$ (32.703 cps) — $B_1$ (61.735 cps) |
| 2 | $C_2$ (65.406 cps) — $B_2$ (123.47 cps) |
| 3 | $C_3$ (130.81 cps) — $B_3$ (246.94 cps) |
| 4 | $C_4$ (261.63 cps) — $B_4$ (493.88 cps) |
| 5 | $C_5$ (523.25 cps) — $B_5$ (987.77 cps) |
| 6 | $C_6$ (1046.5 cps) — $B_6$ (1975.5 cps) |
| 7 | $C_7$ (2093.0 cps) — $B_7$ (3951.1 cps) |

If the tone being tested is in tune with the equally-tempered tone at the pitch standard used to calibrate the Strobotuner, a stationary pattern will be seen for each tone introduced. If a tone is flat (lower in frequency) to the equally-tempered scale frequency, the stroboscopic pattern will rotate to the left. The speed at which the pattern drifts is an indication of how much it deviates from the equally-tempered scale. If it is desired to measure how flat the tested tone is, turn the tuning knob so its pointer moves to the left (counterclockwise) until the stroboscopic pattern becomes stationary. Then read the number of cents flat from the position of the pointer on the tuning scale. Similarly, if the tone being tested is sharp (higher in frequency than the equally-tempered scale frequency) the stroboscopic pattern will rotate to the right and it can be stopped by turning the tuning knob clockwise.

The gain control is provided to adjust the input signal for optimum clarity. If the input signal is too strong for a clear stroboscopic pattern, turn the control counterclockwise. If the input signal is too weak, it will be necessary to move the microphone closer to the tone source or to make the tone louder.

A simple flute-like tone tends to produce a sharper stroboscopic pattern generally, and it will appear distinctly only on one band. If the tone being tested has strong upper partials, they will cause patterns to appear on the higher number bands also. For example, if A2 (110 cps) is being tested, its second harmonic (220 cps) may cause a pattern to appear on the third band from the center of the scanning disc and its fourth harmonic (440 cps) may cause a pattern in the fourth band, and so on for octavely related harmonics.

If the partials in a tone being tested are not whole number multiples (harmonics) of the fundamental frequency, it will be possible to get a stationary pattern for the fundamental of the tone (its lowest frequency) while the patterns formed by the higher partials are drifting. This will be true generally for the piano tones or chime tones.

If the tone being tested is not steady but has a slight variation in frequency, such as produced by vibrato, the pattern on the scanning disc will waver back and forth according to the variation in the tone. This gives an indication of how steady a tone is and also the extent and the balance in a vibrato.

The cover of the Strobotuner can be raised after it has been opened to remove it from the case and used as a base for the microphone. The microphone can be taken from the cover by removing a screw in its base.

### *Principle of Operation*

The signal whose frequency is to be measured is amplified after it is introduced at the signal input. This causes the neon lamps behind the scanning disc to glow in accordance with the frequency of the input signal. If the input signal has 440 alternations per second, for example, the lamps will glow alternately brighter and darker 440 times per second.

The scanning disc is driven by a synchronous motor that receives its power from an internal frequency standard. The internal standard is an electronic oscillator that is quite stable with respect to changes in the power supply line, or changes in temperature, but is adjustable as desired.

There are 12 major adjustment settings conforming with the 12 steps in an octave of the equally-tempered musical scale. A vernier adjustment to get 12 major steps is provided in the tuning knob. While the tuning scale is marked to plus or minus 20 cents (1 cent is .01 half-steps in the equally-tempered scale), to cover most applications, it is possible to turn the tuning knob beyond the 20 cent mark if that is required for certain applications.

The scanning disc has seven concentric bands of dark and light segments. The band nearest the center has two dark and two light segments. The next band has four dark and four light segments to cover a range one octave higher than the No. 1 Band. The third band has eight dark and eight light segments for the third octave range; and so on out to the seventh band, having 128 alternating segments.

The receptacle on the back of the Strobotuner is provided for convenience in checking the instrument during its manufacture, or its servicing, and is not used during the ordinary operation of the instrument.

### *Suggested Uses of the Strobotuner*

As enumerated above, the Strobotuner was designed to measure the flatness or sharpness of a tone against a reference frequency. Many persons or musical groups have need for checking individual notes against the tempered scale; these include bands, orchestras, vocal groups, individual performers, piano tuners, and organ tuners.

### *Suggestions for Instrumental and Vocal Music Teaching*

The Strobotuner in music teaching shows the operator visually whether or not the tone under investigation is in tune with the equally-tempered scale. For the music educator, the Strobotuner provides an accurate visual standard in a tone range which encompasses the range of all the instruments commonly used in the band and orchestra.

It is only necessary for the player or vocalist to alter a tone to produce a stationary disc pattern in the Strobotuner. The tone selector switch, of course, is preset to the tone desired to check after the Strobotuner has been calibrated and prepared for operation.

The tone selector knob is provided with markings to aid in transposition. In setting the knob, point the arrow at the concert pitch desired. If the knob is not moved, instruments built in keys other than C will play the note pointed out for their respective key.

For instance, when B♭ concert is to be measured, the arrow is pointed to A# (B♭). Instruments in C play B♭, B♭ instruments play C, E♭ instruments play G, and F instruments play A.

While the checking of an individual student's tone for accurate intonation is a basic function of the Strobotuner, several suggestions can be made for more extensive use of the instrument.

*Student Operation:* A short explanation of the Strobotuner's operation will usually suffice to get students started on practice with it alone. Caution with regard to care in handling the instrument in order to allow air circulation, etc., should be emphasized. Rough handling, excessive bumping, or dropping could possibly destroy the Strobotuner's factory-set calibration of scale intervals, necessitating its being returned for recalibration.

*Playing Scales:* While the Strobotuner is easily adapted to the checking or measuring of individual tones, chromatic scales can be checked with the help of another individual. It will be necessary, as the player or singer progresses up the scale, for another person to change the tone selector switch for each successive tone. It is recommended, in following this procedure, that each tone be sounded for at least four slow counts in order to allow the instrument to stabilize at the new standard for each change of the selector switch. A four-beat tone is advisable in any case in order to permit an adequate measurement or analysis of the tone.

*Charting Performance:* A strong incentive to students for improvement is the recording of their intonation readings as measured by the Strobotuner for comparison with later tests to determine progress. This is accomplished usually with two or three students working in a group; one playing or singing, one making measurements on the Strobotuner, and the other recording the results on specially prepared charts.

Printed charts are available for each instrument, or they can be designed by the bandmaster or teacher. The charts usually consist of a straight vertical line representing perfect intonation, and the sharp or flat variations from zero are recorded as dots with a connecting line.

The procedure for measuring the sharpness or flatness of a tone is simple. If the pattern is drifting to the right, indicating a sharp tone, for example, the vernier control knob and pointer are moved slowly to the right until the pattern is brought to a standstill. The pointer then shows the number of cents (.01 of a semitone), indicating the tone is sharp. To measure a flat tone, the pointer is moved to the left in the same manner. The pointer reading is then recorded on the chart at a point to the right or left of the zero line corresponding with the number of cents deviation.

Such charts are usually prepared in duplicate, one for the director and one for the player. It is good practice to require the preparation of these charts periodically during the year, checking each new test against the previous chart to note progress.

### *Suggestions for Piano Tuning*

If the piano is to be tuned to the standard tuning frequency of A-440, the Strobotuner should be calibrated accordingly as explained in the section on calibration. If it is to be tuned to any other standard, there are two possibilities. One method is to calibrate the Strobotuner to A-440 and then to turn the tuning knob to the desired pointer setting. For example, if the Strobotuner is calibrated at A-440 with the pointer in the zero position, turning the knob to move the pointer to another position will give the following standards: −20 gives A-435, −10 gives A-437.5, + 10 gives A-442.5, and + 20 gives A-445. Of course, the pointer can be set in between the scale marks as well as directly on them.

A second method is to calibrate the Strobotuner to whatever standard is to be used instead of A-440. Any source of sound can be used as a standard. When sound is picked up by the microphone, remember that the "calibrate" switch is *not* used when calibrating to an external source. This is explained in the section on calibration. For example, it may be decided that a piano which is rather flat is not to be raised to A-440 tuning, and one string on the piano is to be used as a reference standard. In such a case, set the tone selector knob for whatever tone is to be used as a standard and proceed with the method for calibrating the Strobotuner with an external sound source.

After the Strobotuner has been calibrated and the piano prepared for tuning, place the microphone in a suitable location for the best pickup of the sound from the string being tuned.

*Stretching the Octaves:* Many technicians prefer to start tuning at the "break" in the scale because of the marked change in the inharmonicity of the partials of the tones at this point. The stiffness of piano strings causes the tones produced to have partials that are not harmonically related to each other; that is, the second partial is not exactly twice the frequency of the first partial, or fundamental, of the tone. The third partial is not three times the frequency of the fundamental, and so on. If the partials are to be harmonic, they need to bear a whole number relationship (1,2,3,4...) to the fundamental. The partials in piano tones are nearly always slightly higher (sharp) than the whole number multiples (harmonics) of the fundamental. This has an important bearing upon the tuning of a piano.

When one listens to two piano tones an exact octave apart, the second partial of the lower tone will be sharp with respect to the fundamental of the higher tone. This will cause audible beats to be produced and the listener will not consider the tones to be truly an octave apart even though the fundamental frequency of the top tone is exactly twice the fundamental frequency of the lower tone, as is required for a true octave. In order for the octave of the piano to sound in tune when the two notes are played at the same time, it is necessary to stretch the interval by lowering the bottom tone or raising the top tone. The technique for determining the optimum amount of stretch with the Strobotuner will be explained as we go along.

*The Temperament Octave:* The inharmonicity of piano tone partials is usually smallest in the middle of the keyboard; therefore an octave is chosen there for setting the temperament. Usually care should be taken that the break, or a marked change in string design, does not occur within the temperament octave. All but one string per key is muted with felt or wedges, so only one string at a time sounds when a key is struck.

*Tuning the Treble Strings:* Let us assume that C4 (middle C) is chosen for the starting point. Some other starting point might be preferred and could be used as well. Proceed from C4 up the scale, tuning one string on each key while watching the fourth ring or pattern band. The Strobotuner pointer remains in the position chosen to establish the tuning standard while tuning this octave.

It may be noted while tuning this octave that even though the tension on the string is adjusted to cause the fourth ring pattern to be stopped, the patterns in the fifth and higher rings will move slowly to the right due to the fact that the partials producing those patterns are not exactly in a 2, 4, 8 ... relationship to the fundamental of the tone. If the fifth ring pattern moves to the right for the C4 string, when the fourth ring pattern is not moving, the tuner can note how far to the right he needs to move the Strobotuner pointer in order to make the fifth ring pattern stand still. If this is 1 cent or more, it indicates that C5 should be tuned sharp by at least that amount. Therefore, when tuning C5, the pointer is advanced to the right of the starting position used for tuning the temperament octave. This is the beginning of the octave-stretching process.

It may be that the inharmonicity of the partials in the C4 string is so small that it is negligible. If that is the case, the pointer should be left in the C4 position while tuning C5; this octave is not stretched.

Since inharmonicity of partials is caused by the stiffness or rod-like character of the strings, it is obvious that the short, thick strings will have greater inharmonicity of their tone partials than will long slender strings. Therefore, the degree of inharmonicity will vary from string to string in a given piano and will vary between pianos. The degree of inharmonicity is greater at either end of the piano keyboard than it is in the middle, and it tends to be greater in small spinet pianos than in grand pianos.

As the tuner proceeds to go up the scale from the temperament octave, he gets a good idea of how much to stretch the octave by sounding the tone an octave below the one he is tuning and noting how sharp the second partial is with respect to the true octave. As he goes up the scale, he will note a marked increase in this inharmonicity; so, he finds that the higher he goes the more stretch is required in the octave. Due to the wide variety of piano designs, no set rule can be stated for stretching the octaves, but the Strobotuner gives an accurate measurement of the condition that exists to guide the tuner so that he can tailor the stretch to fit each particular piano.

*Technique for Tuning C8:* The Strobotuner normally is calibrated so that its measurements track the notation indicated by the pointer on the tone selector knob. However, it is possible to calibrate the Strobotuner so it actually reads a half-step higher than the tone indicated by the tone selector knob. To do this after tuning the B7, which normally is the top tone on the Strobotuner, turn the tone selector knob back to A#, sound the B7 tone on the piano, and turn the tuning knob clockwise to cause the stroboscopic pattern in the seventh band to be stationary (about one-half turn). Then turn the tone selector knob back to B and sound the C8 tone on the piano. It can be tuned by watching the seventh band on the scanning disc, for the Strobotuner is now calibrated to read one half step (100 cents) higher than for its regular use. Turning the tuning knob a revolution in either direction does no harm to the instrument.

*Optimum Compromises:* The fundamental is usually the strongest partial in the tones above C4, and the higher partials are progressively weaker. Thus, the fundamental and the second partial are the two most important parts of the tone to consider when tuning octaves. However, the meticulous tuner may find that even though the fundamental is exactly in tune with the second partial of the tone a stretched octave below, some beating between tones exists. If such is the case, he is hearing beats between higher coincident partials, such as the fourth partial of the lower tone and the second partial of the higher tone.

These partials can be noted in the Strobotuner patterns at the same time the lower partials are indicated. Taking the fourth octave tones as an example, the fundamental is indicated in the fourth band, the second partial in the fifth band, the fourth partial in the sixth band, and the eighth partial in the seventh band. Since the higher partials are relatively weak and die out quite rapidly after the tone is sounded, the patterns for the upper partials usually will not be as clear as the lower partial patterns.

If the tuner finds that objectionable beats exist when the fundamental is exactly in tune with the second partials of the tone an octave below, he will note relatively strong patterns for the upper partials and can measure how much mistuning exists between the higher coincident partials. He can then stretch the octave even further by the amount needed to reduce the beats between the higher coincident partials. In so doing, he introduces beats between the lower coincident partials so that the resultant tuning is a compromise which depends upon the degree of inharmonicity and the relative strength of the upper partials. The degree of compromise is determined by the information revealed by the Strobotuner added to what the tuner hears.

Compromise tuning is necessary because of the nature of piano tones, and it is not related to the *method* of tuning. It needs to be understood that a tuner does not turn off his ears while tuning with the Strobotuner, for it is quite important that he correlate the information obtained visually from the Strobotuner with the information he gains through hearing. The eyes and ears working together can give far more information than either can give alone.

The tuner proceeds up the scale from his starting point, following the procedure suggested for stretching the octaves, until he reaches the top key (C8), which is outside the regular range of the Strobotuner. It can be tuned with the Strobotuner, however, by using the technique given later in this chapter.

*Raising the Pitch*: After one string for each key has been tuned, a quick check can be made to determine if the strains produced by a general tightening of the strings caused the first strings tuned to be detuned. If the pitch of the piano has been raised considerably during the tuning process, it is almost certain that the tuner will need to go over the piano several times because of the added tension on the frame and sounding board. Some tuners make a practice of quickly tuning all strings (except the highest octave or so) roughly about 10 cents sharper than the ultimate tuning is to be. The strings above the break add the most change in tension so that they are done first. Then the strings are accurately tuned the second time over. Getting a uniform overtension the first time through is simple with the Strobotuner. The pointer is moved to the right by whatever amount desired during the first rough tuning.

*Tuning the Unisons*: The unison strings are generally tuned aurally, but the Strobotuner can be used in the same manner as on the first string, if desired.

These instructions pertain to the use of the Strobotuner. There are principles and techniques that are important to piano technicians. But the Strobotuner serves as a useful tool for the technician. It can give him a better understanding of the underlying principles of piano tones and tuning. It can instill confidence in the tuner and in his customers because of its accuracy and because it makes use of both the eyes and ears instead of just the ears alone. Skill, good judgment, and careful workmanship are indispensable in the use of any tool and instrument.

### *Suggestions for Use in Organ Tuning*

Many of the suggestions regarding Strobotuner preparation apply also to the tuning of electronic and pipe organs. The microphone is placed for best results directly in front of the proper speaker in the case of an electronic organ, and near the pipes being tuned in the case of the pipe organ. In tuning electronic organs, where direct connection may be desired, a patch cord is recommended in place of a microphone. A patch cord is offered as an accessory to the Strobotuner.

First, both the Strobotuner and the organ should be allowed a 10 to 15 minute warm-up period. Then calibrate the Strobotuner in the manner described under the section headed "Calibration." Before one proceeds, it is advisable to consult the service manual for the make of organ being tuned. Then follow the recommended procedures.

After preparations have been made, adjust the Strobotuner gain control to produce the best pattern contrast. The organ can then be tuned in the usual way, changing the tuning adjustment on the organ to produce a stationary pattern on the Strobotuner disc. The tone selector knob is reset, of course, for each different tone measured.

Instead of tuning successive notes in each octave, some tuners prefer to use this alternate method: First, tune the C's in all octaves with the selector switch set at C, and then proceed with all the C#s, etc. This method reduces the number of tone selector switch settings and may speed the tuning operation. However, we suggest that service manual tuning procedures be followed closely in all cases.

### *Some Observations on the Conn Strobotuner*

For almost as many years as this reliable instrument has been on the market, I have owned and used one, in combination with aural tuning methods in servicing pianos. Without exception, musicians and piano teachers for whom I have tuned have been high in their praise of my tuning work. Therefore, it is reasonable to assume that one can satisfy the most critical performers at the piano when one uses the Strobotuner as suggested.

I have based my instruction on the directions which the manufacturer supplies with the instrument. These directions are the work of an excellent engineering department and apply to the tuning of all piano makes and styles. If one follows these instructions, and uses the various fifths, seventeenths, thirds, and sixths, as all dependable piano craftsmen do, he can feel he is well on his way to becoming well qualified for his chosen profession.

In countless schools throughout America, the Strobotuner has given dependable service to music departments. The general design has not changed over the years, the only exception being that some knobs have been modernized. Perhaps the reason for this is that the Conn Strobotuner has always done the job it was designed to do when in the hands of a conscientious craftsman.

# 6
# Using the Yamaha Portable Tuning Scope Model PT-3

As one may judge by viewing the illustration included herewith, the Yamaha Portable Tuning Scope, with its attractive satin metallic finish, is a very ''scientific'' appearing instrument. The microphone is color-coded to match the tuner—quite an innovation—and the manufacturer has even provided two spare fuses. Extremely well made, it is 9 × 4¼ × 7¼ in. overall, including the protuberances (but excluding the useful chromium handle).

A compartmentalized carrying bag with shoulder strap is included. It contains the tuner and an instruction book, and it is equipped with a pair of snap holders for storing a tuning lever. Also, the bag is spacious enough to carry a tuning kit. Not much larger than a casette tape recorder, it adds a professional touch to the tuner making a call and equips him with all that's necessary to do a first rate job. Unquestionably the unit is splendidly engineered.

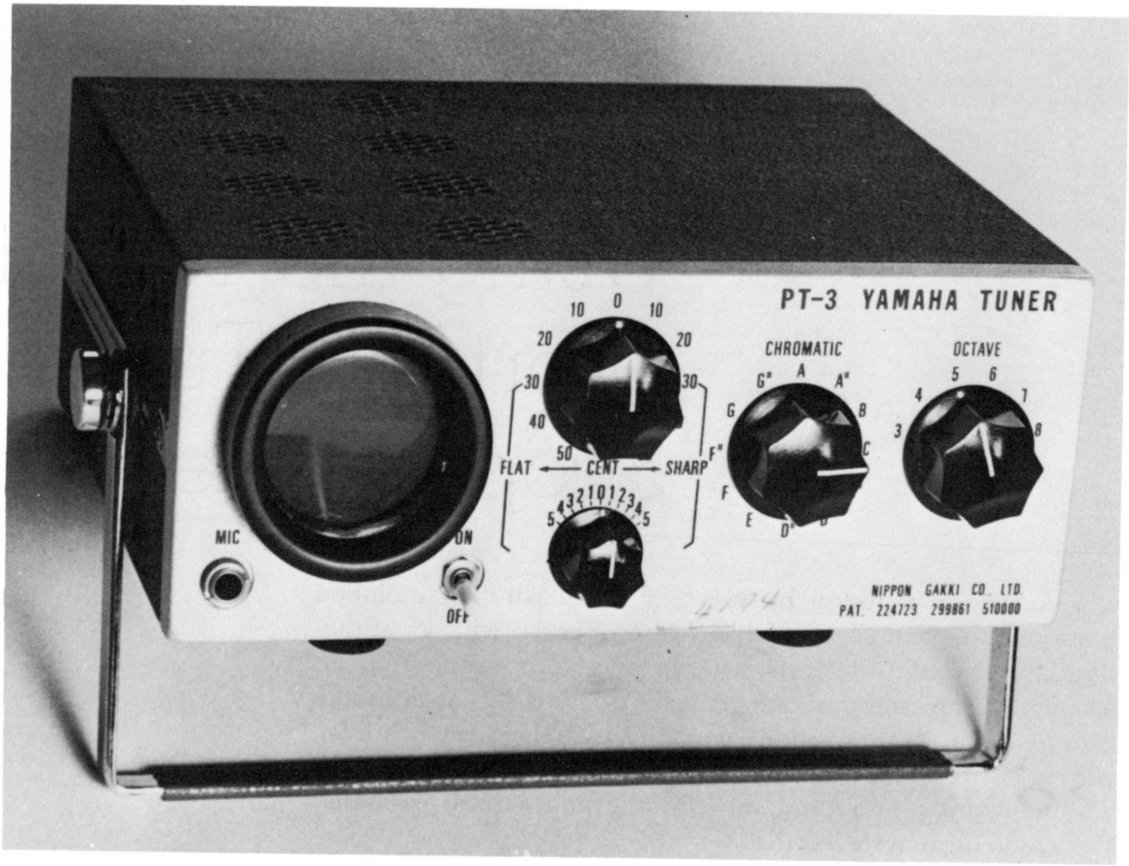


*Figure 6.1* Yamaha Tuning Scope Model PT-3

This tuner operates on 110 volts, 50 or 60 cycles per second, and draws only 10 watts of power. The temperature rise is perhaps from 40 to 50 degrees, no matter how long the instrument is turned on.

The relative error of standard frequency is plus or minus 1 cent or, in other words, .01 of a half tone, which puts it well within the accuracy range we expect of finely-made electronic tuning instruments. The standard frequency can be varied from 55 cents flat to 55 cents sharp, or more than a full half tone. Its total audio range, which is measurable, is from A 27½ cycles per second, which is the lowest A on a piano, to G 6,645 cycles per second.

The basic idea behind the Yamaha tuner is to make one instrument out of two accurate instruments. Basically, an audio generator is used to supply the tones from a standard oscillator through a frequency divider system, to the sweep generator, and then to horizontal plates of a cathode-ray oscilloscope tube. This pattern, which in effect is the output of the basic audio generator, would appear as a single line on the ordinary cathode-ray tube. However, the second instrument used in the Yamaha portable tuner is a microphone-fed filter amplifier and a brightness amplifier; the output from these is fed to the grid of the cathode-ray tube. The end result is that one receives a square wave pattern on the face of the cathode-ray tube when a particular note is set up on the audio generator and a similar note is played on the instrument being tuned.

Harmonic overtones are taken care of in this tuner by a table which comes with the instrument. The table advises the piano tuner as to how many cents flat or sharp he should set each note on the piano, provided that he tunes the piano from the bottom note to the top straight through. In other words, it would not be necessary to know fourths, fifths, thirds, sixths, minor thirds, or other intervals, or to accomplish beat rates if one were to tune a piano with this instrument. It almost seems as if a deaf man could use this tuner, utilizing the spread that is built into the instrument and the instructions that come with the standard piano tuning table.

The advantages of this tuner are many. First of all, the scales on the face of the tuner knob switch control with the percentages of sharp and flat are easy to read and well marked with dark figures on a light background. The octave selector switch is a simple matter to master and the chromatic tone being selected is visible from almost any angle from which the tuner may look. The off-and-on switch and the microphone jack are the only things that remain on the face of the instrument and they, of course, are quite visible.

The pattern which emerges on the face of the Braun cathode-ray oscilloscope tube is easily read and easy to decipher. There are rubber mountings on the back of the instrument and rubber feet on the front portion, so as to avoid marring or scarring the piano or any other instrument one is tuning.

The Yamaha Portable Tuner takes up the same space as an oscilloscope or an audio generator, such as the Peterson. While there is some difficulty in deciding just where to place the instrument on a piano, especially if it is a small spinet, it is still possible, after some trial and error, to determine the location so that the technician can see it and handle it. The microphone compartment, which is in the bottom or back end, so to speak, of this tuner, also serves as a storage space for the electric supply cord. It seemed to me that the compartment is somewhat small for the use for which it was intended. However, after almost a year of using this tuner, I have not had any difficulty in getting everything into the compartment. It's a matter of figuring out where to put the equipment so it fits.

Some additional padding on the chassis and on the cover would be helpful.

Yamaha furnishes a complete set of operating instructions with this instrument. They begin with an informative statement that the Yamaha Tuning Scope Model PT-3 is a portable, easy-to-use instrument requiring mainly the eyes to tune a musical instrument. With this unit tuning accuracy can be verified at a glance for any type of instrument. We are advised to make full use of the precision and convenience the tuning scope affords and to avoid abusing its power. With proper care, the Model PT-3 will give years of dependable service for precision tuning.

A complete block diagram of the circuit layout is supplied. The circuit begins where the calibration signal is fed in to a standard oscillator. It follows through the divider, sweep generator, horizontal amplifier, and Braun tube, including also the vertical oscillator postion in the circuit and the separate microphone jack filter amplifier, brightness amplifier, and power supply. One set of arrows shows the signal path through the instrument; the other shows the control path or the things that are affected by the knobs on the front. Block diagrams with part layouts of the circuit boards are depicted in the owner's manual.

There's a complete schematic diagram which would enable a television or transistor repairman to fix practically anything that went wrong. Also there's a troubleshooting chart in the manual which tells one what to do when such faults occur as a fuse blowing out, no pattern being on the scope, the sound fed into the microphone not affecting the pattern, or no picture being swept horizontally on the tube. There are 18 transsistors in these circuits and two tubes: a 50HB1 and a 6AV6.

Yamaha assures us that the PT-3 will not be affected by ordinary vibrations when being carried in a car or a station wagon but that it would be inadvisable to knock it against something or to drop it. We are cautioned not to place heavy objects on the unit, even when it is in its containing bag. According to the owner's manual, the unit is factory-adjusted for a clear pattern, but if this fades and loses its focus after some use it may be corrected with the intensity and focus adjustments. If the intensity adjustment is set too far to the right, the extreme brightness will eventually burn out the cathode-ray tube. Therefore, we are advised not to use any more brightness than is absolutely necessary. Also, the power should be turned off as soon as the tuner is not being used in order to prolong the life of the circuit parts.

Size and horizontal and vertical positions of the striped pattern may be adjusted, using the horizontal size, horizontal position, and vertical position adjusters, which are located on the left side of the case. There are instructions as to how to remove the chassis from its container and how to calibrate the instrument.

Calibration method: in order to calibrate the PT-3 Portable Tuning Scope, use either a frequency measuring instrument with a range of at least 880 to 1700 cycles per second or a tone or electric signal generator with the same accuracy as plus or minus 5 degrees. The former can be an electronic counter with a crystal-controlled standard frequency, and the latter can be a standard tuning fork or a crystal-controlled audio frequency standard instrument. With the frequency measuring instrument, connect the jack which reads "signal out" located on the right side of the case to the input terminal of the measuring instrument. The input impedance must be over 50,000 ohms. Then adjust the calibrator so that the signal matches its rated setting.

If one uses a signal or tone generator it may be fed into the microphone jack directly or sounded through the microphone, and the selectors and adjusters should be set to the tone and the calibrator adjusted while watching the cathode-ray tube.

Using a Model PT-3 is not difficult. The simplest kind of tuning is that on an organ or similar instruments. To do this, one would set the cent adjusters to zero and the chromatic selector to the note one wished to tune. Then one sounds the note and tunes so that the striped pattern on the cathode-ray tube stops. The octave selector can be turned to any setting where a pattern movement is clearly seen. In other words, lower ranges require lower octave selector settings and vice versa.

And when you tune an electronic instrument, the signal can be fed directly to the tuning scope without using the microphone. This can be done by plugging the signal cord approximately 10 millivolts into the microphone jack, using a coupling condensor. Yamaha suggests that you familiarize yourself with all the controls of the instrument by studying the photo, where they are clearly shown.

Most of the controls do not need to be used in the ordinary work of piano tuning. Only the octave selector, the chromatic selector, the cent adjuster, and the fine cents adjustment are ever used by the piano technician. The microphone must be plugged into the microphone jack and the instrument power switch must be turned on.

To prepare to use the tuner, first remove the unit from the bag by grasping the handle and set it near the musical instrument or on it, depending upon the space and convenience. The handle can be used as a stand by pulling it down under the unit. However, if this makes the scope too high to read comfortably, one can leave the handle up and stand the unit on its rubber feet. After removing the power cord from the microphone and AC compartment in the back of the unit, close it. The door of the compartment, made of metal, will scratch an instrument or furniture on which the tuner is set unless this door is closed and latched. Plug the AC cord into the electric outlet. Plug the microphone into the microphone jack. Then carefully place the microphone in a position to pick up sounds from the instrument to be tuned. Usually it is a good idea to place the microphone upon a folded piece of chamois leather or some similar substance. This will keep vibrations from disturbing the case of the microphone and at the same time prevent possible damage to the finish of the instrument you are tuning. A microphone is delicate; if it is banged against something or dropped its quality may deteriorate. Turn on the power switch. After a few seconds, a green pattern approximately 10 millimeters wide will appear across the face of the cathode-ray tube.

When tuning a piano with the Yamaha PT-3 Tuner, one must keep in mind the same problems of piano tone that have been plaguing tuners since the craft began. Electronic tuning specialists must be especially mindful of the fact that harmonic overtones of piano strings are not simple multiples of basic frequency. This is the most important point to remember when one is tuning a piano, whether doing it by ear or by an electronic instrument. Frankly, if this harmonic content is clearly understood, it matters little whether one tunes by ear or by electronic methods, since the tuning will come out equally well either way.

Conversely, if the harmonic content is misunderstood, no amount of ear training will enable a man to tune a piano better than he did before, and no electronic instrument will result in achieving a well-tuned piano.

Since the harmonic overtones are not simple multiples of frequency, the octave and chromatic selectors and cent adjusters on the Yamaha tuner must be set for each note. Begin in the following manner:

1. Match the chromatic selector setting to the key or note to be tuned.

2. Find the octave selector and cent adjustment settings by referring to the standard piano tuning table. The cent must be set by balancing the two selector settings. This can be seen by considering the settings when tuning the third key from the left on the piano, or in other words, the lowest B on a piano. First, set the octave selector to 3, which means you have chosen the lowest octave on the Yamaha tuner to tune the lowest octave on the piano. Then set it for −18 by turning the cent adjuster to 20 on the flat side and the fine cent adjuster to 2 on the sharp side. In other words, a minus sign corresponds to flat and a plus sign corresponds to sharp.

After considerable experimentation I arrived at a standard piano tuning table with a normal amount of stretch for the average piano that I have encountered in a year's time of tuning. A comparison of my table, which will be found in an earlier chapter in this book, with the standard piano tuning table that is provided by Yamaha leaves few areas that are disparate. As a matter of fact I was pleased that my laboriously-kept figures over a period of a year's time tuning pianos, relating to the amount of stretch required, were almost in perfect accord with the scientific figures determined by the Yamaha engineers as the proper stretch for the average piano.

Now, it is obvious that each piano is slightly different from any other and that the stretch for one piano may be slightly less or more than for another piano. Usually the larger the piano, the less amount of stretch required to make it sound good. However, after using the Yamaha tuner for a year, I have discovered that if one were to stick to the Yamaha table of standard deviation of frequency from the first note on the lower left on the keyboard to the top note, No. 88 at the top of the keyboard, he would tune a piano very well and would have a fine-sounding instrument, no matter what its size. Individual tuners may make individual adjustments, of course, depending on what their ear and their general taste may dictate in the far reaches of the bass and the upper reaches of the treble, and in the amount of stretch they care to put into a piano. Nevertheless, the standard piano tuning table of stretch as supplied by Yamaha will in almost every instance make a fine-sounding piano out of every one the tuner tunes. A glance at the standard piano tuning table shows that the lowest B, or key 3, has to be set 18 cents flat. You will notice that the lowest key on the piano, A, has to be set 20 cents flat. One of the great advantages of the Yamaha tuner, it seems to me, is that it does show you the lowest notes on the piano in a clear manner.

3. Strike only one string for each note, muting the others

## Yamaha Standard Piano Tuning Table

| OCTAVE SELECTOR | KEY NO. | CHRO-MATIC | OFF SET (CENT) | OCTAVE SELECTOR | KEY NO. | CHRO-MATIC | OFF SET (CENT) |
|---|---|---|---|---|---|---|---|
| 3 | 1 | A | –20 | 4 | 25 | A | – 3 |
| | 2 | A# | –19 | | 26 | A# | – 3 |
| | 3 | B | –18 | | 27 | B | – 3 |
| | 4 | C | –17 | | 28 | C | – 3 |
| | 5 | C# | –16 | | 29 | C# | – 3 |
| | 6 | D | –15 | | 30 | D | – 3 |
| | 7 | D# | –14 | | 31 | D# | – 3 |
| | 8 | E | –13 | | 32 | E | – 3 |
| | 9 | F | –12 | | 33 | F | – 3 |
| | 10 | F# | –11 | | 34 | F# | –2.5 |
| | 11 | G | –10 | | 35 | G | –2.5 |
| | 12 | G# | – 9 | | 36 | G# | – 2 |
| 4 | 13 | A | – 8 | | 37 | A | – 2 |
| | 14 | A# | – 7 | | 38 | A# | – 2 |
| | 15 | B | – 6 | | 39 | B | – 2 |
| | 16 | C | – 6 | | 40 | C | – 2 |
| | 17 | C# | – 5 | | 41 | C# | – 2 |
| | 18 | D | – 5 | | 42 | D | – 2 |
| | 19 | D# | – 4 | | 43 | D# | –1.5 |
| | 20 | E | – 4 | | 44 | E | – 1 |
| | 21 | F | – 4 | | 45 | F | – 1 |
| | 22 | F# | – 4 | | 46 | F# | – 1 |
| | 23 | G | – 4 | | 47 | G | – 1 |
| | 24 | G# | – 3 | | 48 | G# | – 1 |

| OCTAVE SELECTOR | KEY NO. | CHRO-MATIC | OFF SET (CENT) | OCTAVE SELECTOR | KEY NO. | CHRO-MATIC | OFF SET (CENT) |
|---|---|---|---|---|---|---|---|
| 5 | 49 | A | 0 | 7 | 73 | A | 6 |
| | 50 | A# | 0 | | 74 | A# | 7 |
| | 51 | B | 0 | | 75 | B | 8 |
| | 52 | C | 0 | | 76 | C | 9 |
| | 53 | C# | 0 | | 77 | C# | 10 |
| | 54 | D | 0 | | 78 | D | 11 |
| | 55 | D# | 1 | | 79 | D# | 12 |
| | 56 | E | 1 | | 80 | E | 13 |
| | 57 | F | 1 | | 81 | F | 15 |
| | 58 | F# | 1 | | 82 | F# | 17 |
| | 59 | G | 1 | | 83 | G | 19 |
| | 60 | G# | 2 | | 84 | G# | 21 |
| 6 | 61 | A | 2 | 8 | 85 | A | 23 |
| | 62 | A# | 2 | | 86 | A# | 25 |
| | 63 | B | 2 | | 87 | B | 27 |
| | 64 | C | 2 | | 88 | C | 30 |
| | 65 | C# | 3 | | | | |
| | 66 | D | 3 | | | | |
| | 67 | D# | 3 | | | | |
| | 68 | E | 4 | | | | |
| | 69 | F | 4 | | | | |
| | 70 | F# | 5 | | | | |
| | 71 | G | 5 | | | | |
| | 72 | G# | 6 | | | | |

with either a felt strip or rubber mutes, and tune so that the striped pattern stops moving.

4. Lift the mute from the string on one side of the one you have tuned. Tune this other string of the unison by ear so that all beats between the two strings are eliminated. Then lift the mute from the other string of the unison, if there are three strings in the unison, and tune the third string to the two strings you have just tuned so that there is no discernible beat.

5. If you glance at the Yamaha tuning standard table you will see that some notes in the same octave have the same cent marks. For example, the cent for notes 36 through 39 is zero. In such a case, if one desires to tune more pleasingly to the ear, it is better to tune the higher notes *above* the setting, or, in other words, so that the striped pattern moves slightly to the right, rather than to tune the lower ones lower than the setting which the table suggests.

6. In the eighth octave it is sometimes difficult to ascertain in which direction the pattern is moving if there is a large difference between the string's frequency and the cent setting of the tuning scope. In this case, move the adjusters back and forth to find in which direction the pattern is moving. Be sure to reset the adjusters to their correct positions before tuning the string. Repeat the adjustment two or three times to be sure there is no mistake. Pattern movement to the left means the note is flat. Pattern movement to the right means the note is sharp. Always tune to stop the movement.

One of the easier ways to tune the top 12 notes on the piano is to strike the note an octave below the note you intend to tune and to listen very carefully as you manipulate the top treble string which corresponds to the note you are trying to tune. When you have trained your ear sufficiently, you will discover that you can hear the echo, or the sympathetic vibration of the proper harmonic in the highest treble wire, one octave above the note you have just tuned.

This means that you can tune the top 12 notes on a piano without ever striking them by simply striking the corresponding notes an octave lower and listening for the harmonic overtones to vibrate the string you are tuning when you have it in proper pitch. This is a trick of the trade which few tuners use or know about. But it is an excellent way to tune the top treble to perfect harmonic fidelity with the octave just below it. After this is done, one can easily check with the Yamaha PT-3 and determine whether he has given the stretch the table would suggest. For all intents and purposes, he will find that the stretch that has been given to the upper treble harmonics is precisely the amount indicated on the Yamaha table as the proper one for a good-sounding piano.

The Yamaha tuning table shows us that there is no problem in setting a temperament with this instrument. For example, when one looks at note 33, which corresponds with the lower end of the F temperament (which the average tuner would use in aural tuning), he discovers that he is supposed to set this F 3 cents flat as compared with perfect F in a chromatic scale. By setting this lower F in his temperament 3 cents flat, he has actually made it only 1 cent flat compared to middle C, or key 40. One cent flat from key 40 would mean that he had just about the beat rate per second that he would expect when he went down from C to F in a normal aural temperament.

The F above middle C is then set 1 cent flat from standard, which means that it will be 1 cent sharp compared to middle C. So the beat ratio between the F above middle C and middle C, and the F below middle C and middle C, will correspond very closely to what the aural temperament provides. According to the Yamaha piano tuning table, if one were to set A at the proper pitch, one would strike the A fork and set A49 to perfect resonance with it and then drop down to the next A, which is 37, and set it 2 cents flat.

In actual practice most tuners will agree that they begin

to stretch and actually begin a temperament this way in many cases. If one were to set a temperament with a C fork according to the Yamaha tuning table, one would use C52, or one octave above middle C, and bring it to perfect resonance with the tuning fork, and then drop down an octave and make the other C 2 beats flat. In fact, this is what one actually does, because we are working with harmonics the moment we move away from whatever note we have set with the tuning fork.

No doubt it would be possible for those who are gifted in mathematics or physics to find some way to slightly alter the table that Yamaha has given. I am no devotee of arithmetic, nor am I particularly interested in splitting fine hairs or fractions of a cent, or fractions of a semicent, or anything else that would make a table exhaustively precise. Suffice it to say that for the purpose of good piano tuning, and masterful tuning at that, that the Yamaha piano tuning table, when used with the Yamaha scope, makes for accuracy of a high degree indeed. Furthermore, a knowledge of Yamaha's table, or the author's which is based on totally different criteria perhaps, would enable most tuners to do a much finer job of consistently tuning every piano well. The overall stretch ratio as given in these tables will time after time be required if one wants to have a piano that stays stretched as it should and sounds as a piano should. The best way to set temperament with the Yamaha tuner is to do precisely what the Yamaha people suggest.

Turn on the tuner, use the standard piano tuning table, and set the notes accordingly. By using the table to set temperament, and doing each note one at a time without stopping to check the beat rates between intervals in the temperament, the piano technician will discover that he has achieved an acceptable temperament and one which begins to sound thrilling as he moves further and further along going out of it in arpeggios.

This temperament is smooth and even in all its progressions. There are no beat rates within it which seriously contradict the best that we have learned in aural tuning. As a matter of fact, there is little I can say to find fault with the temperament method used with this tuner. It would be just as simple to start with key 1 at the lower end of the piano, observing the Yamaha piano tuning table, and to set the piano going up note after note without ever stopping, using the tuner for the purpose of termperment. However, there are some other factors that should be considered at this particular point.

Some of these have to do with the long-held view on my part that tuning a piano is not simply a matter of tuning all the notes to a particular frequency which corresponds to what they should sound like in their place in the scale. Many tensions and stresses are involved in tuning, and it is possible, if the piano is far out of tune when the tuner arrives, that he is going to add some stresses to different portions to the soundboard and bridges which were not present when he began to tune.

For this reason, I have always felt it best to set the center section of the piano on single strings; to proceed down into the bass and to set the single strings of each unison; to move up into the treble and set the single strings of each unison; and finally to begin again at the center and bass to fill in the additional strings of the unison, bringing them up to proper pitch.

This overall method of tuning a piano, single strings in the center, single strings next in the bass, and then single strings in the treble, allows for one-third of the additional tension which the tuner is placing on the piano to be placed evenly throughout before the additional strings on the unisons are brought into play.

In addition to that, after the single strings are all set at proper pitch, moving down into the bass to bring the strings of the unison in proper harmony with those already set, then moving into the treble, which must accept one-third of the tension, and finally proceeding into the center section, gives the tuner confidence that he has stressed the edges of the bridges farthest removed from the center of the sound board to which he must add tremendous stress. At times, it appears that the piano almost aids in the tuning process, considering how it accepts and distributes the tensions of the strings.

However, what has been said in no way makes less useful the Yamaha tuner. For it is a simple matter for the tuner to begin at the lowest tenor string next to the base-break and to mute the center section of the piano, and from that point on, to use the standard tuning table and to tune all the way up to the treble break, and stop. He then can go down to the first bass string next to the tenor, where the two lengths of string begin to intersect, and to move down on single strings straight on through the bass—actually more rapidly with the use of the PT-3 tuner than by ear.

Following this, the tuner then moves up to the break in the treble and begins to set one string of each unison with the Yamaha, following the table, right on up to C88, and then proceeds to go back and tune in the single string sides to the unisons so as to get an overall piano tuning. By using this method, which to some might seem more complicated, rather than starting at the bottom of the piano and going straight through I find that the Yamaha tuner will cut one-fourth of the time usually required to tune the average piano. Not only that, but the tuner himself is better satisfied that he has been scientifically compensated for the harmonic overtones which can (or cannot) be handled at times by the human ear.

There is also a happy medium that a tuner may use with the Yamaha PT-3. If desired, he can set his temperament with the Yamaha and proceed from there in fifths, thirds, sixths, or whatever system he prefers to make his octave arrangements, and to compensate and to put the proper amount of stretch in the piano which he feels his ear alone might not do accurately. I have tried every method not once, but many, many times with this tuner, and in every instance I have found, without fail, that the final result on the piano ended up close to the settings suggested on the Yamaha table.

Following this table when working on electronic instruments, like organs, may put them in perfect tune with the piano, but perhaps they would not sound exactly as an organ should. But on a piano, following this table is the surest way I have ever discovered to tune a piano accurately, beautifully, and well. If being a master tuner is your ambition, here is the tuning instrument which will rarely fail to turn out a competent job.

As I have stated before, the instrument is compact and professional. There's no reason why the average tuner should not be able to do a perfect job if he follows good tuning practices. By that I mean the proper lifting of the string, the proper springing or setting of the pin, the proper follow-through with an 8 or 9 lb. blow on each string to make sure there will be no further shift after the tuner is through with it. As a matter of fact, no instrument can tune a piano well, unless the man who is using it can set his pins properly and add the tensions to the piano in the process of tuning in a systematic and sensible way, so as to avoid unusual shifts or strains within the framework and body of the piano and its bridges. If the man who is tuning the instrument views himself as a master craftsman, tunes with care, and brings his unisons in with perfect clarity, he may begin where he wishes in the Yamaha table, and by following it religiously, figure for figure, using the PT-3 he will tune a piano so that it sounds better than it did after the last man tuned it.

# 7
# Using the Tune Master

The cooperation that I received from Marvin Masel, president of Berkshire Electronic Instruments, the manufacturer of the Tune Master, leads me to assume that the technician who buys a Tune Master will find a factory behind it that will help make him proficient in its use and one that should follow up with additional sophisticated information in the years ahead.

Thoroughness seems to be one of Mr. Masel's habits. While his attitude was in no way different from that shown by other manufacturers whose products are discussed in this book, it seems worthy of mention because the Tune Master is a recent arrival on the market, and tuners and technicians should be informed as to what to expect if they purchase it.

The Tune Master is an electronic instrument that gives an accurate indication of the frequency of a sound or electrical signal. It compares the frequency to be measured with stable internal frequency standards based upon the equally-tempered musical scale. The frequency deviation is shown on a meter movement calibrated in cents (hundredths of a half tone) sharp or flat.

It is possible to measure the frequency of a selected overtone, as well as the fundamental. A front panel control modifies the internal frequency reference from equal temperament to the stretched temperament needed for proper tuning of pianos.

The basic system is built around a meter movement which indicates deviation from a basic standard, with the meter movement going to the right for sharp and to the left for flat. In using this instrument, I found it a little difficult to stabilize the meter movement for any sustained period of time in order to get a reading which would enable me to make the slight movements of the tuning process necessary for extremely fine tuning. However, with considerable practice, and as one becomes familiar with the methods used in tuning with this instrument, it is possible to anticipate the direction in which the meter will move next.

Piano tones, as most tuners know, do not remain constant in pitch from the start to the finish of their audible duration. There is a pronounced flatting of the tone at the moment the hammer strikes the string, followed by a gradual rise to higher pitch; this might be compared to a 90 degree curve on a graph. This rise is followed by a deterioration of tone into many partials which offer random impulses to any meter system. It is essential that the technician be guided by the indicator light on this unit, which glows brightly at the proper moment for adjusting the tone of the string.

### *Operating Instructions*

To operate the Tune Master, connect the line cord to a 115 volt, 60 cycle outlet and turn the power switch on. To make a measurement, the internal standard is selected by the octave switch, tone switch, and cents control.

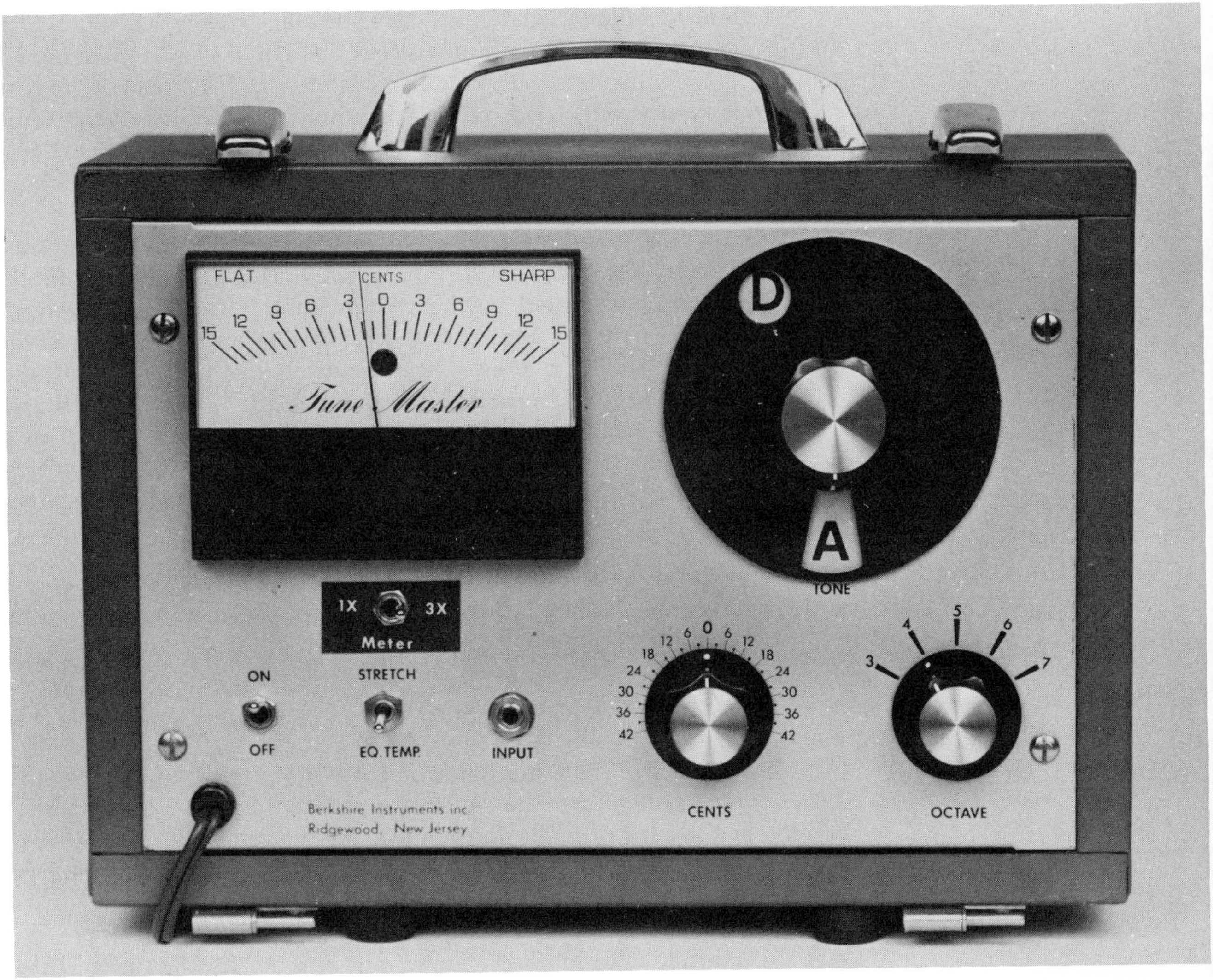


Tune Master *Figure 7.1*

Frequency deviation from the internal standard is displayed on the meter, which is divided into cents (.01 of a half tone). A lamp located on the meter face glows steadily when the input signal is sufficiently strong to give a valid reading.

The stretch switch will be set to the E.T. position (equal temperament) for organs. For tuning pianos or harpsichords, setting the E. T.-stretch to stretch modifies the internal frequency standards slightly, but in a musically significant manner.

The tone switch has 12 positions with C the lowest frequency and B the highest frequency. There are two windows in the disc rotated by the switch knob. The larger wedge-shaped window, shown in the picture as displaying an A tells us that the Tune Master is measuring the frequency of any input signal which is approximately an A. The smaller round window, is displaying a D. As one tunes the bass strings of a piano, the round window is useful, as discussed later.

The octave switch enables selection of any of five octaves beginning with:

C3 = 130.81 cps
C4 = 261.63 cps (middle C)
C5 = 523.25 cps
C6 = 1046.5 cps
C7 = 2093.0 cps

In order to provide complete frequency coverage, the cents control may be set over a plus or minus 42 cents range. In the zero position, the internal frequency standard is A-440 cps. Note that 1 beat per second at A-440 corresponds to about 4 cents.

A jack is provided for the use of a pickoff other than the internal microphone. Inserting a plug in this jack automatically disconnects the internal microphone.

All Tune Masters are supplied with an external microphone, which is particularly useful for tuning the treble octaves.

There is a special magnetic pickoff which is sensitive to nearby vibrations of a piano string. This pickoff is convenient when tuning in a noisy environment as it is insensitive to acoustic inputs.

### *Measurement of Overtone Frequency*

For most applications, the Tune Master's input will not be a pure tone of a single frequency, but rather a complex mixture of fundamental plus many partials, or overtones. In order to analyze such an input, the Tune Master attenuates any frequency more than a half tone distant from the frequency selected by the tone and octave switches. Suppose concert A (A4) is tuned to 440 cps with the octave switch on 4. The frequency of the second partial of the evoked sound may be measured by setting the octave switch to 5. It is possible to measure the frequency of the third partial (an octave plus a fifth above A4) by setting the octave switch to 6 and the round window of the tone switch displaying A (the wedge-shaped window is then displaying E). In the case of a piano string, the upper partials are found to be sharp: in the neighborhood of 2 cents for the second partial of A4, 5 cents for the second partial, 10 cents for the third partial, etc. (Note: the fifths in equal temperament are 2 cents flat; hence, in measuring the sharpness of a third partial it is necessary to subtract 2 cents from the Tune Master's reading.) The increased sharpening of higher partials as we know, is sometimes referred to as inharmonicity. Inharmonicity of overtones is, of course, much greater for short treble strings than for long bass strings.

The tuning schedule shown in the table which follows this chapter provides the 3 cents per octave stretch, with a little extra in the highest octave. In the fourth octave and higher, fundamentals are used for tuning. The bass is more easily tuned by using upper partials. For C3 through B3, note that the octave is used for tuning, with the octave switch set to 4. The meter target is set at flat 3. (On some pianos, the highest few notes of the third octave are difficult to read with the octave switch at 4. If so, turn the octave switch to 3 and set the meter to flat 3 as before.)

Below C3 it is usually easier to obtain steady and reliable readings by tuning the third partial (octave plus a fifth) or in the extreme bass, the sixth partial (two octaves plus a fifth). For example, B2 may be tuned with the octave switch at 4 and the round window of the tone switch displaying B (the wedge-shaped window then displays an F). The desired stretch is maintained with the meter reading at zero. Typical inharmonicity of upper partials was taken into account in deriving the suggested meter readings.

An added stretch is provided in the seventh octave by setting C7 to sharp 9, C#7 to sharp 10, etc., adding 1 cent for each semitone. Alternately, the cents control may be rotated 9 cents sharp (clockwise) of its prior setting and the meter target setting is zero for C7, sharp 1 for C#, etc.

The Tune Master's internal microphone is generally more convenient to use except in the sixth and seventh octaves. However, keep the external microphone handy for an occasional hard-to-read string in the bass section of a vertical piano. It is difficult to attain a tuning of concert quality when changing pitch more than 10 cents. The piano structure readjusts itself to the changing stresses. However, if the pitch changing process is begun in the extreme bass and continues string by string until the highest treble note, the tuning accuracy is affected less by yielding of the structure.

If there is no time for preliminary pitch changing, followed by a fine tuning, it may be necessary to tune the piano above or below A-440. This is accomplished by adjusting the cents control until one of the untuned strings in the fourth octave reads zero. Then continue the tuning according to the table.

The Tune Master user has a significant advantage over even a skilled aural tuner in that each string is adjusted to an absolute standard of pitch. Therefore, any inaccuracy of setting a string, or subsequent slippage, causes only one error. In aural tuning, one single error can propagate through the whole tuning process so that continual rechecking is necessary.

Of course, only a careless tuner would fail to check his notes while tuning the piano, wherever he goes. An electronic tuning device should not take the place of skilled tailoring of the octaves by checking with fifths, thirteenths, and seventeenths. The best possible tuning of a piano is not done by strict adherence to a mathematical progression of frequencies, but rather by an intelligent shading of the octave intervals through the use of other intervals as standard checking points. Since pianos differ markedly in the amount of stretch which is required to make them sound musically in tune, slight deviations from an electronic frequency standard are absolutely necessary for first class tuning.

This is not to say that a piano cannot be tuned by strict adherence to a planned deviation from the norm, when worked out according to a table of average stretch required. That is, the table itself must in all cases be amenable to shading on individual notes, dependent upon the actual piano being tuned. We cannot turn off our ears when tuning a piano electronically without causing detrimental practices in our tuning process and less than perfect results in our finished work.

## *Suggestions for Piano Tuning with Tune Master*

It is well known that tuning a piano to equal temperament gives poor results. Professor Meinel* has demonstrated that

*Meinel, H., Musicinstrumenstimmungen und Tonsysteme, Acustica. Volume 7, No. 3, 185–90 (1957).

expert aural tuners develop a stretch of 3 cents per octave over the whole scale, except for a possible increased stretch in the highest octave. He notes that the 3 cents per octave stretch (which is proper for uprights or consoles as well as grand pianos) causes the excessively narrow equal temperament fifths to be expanded and makes piano tuning compatible with orchestral instruments. Stretching of octaves also tends to make the upper partials of bass semitones more nearly consonant with the fundamentals in the higher octaves.

By setting the E.T.-stretch switch to stretch, the Tune Master's internal frequency references are altered to a slight extent. The frequency difference between adjacent half tones is widened to 100¼ cents instead of 100 cents, while maintaining the frequency of A unchanged. Thus C is 2¼ cents flat of the equal temperament value and B is ½ cent sharp of the equal temperament value.

To maintain a 3-cents-per-octave stretch, assume that the octave from C4 through B4 is tuned so that the meter is set to zero for each tone. If the octave C5 through B5 is tuned so that the meter movement is set to + 3 cents for each tone, a little arithmetic will show that C5 will actually be tuned ¾ cent sharp of A4. The 3-cents-per-octave stretch is thereby distributed evenly from half tone to half tone without sudden jumps.

If you are skilled at tuning unisons by ear, strip mute all but one string of each unison throughout the piano. Otherwise, the Tune Master may be used for tuning the strings of each note, in sequence.

Plug the Tune Master into a power outlet and place it on the piano. Turn the on-off switch to on, the stretch-eq. temp. switch to stretch, the octave switch to 4 and the wedge-shaped window of the tone switch to C. Observe that the letter C is in a light background. The black keys, as for example C#, are in a dark background. The cents control should be at zero. If your Tune Master has a meter switch, set it at 1X.

Mute two of the strings of the middle C (C4) unison, strike

the piano key a medium blow, and observe the meter. If the pointer indicates off scale, you may return it to zero by turning the cents control while the light is on. Note that a valid reading light glows steadily on the meter face within a fraction of a second after the key is struck. As the sound dies away, the light will flicker and the meter may move erratically. Ignore the pointer while the light is flickering.

If the middle C pitch reading is on scale, you may proceed to fine tune the piano to standard pitch (A-440). Where the existing piano pitch is more than about 15 or 20 cents sharp or flat, two or more tunings may be needed for adequate stability. If there is no time for multiple tunings, you may set the cents control for only a partial pitch raising or lowering.

You may begin tuning. The C below middle C is a good place to start. Looking at the keyboard chart, we see that the octave switch should be at 4 and the wedge-shaped window of the tone switch at C. With one string of the unison unmuted, strike the key a medium blow. The pointer will show the pitch reading within a fraction of a second. If you strike the key a hard blow, you may have to wait longer for the reading to stabilize.

The keyboard chart shows that the pitch of C3 should be set at flat 3. When raising pitch of a string, pull the pitch about 3 or 6 cents sharp off its target setting and then ease it back. Smooth rather than jerky movements of the tuning hammer are preferred. Some piano strings have false beats, causing the pointer to waver somewhat. In such cases, set the pitch so that the midpoint of the meter swing corresponds to the recommended setting on the keyboard chart. Feed-through of sound from inadequately muted strings can also cause wavering of the pointer.

After C3 (one string if you have strip muted the piano, all strings otherwise) proceed to C3#, D3, etc., to B3, setting the pointer to flat 3. In each case, make sure the wedge-shaped window of the tone switch is over the note. When you reach

C4, begin to set the meter pointer to zero. Continue in sequence to B4. When you reach C5, advance the octave switch to 5 and tune for meter reading of sharp 3. At C6, turn the octave switch to 6 and advance the meter target to sharp 6. Continue until B6. Next, begin tuning the bass, with the intent of finishing the seventh octave later. Return the octave switch to 4 and place the round window of the tone switch over the letter B. Now tune B2, setting the meter pointer to zero. Next, tune A2#, A2, etc., through F2, always using the round window over the note being tuned. When you reach E2, rotate the octave switch to 3 and set the meter reading to flat 3. Below F1 of the piano, tune to flat 6 all the way down to the lowest key.

For steady readings in the lowest octave, use a light blow of the key. If you have difficulty with any note, try plucking the string lightly. Plugging in the external microphone may also improve the reading for an occasional difficult bass note.

The Tune Master will not give a reading if the note is out of tune more than about one semitone. There is also a hazard in the extreme bass of getting a pitch reading of the wrong partial if the note is mistuned by a major third or more. Therefore, the piano must be set in approximate tune aurally before fine tuning with the Tune Master.

After finishing the bass tuning, we return to the highest octave. Use the external microphone and place it near the treble string. From the keyboard chart we note the C7 is tuned at sharp 9 with the wedge-shaped window over the C and the octave switch at 7. However, sharp 9 is inconveniently close to the edge of the meter, so we rotate the cents control by 9 cents clockwise from its previous position and tune C7 so that the pointer is at zero. Next tune C7#, to sharp 1, D7 to sharp 2, etc., sharpening each note by 1 cent. At F we may rotate the cents control 6 cents clockwise and tune until the pointer is at zero. Continue tuning each note 1 cent sharper until B7. C8 should then be tuned aurally.

At this point remove the strip muting and tune all unisons aurally. If you have previously tuned the unisons with the Tune Master, recheck them aurally and correct any that have drifted.

***Meter Switch and Audio Output Options***

The Tune Master II-E and II-EA have a meter switch with 1X and 3X positions. On the 1X position, one division of the meter corresponds to 1 cent frequency deviation; on the 3X position, one division corresponds to 3 cents frequency deviation. The 1X sensitivity is needed for fine tuning of pianos; for rough tuning of pianos or for tuning most other instruments, the 3X sensitivity is more convenient.

The Tune Master II-EA also has an added jack with volume control for audio output. Either a monaural or stereo 1/4 in. plug can be plugged into the jack and one listens with earphones. Any type of earphones may be used provided the impedance is in the range of 8 ohms to 2,000 ohms. Padded hi-fi earphones are fine for educational applications but are somewhat bulky and uncomfortable for long hours of tuning. Some users have reported that the Allied Radio Shack's Realistic Model No. 33-196 is satisfactory.

The audio output option is useful for demonstrating the decomposition of a musical tone into fundamental and upper partials. Thus, if you sound middle C, you may isolate each partial as follows:

| Partial Description | No. | Octave Switch | Tone Switch |
|---|---|---|---|
| Fundamental | 1 | 4 | C |
| Octave | 2 | 5 | C |
| Octave plus a fifth | 3 | 5 | G |
| Double octave | 4 | 6 | C |
| Two octaves plus a major third | 5 | 6 | E |
| Two octaves plus a fifth, etc. | 6 | 6 | G |

You may also listen to the significant beating partials when playing an interval. Thus, play middle C and the E above with the octave switch at 6 and the tone switch at E. The fifth partial of the C may be heard beating with the fourth partial of the E.

By setting an exact bearing with the Tune Master meter, then listening to the progression of the major thirds and cross-checking with fourths and fifths, you can rapidly improve your aural tuning ability. You will also be amazed at how your aural unison tuning improves when listening to the proper upper partials.

Even the most skilled of aural tuners can profit from the audio output when tuning in concert halls, schools, homes, or other places which sometimes are noisy.

### *Application of Tune Master to Meantone Temperament*

Traditional tuning of meantone is performed by setting four notes: D, A, E, and B so that the fifths are even narrower than in equal temperament (by 3.4 cents) and the fourths wider by the same amount. All other notes are then tuned so that the major thirds are beatless (i.e., with an exact 5.4 frequency ratio).

Accurate meantone tuning exceeds the capability of all but a select group of aural tuners. The Tune Master, on the other hand, provides a direct readout of frequency offset without a need for knob turning.

The simplest method of setting a meantone temperament using the Tune Master is to follow the chart below. Please note that other meantone temperaments, interchanging sharps and flats, are possible.

The Tune Master-III has a meter range of + or −30 cents so that it is possible to read the maximum deviation from equal temperament directly in cents. The Tune Master II-EA range is + or −15 cents, so it is necessary to set the meter switch to 3X. The third column gives the dial reading to the nearest

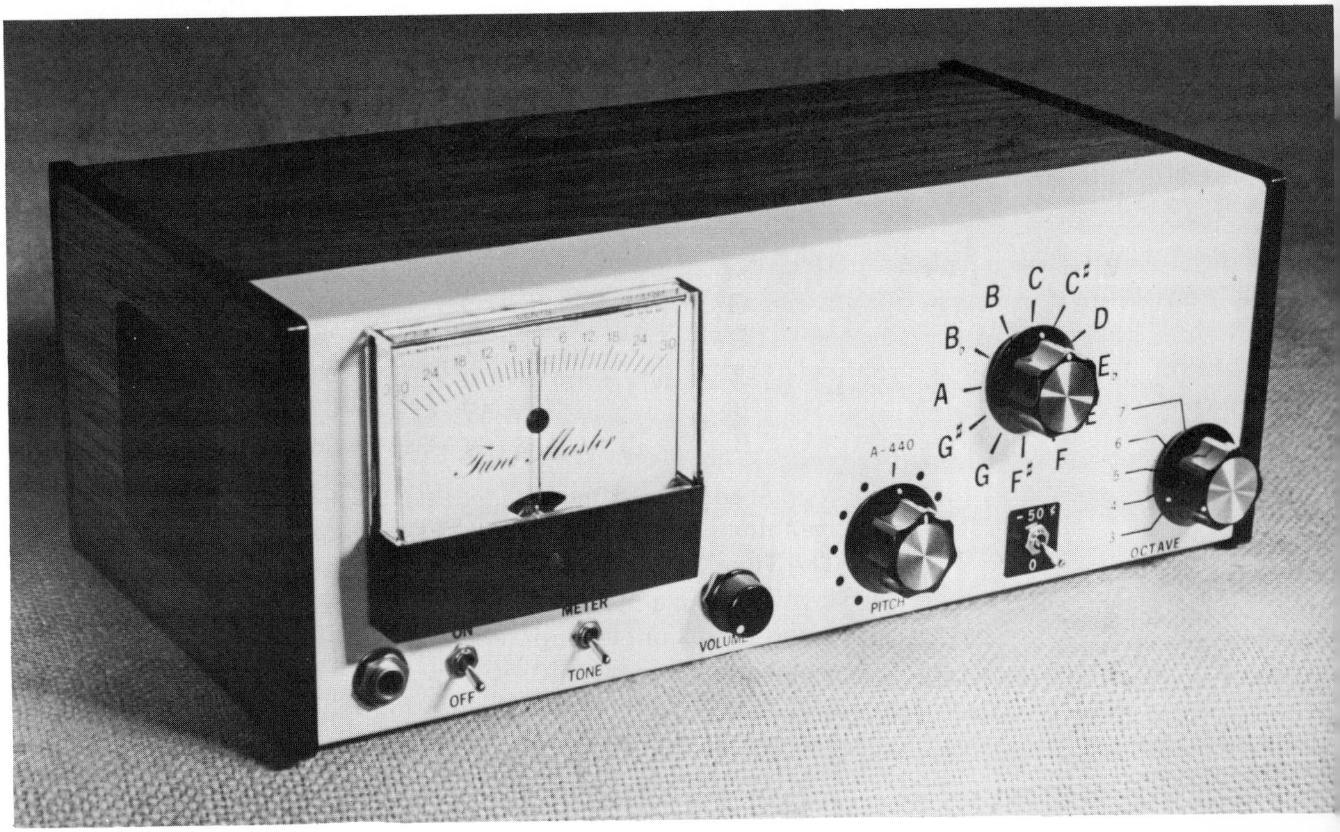


Tune Master III *Figure 7.2*

integer. (The Tune Master II-EA's E.T.-stretch switch should be set to E.T.)

| Note | Cents sharp (+) flat (−) | Dial Reading on 3X scale |
|---|---|---|
| C | + 10 | + 3 |
| C# | − 14 | − 5 |
| D | + 3 | + 1 |
| Eb | + 21 | + 7 |
| E | − 3 | − 1 |
| F | + 14 | + 4 |
| F# | − 10 | − 3 |
| G | + 7 | + 2 |
| G# | − 17 | − 6 |
| A | 0 | 0 |
| Bb | + 17 | + 6 |
| B | − 7 | − 2 |

A somewhat more accurate method of developing the meantone is to set D, A, E, B, to the values shown in the chart. The Tune Master is then used to match the fifth partial of the lower note of a major third with the fourth partial of the upper note. For example, suppose A3 has been tuned to zero cents, with the octave switch set at position 3 or 4. If the octave switch is then rotated to 5, the fourth partial of A3 may be measured. In the case of a piano, the fourth partial will be sharp on the zero reading because of inharmonicity effects. If F3 is sounded next, its pitch may be adjusted so that the meter pointer is at the same position as for the A3 partial. The second partial of A4 could then be tuned in the same manner, insuring the beatless 5.2 ratio of the minor sixth.

The major thirds as tuned above sound quite differently from the equal temperament intervals to which we are accustomed. They are about 14 cents narrower and the minor sixths are correspondingly wider.

In meantone, C# does not mean the same as D♭. To tune C#4, set the fourth partial to C#4 coincident with the fifth partial of A3. However, to make the same note a D♭3, set its fifth partial coincident with the fourth partial of F4.

The external microphone accessory of the Tune Master II (available at extra charge) should be used when measuring upper partials; its excellent treble response enhances the selectivity of the Tune Master's tunable filter.

## *The Tune Master II Series*

Tune Master II-EA has all the features of Tune Master II-E plus a unique provision for audio output. Only the selected frequency components are heard through an external headset. Other frequencies are suppressed.

## *Applications of Audio Output*

It blocks out interfering sounds when tuning in noisy places; concentrates hearing on desired partials while tuning intervals; demonstrates decomposition of musical tone into fundamental and upper partials; helps in explaining different tuning methods: equal temperament, meantone, just, stretched piano; and, in research and manufacturing, the audio output signal may be used to excite reed, string, or air column, in steady state. Frequency error signal from meter may be provided on special order.

## *Examples*

To isolate beating partials of the major third middle C and the E above, set Tune Master for two octaves above the E. The fifth partial of the C may be heard beating with the fourth partial of the E.

Similarly, beats of the fourth may be heard by setting the Tune Master for two octaves above the lower note. For listening to beats of the fifth, set the controls for one octave above the higher note of the interval.

Octave and unison tuning can often be made more precise by listening to upper partials.

*Useful Hints*

To practice aural tuning, the beginner may tune an accurate bearing with the Tune Master meter, then listen to beating partials of thirds, fourths, and fifths. The use of a Y adapter will permit an apprentice and his teacher to listen with earphones to the same Tune Master.

*Tune Master Magnetic Pickoff*

The magnet at one end attaches to the piano strings or steel plate; the other end senses vibration of a piano wire in the vicinity. The pickoff is completely insensitive to sound or the vibration of nonmagnetically permeable objects.

You can tune easily in the noisiest places. The pickoff blocks interference from public address systems, lawn mowers, pneumatic hammers, air conditioners, vacuum cleaners, barking dogs, noisy children, or other musical instruments.

The pickoff has excellent treble response: you can tune the highest piano octave while tapping piano key repeatedly to equalize tension.

If you have a Tune Master II-EA, plug the magnetic pickoff into the input jack, and any loudspeaker into the audio output jack. The selected partial of the piano string is amplified and some of its energy is fed back to keep the piano string excited.

The Tune Master external microphone may be used in reverse as a loudspeaker. With each magnetic pickoff an adapter is supplied for inserting the external microphone into the audio output jack. The external microphone used in conjunction with the magnetic pickoff is particularly useful in tuning the highest piano octave; for best results, place the microphone near the treble strings. You may use the Tune Master meter or benefit from the prolonged sound of aural tuning.

The prolonged amplified audio signal is useful in music education. A teacher may demonstrate to a whole class the decomposition of a single piano tone into the complete harmonic series. The Tune Master magnetic pickoff includes an adapter for the external microphone.

### *Bridge Adjustment for Guitars for Proper Intonation*

Guitars may be tuned either by using an acoustic input to the Tune Master or by connecting a guitar pickup to the input jack. (In the case of the Tune Master III, a monaural plug should be inserted halfway, a stereo plug all the way. A Tune Master II requires a plug adapter.) Volume and tone controls of the guitar should be at maximum clockwise rotation. The capability of silent tuning is of particular interest during stage or broadcast work.

The standard guitar tuning is E2, A2, D3, G3, B3, and E4, where the number refers to the piano octave. However, you will generally get the most satisfactory pitch readings with the Tune Master's octave switch set at 4. The Tune Master is thus sensing the fourth harmonics (more properly called partials) of the low E and A strings, the second harmonics of the D, G, and B strings, and the fundamental frequency of the high E string.

To obtain a steady and precise measurement, it is useful to maximize the amplitude of the desired harmonic and to damp unwanted modes of vibration. Thus, to excite the fourth harmonic of an open string, pluck the string near the bridge and then briefly give the string a light touch at the fifth fret. To measure the second harmonic of the open string, touch at the twelfth fret. The fundamental is emphasized by plucking the midpoint of the vibrating section.

An electric bass may be tuned by the same method as above, but with the octave switch set at 3.

The adjustment of an individual string length is best performed by a comparison of the pitch of a harmonic of the open string with the pitch of the shorter section that results when pressing firmly behind the twelfth fret. The musical ear prefers the treble tuning to be slightly sharper than the theoretical equal temperament scale. This octave stretching is accomplished by adjusting the bridge so that the pitch of the shorter section reads about 3 cents sharp compared to the pitch of the open string harmonic. Some musicians prefer even more than 3 cents stretch, particularly in the adjustment of the high E string.

You will note that moving the bridge toward the neck causes the pitch of the stopped string to sharpen compared to the harmonic of the open string. After each displacement of the bridge, the string should be retuned, approximately, so that the comparison may be made.

After perfecting the intonation as described above, the guitar may be retuned. In accord with the 3-cents-per-octave stretch, the approximate cents setting for the six strings are zero for low E, sharp 2 for A, sharp 3 for D, sharp 4 for G, sharp 5 for B, and sharp 6 for high E. If the guitar is to be played together with an electric bass, the bass tunings could be flat 3 for E, flat 1 for A, zero for D, and sharp 1 for G. The A of the lead guitar should be 440 cycles per second, in general. However, it is sometimes necessary to rotate the Tune Master's pitch control before tuning, so that the guitar will agree with the fixed tuning of an organ or piano.

The Tune Master can also be used to check the guitar's fret accuracy and freedom from neck warpage. Simply play the notes of each string chromatically and record the Tune Master's cents reading. There are also promising applications to design and quality control of strings. The Tune Master can be used to compare the frequencies of the various partials with great precision.

The component parts of this instrument are held to standards of plus or minus ¼ of 1%. That is to say that resistors, condensers, etc., are made to some of the highest specifications in the industry.

This device is especially useful in proving aural tuning. For example: most aural tuners know that the interval of a third, from F33 on a piano to A37 should always beat 7 beats per second. This interval beat rate is often used as the beginning check on an aural tuning temperament. Obviously, since the beat ratios going up from this bottom point of an F temperament must increase at an even rate, and if the lowest beat rate, between F33 and A37, is slightly wrong and more or less than 7 beats per second, all following checks will be slightly wrong as well as we proceed up through the temperament in thirds. For this reason, it is essential to get a solid 7 beat rate in the third mentioned.

In tuning to the fundamentals of the previously mentioned F and A, the tuner will often find that the 7 beat rate will not always be dependable. But if one will set the indicator of this device on A37 and then play F33, he will instantly be able to see how flat or sharp F is in relation to the A. Usually, he will find that it is running flat. By spreading the F to A ratio by 14 cents, he will discover one of the clearest beat rates of 7 per second in this interval that his ears have ever heard. Playing F33 while setting the instrument for A61, you can see the fifth partial tone of F33. Playing A37 with the instrument set at A61, one can see the fourth partial tone of A37. One can then widen them by 14 cents precisely using an electronic instrument, and get an exact 7 beats per second spread in the F33 to A37 interval.

In addition to this, we can check the fourths and fifths of our temperament, too. By playing C40, for example, while setting the instrument for C52, you can view the second partial of C40. Then by playing F33 with this same setting, one can view the third partial tone of F33. These coincident partials are used to tune the fifths when doing aural tuning, and can be precisely used in the following way: Set for C52, view the 3rd partial of F33 and narrow it by 2 cents. Set for the fourth, and widen by 2 cents.

While most users will not want to spend time in the client's home engaging in these experiments, it is a good idea to perform them in the shop in order to satisfy one's mind as to the accuracy of the temperament he may set with an electronic device. Also, it will develop more precise beat rate hearing on the part of those tuners who rely on instruments at the possible expense of their keen sense of aural perception.

This simple test system will also enable the electronic tuner to more easily demonstrate to his aural-tuning friends that he is trying to make as accurate a temperament as possible and not just using the instrument as a crutch.

A number of illustrative forms come with the Tune Master, including intonation charts, which will be useful when scientifically measuring the intonation of a particular instrument or a particular student musician. I used one of these to chart a piano which I had tuned aurally and was gratified by the performance of the Tune Master when set on stretch to very closely approximate the efforts of an aural tuning. An intonation chart is included at the end of this chapter.

Also, there's a clear tuning schedule chart. Dial apertures showing each octave in tuning a piano are included with the device. It appears at the end of this chapter. This chart must, perforce, be gradually compromised when tuning with equal temperament, but by putting the switch on stretch, no alterations are necessary.

The applications are many for this instrument, and some of them have been implemented by instructions accompanying the device. Others occur to me, but we are basically interested in its performance as a piano tuning device. In this category, we must conclude that it is an adaptable instrument which will quickly enable a person to set a temperament and to prove the intervals therein without fear of loss of accuracy.

It is light in weight, far lighter than any other instruments reviewed in this book, and easy to carry and to set up on the job. The case, being metal, may scar or scratch a piano; thus, some leather-like covering should be applied if it is to be used in the home of a client.

The microphone supplied with the unit is more than adequate. The magnetic pickoff improves the tuning on grands especially, and offers many other advantages when used with any other electronic tuning device. The factory stands ready to check and calibrate the unit at any time.

In an effort to insure satisfaction, the factory from time to time sends out bulletins which cover maintenance procedures to be followed in the field.

I found the unit to be precise and carefully made. The only trouble encountered was that the indication of the needle was too rapid for sustained manipulation of the tuning lever while fine tuning. It is essential that the technician only tune when the indicator bulb glows brightly. This seemed a drawback to me, but possibly would diminish when one has had sufficient time to work constantly with the instrument and becomes adept at gauging the time lag required for good indication and tuning. An AVC (automatic volume control) circuit might stop this problem.

Tune Master instruments also include the Model Tune Master III-EM. This is designed especially for the ethnomusicologist and others who might be interested in microtonal tuning. The addition of a switch for the purpose of depressing the internal frequency reference by exactly one-quarter of a tone makes it possible to divide the octave into 24 equal parts with better than .01 of a half tone accuracy.

The duration of the input signal must be ¼ of a second or more but lack of such a duration may be overcome by tape recording the signal desired for measurement and then playing the recording at half or quarter speed.

This instrument incorporates a sensitive meter with a plus

30 cents (.30 of a halftone) and minus 30 cents range. The range is from C3 (130.8 Hertz) to B6 (1975.5 Hertz). If one wishes to measure input signals lower than 130.8 Hertz, he may set the note and octave switches for one of the upper partials.

The Tune Master III-EM also puts out a tone which can be ranged by the operator from C3 to B4. The instrument can be wired for 220 volt operation if desired on a special order. It is normally available in two models; one for 120 volt AC operation, the other battery-powered.

For use in piano tuning, the Model III-EM can be ordered with the E.T.-stretch switch option, and the stretch switch will widen the interval between half tones by .25 cents. In other words, the interval would normally be 100 cents, but with the stretch switch on, the interval becomes 100.25 cents between semitones. The magnetic pick off will work with this model as well as the others.

**For Tuning Pianos With Tune Master;**
**E. T.—Stretch Switch at STRETCH**

| *Piano Key* | *Octave Switch* | *Meter Reading* |
|---|---|---|
| A0 thru E1 | 3 (tuning to two octaves plus a fifth) | Flat 6 |
| F1 thru E2 | 3 (tuning to octave plus a fifth) | Flat 3 |
| F2 thru B2 | 4 (tuning to octave plus a fifth) | 0 |
| C3 thru B3 | 4 (octave tuning) | Flat 3 |
| C4 thru B4 | 4 (Fundamental tuning) | 0 |
| C5 thru B5 | 5 (Fundamental tuning) | Sharp 3 |
| C6 thru B6 | 6 (Fundamental tuning) | Sharp 6 |
| C7 | 7 (Fundamental tuning) | Sharp 9 |
| C#7 | 7 (Fundamental tuning) | Sharp 10 |
| B7 | 7 (Fundamental tuning) | Sharp 19 |

*Note:* For A0 through B2 place the round window of the Tone Switch above the note being tuned.

For C3 through B7 use the wedge-shaped window.

## Tune Master Intonation Chart
(for use with calibration systems when testing and analyzing musical instruments)

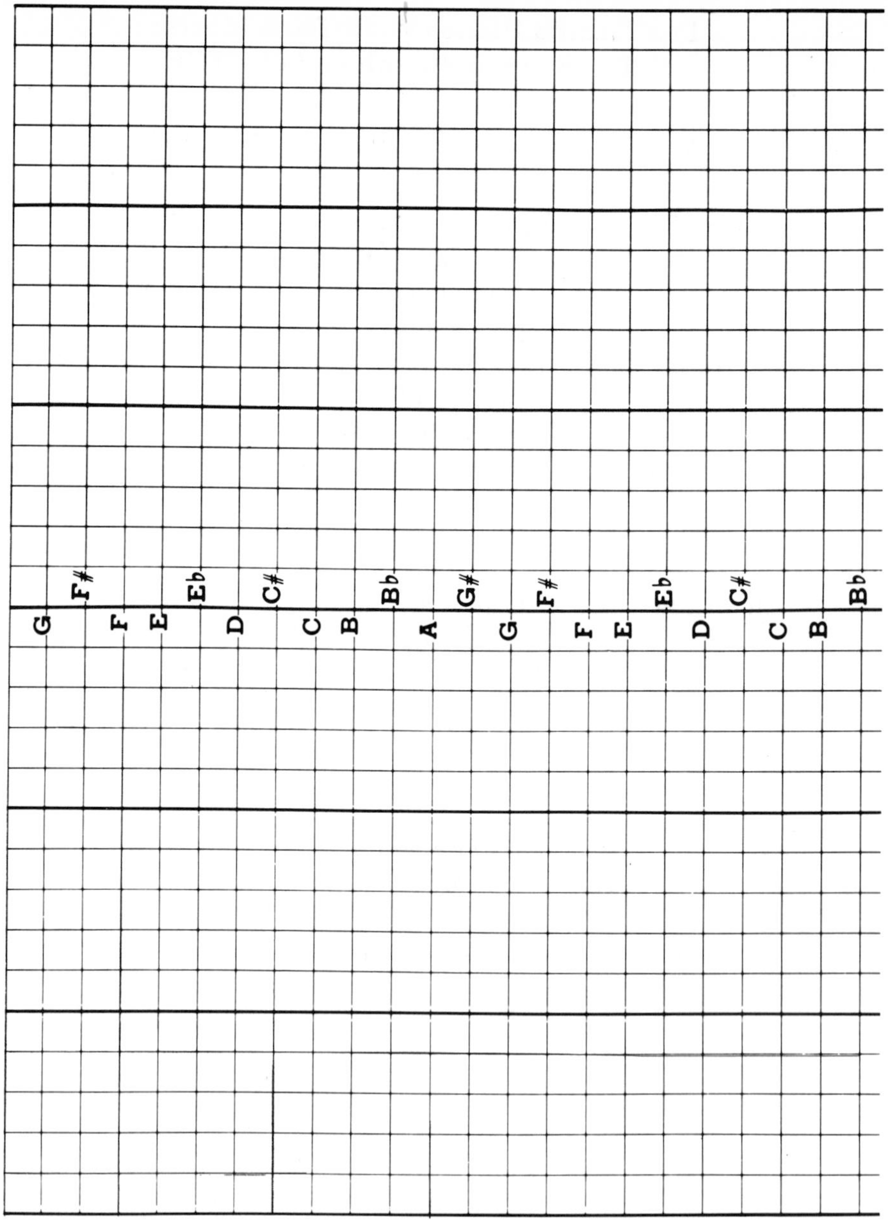

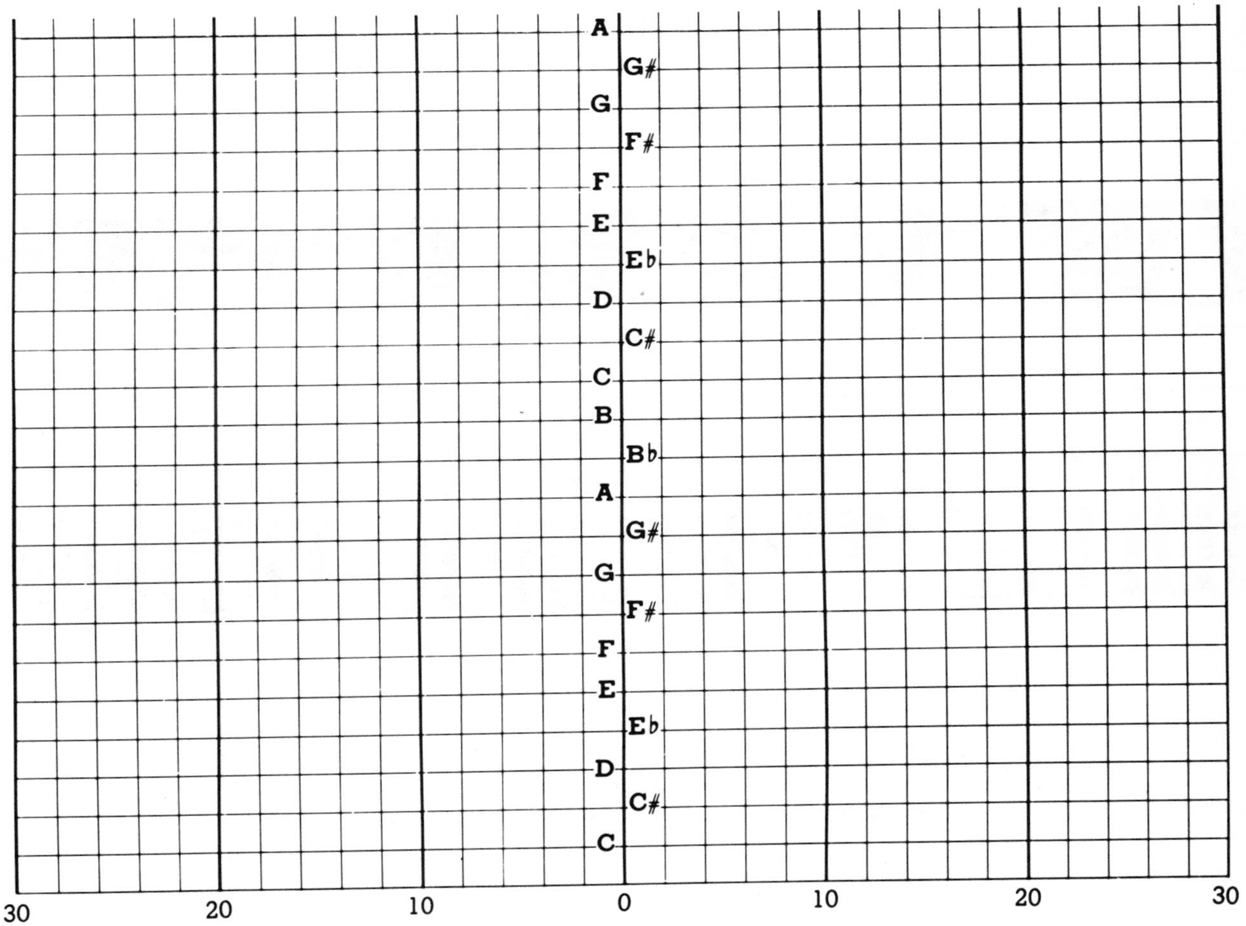


*Cents Flat* *Cents Sharp*

Instrument ____________

Pitch Center: A =

________ Cycles Per Second

Played By ____________

Recorded By ____________

Date: ____________

Tune Master's suggested tuning schedule for pianos indicating which tone window to use for various notes on the piano.

Eq. temp. stretch switch on stretch; meter switch on 1X.

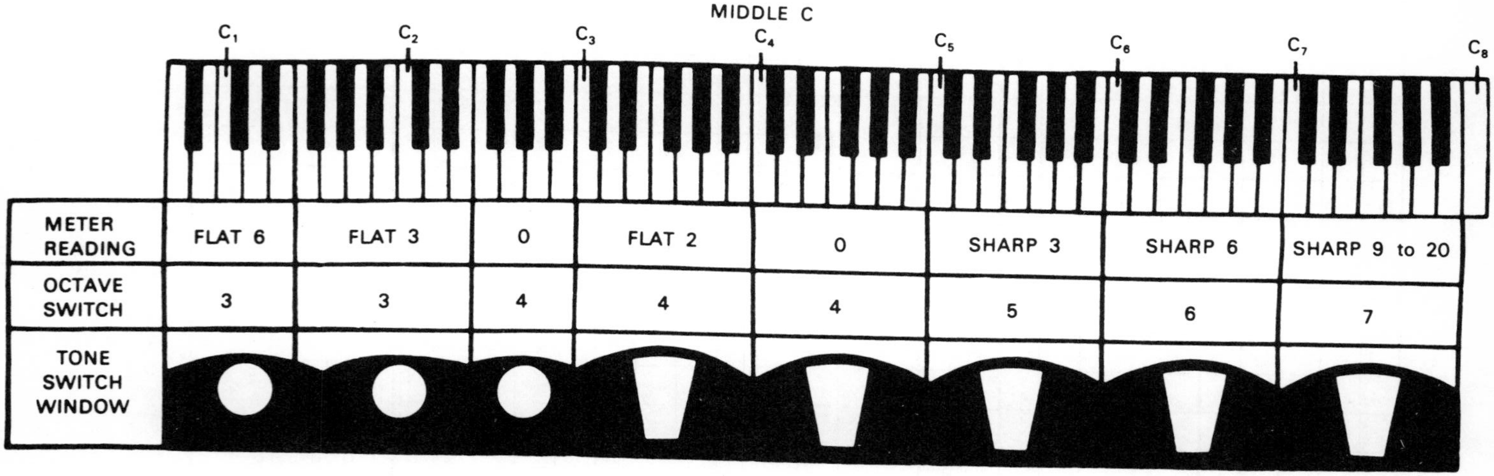

# 8
# Using the Hale Sight-O-Tuner

The instruction manual for the Hale Sight-O-Tuner describes it as a little box with perfect pitch. Certainly, it is the smallest unit in actual size I have worked with or found available in the field of electronic tuning devices. The Sight-O-Tuner is only 3½ in. high by 7 in. wide and 6 in. deep. It weighs only 2½ lbs. Easily placed in a briefcase or small tool case, this self-contained, battery operated unit can truly go anywhere. Since the microphone is internal, there are no cords to be hooked up, and no outside power source is required.

Covering nine full octaves, with an accuracy of plus or minus ½ cent, the Sight-O-Tuner has internal calibration, which gives freedom from tuning forks or line frequency deviations.

Only the note you select activates the tuning display, an important feature. And tones from as far away as 30 ft. from the tuner can be registered on its sensitive system. Mixture stops on organs can be tuned with this unit without cottoning-off individual organ pipes.

A rechargeable battery pack is available, along with a carrying case. An additional feature: the internal battery level is registered by a red light which comes on when there are about six hours of service left in the batteries. Two 9-volt transistor batteries will operate the unit for approximately 18 hours continuously.

The unit which I tested was from a small stock of beginning sales, and time for testing was limited to two weeks. Even so, the Sight-O-Tuner made a most powerful impression when used in tuning pianos and organs. This unit has the intervals of the equally-tempered scale locked precisely and permanently into its memory. Warm-up time is but two minutes, and realignment or correction should never be required, according to the manual. There are no motors, no tubes, no lamps, no moving parts to break, wear out, or burn out. The light indicators are unbreakable, solid state devices such as one sees in computer programming boards.

Using the Sight-O-Tuner is quite simple once you get acquainted with the method Hale suggests for setting pianos, and it can greatly cut down the time required for commercially tuning a piano. Also, the artful refinements required to put a concert piano in fine tune are easily possible with this excellent device.

Of course, piano tuning remains an art requiring intuition, aural sensibilities, and some advanced understanding of piano tones, while working with any electronic device. I always want this statement to be carefully considered when I talk about methods of tuning pianos with the Sight-O-Tuner or any of the other instruments I have reviewed in this text.

### *Description*

The front panel view of the Sight-O-Tuner is shown in Figure 8.1. The microphone is mounted on the right-hand side

The Hale Sight-O-Tuner *Figure 8.1*

of the instrument, and on the back panel is a female input jack for directly connecting electronic musical instruments.

The four control knobs set the internal standard of pitch. The two pitch selector knobs select the note and octave of the tone to be measured. The note switch is labeled from A to G. The black lines between the letters indicate the intermediate sharps or flats. Number 1 on the octave switch corresponds to the bottom octave on the scale (the lowest full octave on the grand piano and the bottom octave of the 16 ft. stop of a pipe organ). The first octave begins at C1 at 32.7 cycles per second and ends at B1 at 61.7 cycles per second. The highest tone that can be measured is B9 at 15,804 cycles per second. Turned as far as it will go to the left (counterclockwise) the octave switch also turns the unit on and off.

The cents deviation dials extend the range of tuning to any frequency in the applicable spectrum. They are calibrated in terms of the cent which is .01 of a semitone. The coarse cents control reaches in 5 cent graduations 55 cents sharp or flat, thereby reaching more than half-way into the range of a neighboring semitone.

The fine cents dial reaches 6 cents in either direction in ½ cent graduations. This makes it possible to establish the accuracy of a desired semitone to within .005 of a semitone at any point on the scale. The effect of the fine and coarse dials is additive. That is, a setting on the coarse dial of 10 cents sharp and a 2½ setting on the fine dial indicate an overall cents deviation of 12½ cents sharp.

The nine lights of the circular visual display indicate the frequency difference between the internal standard of pitch (the setting of the pitch, octave, and fine and coarse cents dials) and the pitch of the musical tone being received. These lights are normally off and are turned on only by the presence of a musical tone with a fundamental or harmonic that falls within approximately 25 cycles per second of the selected settings of the four control knobs.

When the correct frequency is present, some or all of the lamps are turned on to create a visual moving display that allows the tuner to tell immediately whether the tone is sharp or flat or exactly in tune. The eight lights in the outer ring turn off and on rapidly to create the illusion of rotating light bands. These bands appear to rotate clockwise for sharp tones and counterclockwise for flat tones. The speed of rotation is directly in proportion to the frequency error of the received note. That is, 2 cycles per second difference between the tone to be tuned and the reference tone inside the Sight-O-Tuner is indicated by the light display appearing to rotate completely once each second. The pattern appears to be stationary only when the note is exactly in tune.

The central light of the visual display is the sharp light. It tells the tuner when the received tone is sharp by flashing twice per clockwise revolution of the light bands. It does not flash when the bands are revolving counterclockwise. This is helpful, primarily, when the bands are rotating so rapidly (that is, the note to be tuned is so far "out") that it is impossible to determine by eye whether they are rotating in the sharp or flat direction.

### *Piano Tuning*

In order for reference frequencies to become stabilized the Sight-O-Tuner should be turned on at least two minutes before its intended use. Because of its high sensitivity the Sight-O-Tuner can be placed anywhere reasonably near the piano being tuned. In general, of course, the microphone on the side of the instrument should have an unobstructed view of the sound source.

### *Stretching*

Depending upon the type and size, pianos have been found to sound best if the normal scope of the keyboard is expanded slightly beyond an equally-tempered tuning. This is called stretching. Notes above middle C are tuned very slightly and progressively sharper as the scale is ascended, and those below C4 are tuned slightly flat. The amount of deviation is additive and is greatest at the extremes of the keyboard. The amount of stretch required for a given piano to sound its best depends upon the way the piano is designed and made. In general, the better the piano, the less stretch is required to make it sound its best. Using the Sight-O-Tuner to determine the amount of stretch required for a given piano is covered in detail below.

### *Concert Tuning and Chart Tuning*

There are two somewhat different procedures one can use to tune a piano with a Sight-O-Tuner.

Chart Tuning will provide serviceable tuning in a short period of time. It can be employed successfully by commercial tuners working with pianos of less than concert quality.

Concert Tuning should provide results that are virtually optimum for a given piano, large or small, and which should satisfy the most discerning ear. The procedure, although seemingly somewhat involved, is straightforward and, once learned, gives superior results. The tuner should not be discouraged from trying and mastering the technique.

The main difference between the two types of tuning concerns the precision with which the stretch is determined and apportioned out among the notes of the instrument. Concert tuning uses a precise method which will give exactly the right amount of stretch for each individual piano. Chart tuning uses tables giving the average amounts of stretch for three general categories of pianos.

### *Harmonics*

Another difference between Chart Tuning and Concert Tuning concerns the use of harmonics. When a string is excited (the same holds true for pipe organs), it sounds the fundamental tone corresponding to the length and the tension of the string. Although sometimes not immediately apparent to the ear, it also sounds several notes higher which are mathematically related to the fundamental. These tones correspond to the fractional vibrations of the string, and are called harmonics.

### *String and Harmonics*

As illustrated in the table on p. 191, a string vibrating at the fundamental pitch of C1 will also sound notes at C2 (one octave above, the *second harmonic* of the fundamental), G2 (the *third harmonic,* sounding at an octave and a fifth above the fundamental), C3 (the *fourth harmonic,* two octaves above the fundamental), E3 (the *fifth harmonic,* two octaves and a major third above the fundamental but not important to the use of the Sight-O-Tuner for tuning), and G3 (the *sixth harmonic,* two octaves and a fifth above the fundamental tone).

Harmonics are useful to the piano tuners for two reasons. Low strings often have a faint fundamental tone, which makes unison tuning difficult. The very low tones, in fact, produce practically no fundamental tone; what you hear is almost all harmonics. By tuning to more distinct upper harmonics, a more accurate tuning can be achieved. A more important reason to use harmonics has been furnished by Mother Nature with help from her friends. The notes on the scale increase geometrically with frequency while increasing only numerically by note. The frequency difference between low A1 and B1, for example, is only about 7 cycles per second while the difference between A4 and B4 is about 54 cycles per second and between A6 and B6, it is up to 216 cycles per second.

Any 1 cycle per second difference between the reference tone and the tone being tuned causes one light band per second of the light display of the Sight-O-Tuner to appear to pass a given point (the same as simultaneously sounded notes "beat" together one time per second). The greater tuning precision gained by dividing the interval between adjoining notes as finely as possible becomes apparent. One band per second of the Sight-O-Tuner display tuning a string C3 at the fundamental represents an error of $\frac{1}{8}$ of the interval between adjoining notes, while one band per second of the Sight-O-Tuner display tuning sixth harmonics of the same fundamental represents an error of less than $\frac{1}{48}$ of the interval, an increase of six times in accuracy.

Chart Tuning makes use of harmonics only in the two bass octaves where the second harmonics are used. Concert Tuning on the other hand makes use of harmonics throughout the scale. Harmonics as high as the sixth and eighth above the fundamental are commonly used in the bass octaves.

### *Concert Tuning*

The Sight-O-Tuner is capable of precise concert tuning. With care, the method described below will determine the optimum stretch for any piano and apportion it equally among all the notes.

### *Measuring Optimum Stretch (Using Temperament Octave F3–F4)*

Step 1. Set the Sight-O-Tuner to F4 with coarse and fine cents dials set to zero. Mute all but the one string of F4 and tune it so that the pattern on the Sight-O-Tuner remains as nearly stationary as possible. Note: A rule to remember when using the Sight-O-Tuner for tuning pianos is to oppose the motion of the display lights with the motion of the tuning hammer. If the motion of the Sight-O-Tuner display is to the right (clockwise, indicating sharp) then the hammer is used to rotate the pin to the left (counterclockwise) until the lights on the display are almost or exactly stationary. Of course, the opposite procedure applies when the Sight-O-Tuner indicates flat.

Step 2. Switch the Sight-O-Tuner to F5 and adjust the coarse cents dial to stop the lights of the Sight-O-Tuner while sounding F4. (The fine cents dial must still be exactly on zero.)

Step 3. Switch the Sight-O-Tuner to F6 (move octave dial up one number) and adjust the fine cents dial to stop the pattern while again sounding F4. Note: If the range of the fine cents dial is exceeded, repeat Step 1 with fine cents on 5 cents flat and coarse cents on 5 cents sharp. Then repeat Steps 2 and 3.

It is especially important to check the octave interval after this sequence of operations, since, if there is a beat within the octave, you have to set the fine tuning control so as to wipe out the beat. In other words, make sure your octave between the F4 and F5 is beatless and correct the stretch factor in your overall octave accordingly.

***Apportioning Stretch***

Step 4. We now wish to apportion this stretch among all 12 notes of the temperament octave. The optimum stretch figure obtained as a result of Step 3 must be divided by 12 and subtracted cumulatively from each descending note. For example, if at the end of Step 3 the fine cents dial were to read + 6, the optimum stretch for that particular piano would be determined to be 6 cents for the temperament octave. To distribute the 6 cents among all the notes of the octave, one would divide the total stretch by 12 and subtract that amount ($\frac{6}{12}$ or $\frac{1}{2}$ cent) from the fine cents dial with each successively lower note. F4 would be tuned with the fine cents dial on + 6, E4 with the fine cents dial on + 5½, D#4 with the dial on + 5 and so forth until, when the tuner reaches F3, the fine cents dial will again read zero.

Step 4 is a crucial step and the care with which it is carried out will ultimately determine the quality of the entire tuning. You may wish to make a "dry run" with the fine cents dial and the note and octave switches to make sure that the dial does in fact return in as even steps as possible to zero upon reaching F3. When satisfied with your understanding of the procedure, you should then feel confident to proceed with the hammer.

Note: In determining the optimum stretch for a piano it

has been found that, in general, it is better to stretch too much rather than too little. If the figure determined for optimum stretch is fractional (3.7 for example), a general rule is to round the number up to the next highest whole number (4). This would apply to fractional amounts over about .3 of a cent. Three-tenths or under can successfully be rounded off to the next lowest number. *This applies only to the overall amount of stretch.* When one subtracts the incremental amount of stretch, every effort must be made to keep the settings as precise as possible: 3 and exactly $^7/_{10}$, 3 and exactly $^3/_{10}$, and so forth on down to zero.

***Tuning the Temperament Octave***

Step 5. Make sure that the fine cents dial is exactly where it was when the optimum stretch was determined (or where it should be according to how much you have rounded off or up). The Sight-O-Tuner should be set at F6 and all three strings of F4 should be tuned individually to stop the pattern of the Sight-O-Tuner. (One string should be exactly or very close depending upon how much rounding off was done with the optimum stretch amount.) Keeping the Sight-O-Tuner at the same setting, all the strings of F5 and F6 can be tuned individually to stop the pattern of the Sight-O-Tuner. Note: If appreciable adjustment is necessary it is wise to recheck all the strings of a given note after bringing them into tune. Often individual strings will have been found to have slipped out again during the tuning process.

Step 6. Switch the Sight-O-Tuner to E6 and reduce the fine cents dial by exactly $^1/_{12}$ of the optimum stretch amount. (For a 6 cents overall stretch figure the dial would be reduced from 6 to 5.5.) Tune all the strings to E4, E5, and E6 individually to stop the pattern of the Sight-O-Tuner.

Step 7. Switch the Sight-O-Tuner to D#6 and reduce the fine cents dial by an additional $^1/_{12}$ increment (down to 5 cents in our example). Tune all strings of D#4, D#5, and D#6 individually to stop the pattern of the Sight-O-Tuner.

Step 8. Tune the remainder of the temperament octave and the two octaves above it, using this method. Note: When going below C downward on the note switch, the octave switch is reduced for each setting by 1. When tuning B3, B4, and B5, for example, the octave switch is stepped down from 6 to 5. (Going upward the octave switch is increased when going from B to C.)

Step 9. The last step in tuning the temperament octave is made with the fine cents dial back to zero (after having been reduced successively by steps equal to 1/12 of the overall optimum stretch amount). Set Sight-O-Tuner to F5 and tune all strings of F3 individually to stop the pattern of the Sight-O-Tuner. This completes tuning of the temperament octave and the two octaves above it.

It is advisable to check the temperament octave aurally at this point to make sure that all intervals are satisfactory before proceeding to tune the rest of the piano.

***Bass Tuning***

Step 10. E4 has already been tuned so it will be used as the reference note for E3. Set the Sight-O-Tuner to E5 and sound E4 and adjust the cents controls (either one or a combination of both) to stop the pattern of the Sight-O-Tuner. (The Sight-O-Tuner is now in unison with the second harmonic of E4 . . . E5.) Tune each string of E3 individually to stop the pattern of the Sight-O-Tuner.

Step 11. Tune D#3 to D#4 by the same method. That is, set the Sight-O-Tuner to D#5 and sound D#4. Stop the pattern with the cents controls and tune each string of D#3 individually to stop pattern.

Step 12. Continue to tune using the above method down to A#2. Always use the reference of the note one octave above the note being tuned and always set the Sight-O-Tuner two octaves higher than the note being tuned.

Step 13. Notes A2 and below are tuned by a different method using 3rd and 6th harmonics instead of 2nds and 4ths.

To tune A2 set the Sight-O-Tuner to E5 which is two octaves and a fifth above the fundamental and represents the 3rd harmonic of the reference note (A3) and the 6th harmonic of the note to be tuned (A2). Sound A3 and adjust cents controls to stop pattern. Tune each string of A2 individually to stop the pattern.

Step 14. Tune the remaining bass notes by the method described in Step 13. That is, set the Sight-O-Tuner an octave and a fifth above the reference note and adjust the cents controls to stop the pattern as the reference note is sounded. Then tune the note below, one string at a time, to stop the pattern.

Note: It is possible that 2–4 tuning may not be satisfactory all the way down to A2 due to excess beating of the 3rd and 6th of the lower notes. In this case, the tuner may wish to switch to 3–6 harmonic tuning several notes higher than suggested.

It is also possible that 4–8 tuning may be preferable in the lowest bass notes. Set the Sight-O-Tuner two octaves above the reference note and adjust the cents controls to stop the patterns. Then tune the note below to stop the pattern.

*Treble Tuning*

The treble has already been tuned through F6. Tune F#6 and above as follows:

Step 15. Set the Sight-O-Tuner to F#6 and sound F#5. (F#5 has already been tuned and will serve as the reference note.) Adjust the cents controls to stop the pattern. Then tune each string of F#6 individually to stop the pattern.

Step 16. Tune G6 by the same method. Set the Sight-O-Tuner to G6 and sound G5, the reference note. Stop the pattern with the cents controls. Then tune each string of G6 individually to stop pattern.

Step 17. Continue tuning the remaining treble notes by the above method. Set the Sight-O-Tuner to the note to be tuned and sound the reference note one octave below. Adjust the cents controls to stop pattern. Then tune each string to stop the pattern on the Sight-O-Tuner. This completes tuning.

## *Chart Tuning*

On p. 192 three average stretch tables are provided corresponding to the three commonly found types of pianos. Table I with 2 cents per octave stretch is best for grand pianos. Table II with 4 cents per octave stretch is good for quality uprights, and Table III with 6 cents stretch per octave would be suitable for small upright and spinet pianos.

To proceed, select the appropriate table for the piano being tuned and then set the Sight-O-Tuner to note and octave of the first note to be tuned. Set the cents deviation dials as determined by the entry in the corresponding line of the table and then tune each string of the note separately until the light pattern becomes stationary. Tune succeeding notes in the same fashion. (It makes no difference in what order the tuner prefers to make his tunings as long as the correct settings for each note are taken from the table.)

Because of the weakness of the fundamental tone in the two bass octaves the Sight-O-Tuner should be set to the second harmonics of the notes to be tuned. This means that the octave setting of the Sight-O-Tuner is one number higher than the octave number of the note being tuned. The stretch deviations, however, should be observed for the note being tuned rather than for the note and octave setting on the Sight-O-Tuner.

For example, to tune A2 of a spinet piano one sets the note and octave switch on the Sight-O-Tuner to A3 and the stretch deviation dials to total −15 cents. The strings are then adjusted individually until the pattern stops. Unison tuning with the Sight-O-Tuner is very satisfactory in general. A poor unison can only be caused by poorly matched strings with different harmonic structures. In these cases the offending harmonics can be tuned individually into exact tune with the Sight-O-Tuner. This should give better results than zero beating the fundamentals because the beat rate will be slower. Strings with "wild" harmonics, however, can never be brought into really perfect unison.

To tune a piano to other than standard pitch, simply subtract a constant number of cents from every reading in the table being used. If the required correction is less than 6 cents, the fine cents dial can be set to this number and left alone while the coarse cents dial can follow the main settings of the stretch tables.

### *Organ Tuning*

Octave stretch is not required in tuning an organ. With the exception of mixture stops, tuning an organ is completely straightforward. To proceed, set coarse and fine cents dials to zero (or set them to compensate for whatever deviation from A-440 may be desired) and set note and octave switches to the fundamental frequency of the pipes to be tuned. The pipe is then adjusted to stop the rotation of the visual display on the Sight-O-Tuner. With overall range of nine octaves the Sight-O-Tuner is able to encompass the entire range of even the largest instruments. Pipes in the zero octave (the lowest octave of 32 ft. pitch) are tuned with the Sight-O-Tuner set for the first octave.

When using the Sight-O-Tuner, the tuner may want to employ one slight deviation from standard tuning technique. When tuning a chest with more than one rank of similarly pitched pipes, you may find it desirable to tune all the pipes playing at the same pitch and note at the same time, with one setting of the Sight-O-Tuner. This avoids switching the Sight-O-Tuner up and down for each individual rank. As it turns out to be a matter of changing knobs as well as keys, one would suppose that the choice would depend mainly on the willingness (and nimbleness) of the key holder at the console.

### *Mixture Stops*

Because the selectivity of the Sight-O-Tuner enables it to pick out and measure individual tones even when sounded simultaneously with other notes, it is *not* necessary to stop the speech of all but one pipe when tuning a mixture. To tune a mixture, start with the lowest note of the lowest pitch and bring it into unison tuning with the Sight-O-Tuner. Proceed upward, tuning all the pipes of the lowest pitch.

In tuning the harmonics of mixture pipes, it is necessary to remember that such pipes are *not tempered* in relation to the fundamental; the intervals are "Just." The Sight-O-Tuner, however, is calibrated to the equally-tempered scale and a problem is immediately presented. To correct for this discrepancy, the quint pipes (third harmonics) are tuned 2 cents sharp with respect to the fundamental and octave pipes, and the tierce pipes (fifth harmonics) are tuned 14 cents flat with respect to the tuning of the fundamental.

In tuning a 4 rank mixture, for example, composed at a certain point of a fundamental playing at 4 ft. (C4, for example), a quint playing at $2\frac{2}{3}$ ft. (G4), an octave playing at 2 ft. (C5), and a tierce playing at $1\frac{3}{5}$ ft. (E5), the following procedure should be employed:

Assuming that the bottom note C4 has been brought into proper tune with the Sight-O-Tuner (cents deviation dials set to zero), set the Sight-O-Tuner to G4 and set the fine cents deviation dial to 2 cents sharp and tune the pipe. To tune the tierce set the Sight-O-Tuner at E5 and set the coarse cents deviation dial to 10 cents flat and the fine cents deviation dial to 4 cents flat and tune the pipe. (The octave playing at 2 ft. is tuned to the fundamental tone one octave above the lowest note.) The same amount of cents deviation applies to ranks playing quints or tierces, regardless of where they are pitched in relation to the fundamental.

In practice, of course, you will find it more convenient to tune all the pipes of a given mutation at once, running up (or down, if it is your preference) the scale while keeping the cents deviation dials at the same setting.

### *Other Instruments*

The Sight-O-Tuner is able to measure the pitch or to tune any musical instrument. Its sensitivity is such that it is not necessary for the instrument being tuned to be close to the

Sight-O-Tuner, and it is even possible to tune the instruments of an entire orchestra from the conductor's podium.

The harpsichord and other lightly strung instruments have no stretch and are tuned in the manner described for the organ.

Musical instruments with electrical audio outputs, such as electronic organs and guitars, may be tuned silently. Simply feed the audio output of the instrument into the phono jack on the rear panel of the Sight-O-Tuner and tune as above.

### *Maintenance and Battery Replacement*

No routine maintenance is required for the Sight-O-Tuner other than battery replacement, which is necessary when the low battery light, marked by L in the lower left of the visual display, comes on and remains on even without the presence of any incoming signal. It is a good practice to replace the batteries as soon as possible after this light starts to flash during normal operation, but there are still several hours of use left at this point, giving the operator plenty of time to obtain fresh batteries.

To replace the batteries, remove the *bottom* cover plate from the Sight-O-Tuner. This is held in place with three Phillips screws. The two 9-volt transistor batteries are located on the back panel, and are held by snap clips. Always turn the Sight-O-Tuner off before replacing the batteries. Always replace both batteries at the same time, then replace the bottom cover. Suitable batteries are Burgess 2U6, Eveready #216, and RCA VS323.

After completing a dozen tunings with this instrument, I was especially impressed with the ease with which it may be used. After the first few times, the Sight-O-Tuner is no trouble at all to set up on the piano and to observe while tuning the temperament octaves. Both tuning the piano note by note with the Sight-O-Tuner, completing the whole piano from top to bottom in this manner, as well as tuning only the two tempera-

## Fundamentals & Harmonics

*Showing the Interaction of Harmonics of Two Tones Sounded One Octave Apart*

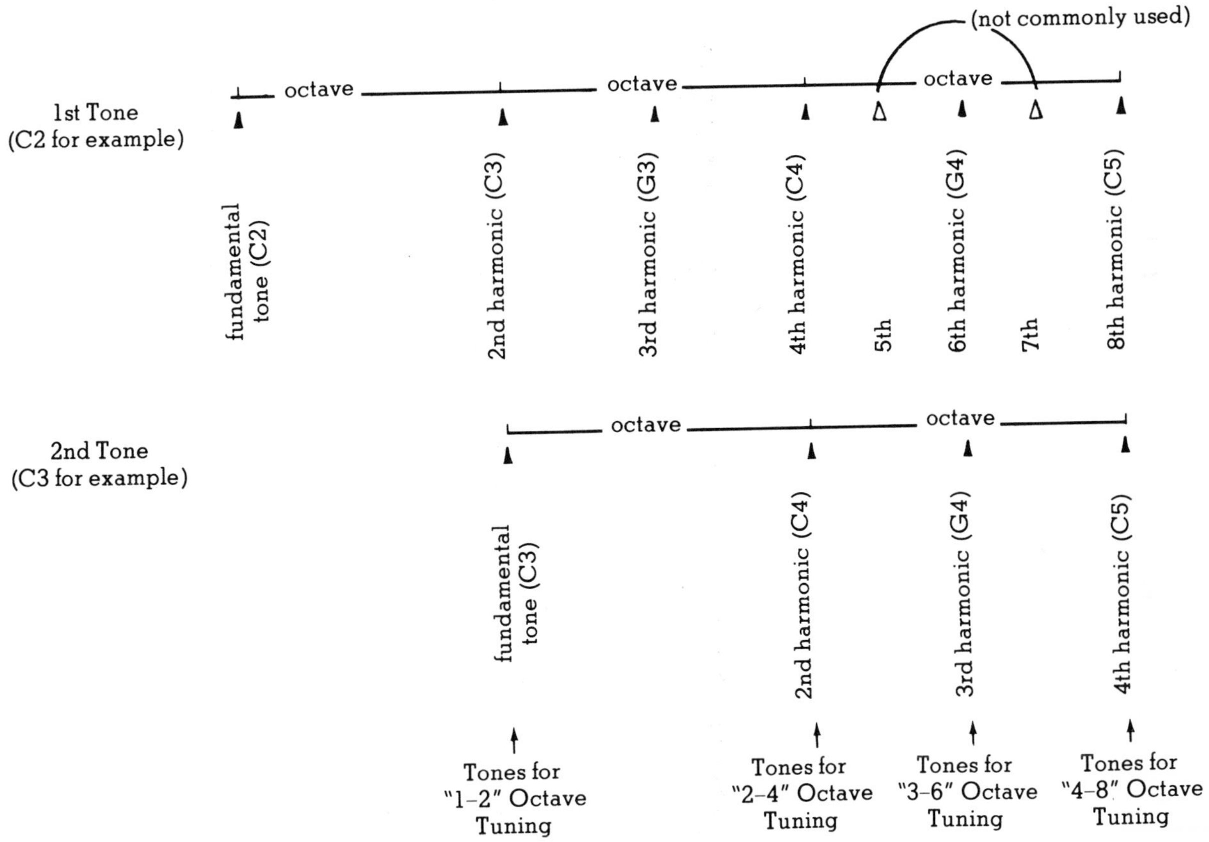

## Average Stretch Tables

| Note Tuning | Ref. Note | Sight-O-Tuner Setting |
|---|---|---|
| $A_2$ | $A_3$ | $E_5$ |
| $G\#_2$ | $G\#_3$ | $D\#_5$ |
| $G_2$ | $G_3$ | $D_5$ |
| $F\#_2$ | $F\#_3$ | $C\#_5$ |
| $F_2$ | $F_3$ | $C_5$ |
| $E_2$ | $E_3$ | $B_4$ |
| $D\#_2$ | $D\#_3$ | $A\#_4$ |
| $D_2$ | $D_3$ | $A_4$ |
| $C\#_2$ | $C\#_3$ | $G\#_4$ |
| $C_2$ | $C_3$ | $G_4$ |
| $B_1$ | $B_2$ | $F\#_4$ |
| $A\#_1$ | $A\#_2$ | $F_4$ |
| $A_1$ | $A_2$ | $E_4$ |
| $G\#_1$ | $G\#_2$ | $D\#_4$ |
| $G_1$ | $G_2$ | $D_4$ |
| $F\#_1$ | $F\#_2$ | $C\#_4$ |
| $F_1$ | $F_2$ | $C_4$ |
| $E_1$ | $E_2$ | $B_3$ |
| $D\#_1$ | $D\#_2$ | $A\#_3$ |
| $D_1$ | $D_2$ | $A_3$ |
| $C\#_1$ | $C\#_2$ | $G\#_3$ |
| $C_1$ | $C_2$ | $G_3$ |
| $B_0$ | $B_1$ | $F\#_3$ |
| $A\#_0$ | $A\#_1$ | $F_3$ |
| $A_0$ | $A_1$ | $E_3$ |

## Summarized Concert Tuning Procedure

(for details see text)

| Step | Sight-O-Tuner Procedure | Note (Playing/Tuning) | Sight-O-Tuner Cents Settings Note/Octave | Coarse | Fine |
|---|---|---|---|---|---|
| 1. | Tune F4 | F4 (one string) | F4 | 0 | 0 |
| 2. | Tune (coarse cents only) to 2nd Harmonic of F4 | F4 (one string) | F5 | X | 0 |
| 3. | Tune (fine cents only) to 4th harmonic of F4 | F4 (one string) | F6 | X | Y |
| 4. | Round "Y" to nearest applicable whole number: result is Yr (see text) Divide Yr by 12 (see table) | | | | |
| 5. | Tune all strings of F4 with fine cents at Yr | F4 (all strings) | F6 | X | Yr (rounded stretch) |
| 6. | Tune all strings F5 & F6 @ same setting as Step 5 | F5 & F6 (all strings) | F6 | X | Yr |
| 7. | Tune all strings E4, E5, E6 with Yr- 1/12 Yr on fine cents dial | E4, E5, E6 (all strings) | E6 | X | Yr−1/12 Yr |
| 8. | Tune all strings D#4, D#5, D#6 with Yr-2/12 Yr on fine cents dial | D#4, D#5, D#6 (all strings) | D#6 | X | Yr−2/12 Yr |
| 9. | Complete temperament octave (switch octave to five when dropping below C4) | | | | |
| 10. | Tune all strings F3, fine cents at 0 | F3 (all strings) | F5 | X | 0 Yr−12/12 Yr = 0 |
| 11. | Check tuning of temperament octave aurally | | | | |
| Bass | | | | | |
| 12a | Tune to 2nd harmonic E4 | E4 (reference only) | E5 | tune to stop pattern | |
| 12b | Tune E3 to stop pattern | E3 (all strings) | E5 | no change | |
| | Continue down through A#2 | | | | |
| 13a | Tune to 3rd harmonic of A3 | A3 (reference only) | E5 | tune to stop pattern | |
| 13b | Tune A2 to stop pattern | A2 (all strings) | E5 | no change | |
| | Continue to bottom (see chart at back of manual for 3rd and 6th harmonic sequence) | | | | |
| Treble | | | | | |
| 14a | Tune to 2nd harmonic of F#5 | F#5 (reference only) | F#6 | tune to stop pattern | |
| 14b | Tune F#6 to stop pattern | F#6 (all strings) | F#6 | no change | |

| PIANO OCTAVE | | 0 | 1 | 2 | 3 | 4 | 5 | 6 | 7 | 8 |
|---|---|---|---|---|---|---|---|---|---|---|
| SIGHT-O-TUNER OCTAVE | | 1 | 2 | 2 | 3 | 4 | 5 | 6 | 7 | 8 |
| NOTE | C | | | | | | + 2 | + 8 | + 15 | + 32 |
| | C# | | –15 | –6 | | | | | | |
| | D | | | | –2 | 0 | + 3 | + 9 | + 17 | |
| | D# | | | | | | | | | |
| | E | | –10 | –5 | | | + 4 | + 10 | + 20 | |
| | F | | | | | | | | | |
| | F# | | | | | | | | | |
| | G | | –8 | –6 | | | + 5 | + 11 | + 23 | |
| | G# | | | | | | | | | |
| | A | | | | –1 | + 1 | + 6 | + 12 | + 26 | |
| | A# | | | | | | | | | |
| | B | –20 | –7 | –3 | | | + 7 | + 13 | + 29 | |

**Table I Average Tuning Chart for Grand Pianos**

| PIANO OCTAVE | | 0 | 1 | 2 | 3 | 4 | 5 | 6 | 7 | 8 |
|---|---|---|---|---|---|---|---|---|---|---|
| SIGHT-O-TUNER OCTAVE | | 1 | 2 | 2 | 3 | 4 | 5 | 6 | 7 | 8 |
| NOTE | C | | | | | | | | | |
| | C# | | –22 | –10 | | | + 4 | + 10 | + 17 | + 35 |
| | D | | | | –4 | 0 | | | | |
| | D# | | –20 | –9 | | | + 5 | + 11 | + 20 | |
| | E | | | | –3 | + 1 | | | | |
| | F | | –18 | –8 | | | + 6 | + 12 | + 23 | |
| | F# | | | | | | | | | |
| | G | | –16 | –7 | | | + 7 | + 13 | + 26 | |
| | G# | | | | –2 | + 2 | | | | |
| | A | –30 | –14 | –6 | | | + 8 | + 14 | + 29 | |
| | A# | | | | –1 | + 3 | | | | |
| | B | –25 | –12 | –5 | | | + 9 | + 15 | + 32 | |

**Table II Average Tuning Chart for Consoles & Large Upright Pianos**

**Chart 1 Fine Cents Settings for Rounded Optimum Stretch Figures . . . . . Temperament Octave**

| Optimum stretch, rounded cents | F4 | E4 | D#4 | D4 | C#4 | C4 | B3 | A#3 | A3 | G#3 | G3 | F#3 | F3 |
|---|---|---|---|---|---|---|---|---|---|---|---|---|---|
| 1 | 1 | .9 | .8 | .75 | .7 | .6 | .5 | .4 | .3 | .25 | .2 | .1 | 0 |
| 2 | 2 | 1.8 | 1.7 | 1.5 | 1.3 | 1.2 | 1 | .8 | .7 | .5 | .3 | .2 | 0 |
| 3 | 3 | 2¾ | 2½ | 2¼ | 2 | 1¾ | 1½ | 1¼ | 1 | ¾ | ½ | ¼ | 0 |
| 4 | 4 | 3.7 | 3.3 | 3.0 | 2.7 | 2.3 | 2.0 | 1.7 | 1.3 | 1.0 | .7 | .3 | 0 |
| 5 | 5 | 4.6 | 4.2 | 3.7 | 3.3 | 2.9 | 2.5 | 2.1 | 1.7 | 1.3 | .9 | .4 | 0 |
| 6 | 6 | 5.5 | 5.0 | 4.5 | 4.0 | 3.5 | 3.0 | 2.5 | 2.0 | 1.5 | 1.0 | .5 | 0 |
| 7 | 7 | 6.4 | 5.9 | 5.3 | 4.7 | 4.1 | 3.5 | 2.9 | 2.3 | 1.8 | 1.2 | .6 | 0 |

(Fine cents dial is placed at indicated setting for F4 when starting to tune the temperament octave. For each subsequent lower note, appropriate FINE CENT settings are shown.)

| PIANO OCTAVE | | 0 | 1 | 2 | 3 | 4 | 5 | 6 | 7 | 8 |
|---|---|---|---|---|---|---|---|---|---|---|
| SIGHT-O-TUNER OCTAVE | | 1 | 2 | 2 | 3 | 4 | 5 | 6 | 7 | 8 |
| NOTE | C | | | | | | | | | + 38 |
| | C# | | -35 | -16 | -6 | 0 | + 6 | + 12 | + 24 | |
| | D | | | | | | | | | |
| | D# | | -30 | -14 | -5 | + 1 | + 3 | + 14 | + 26 | |
| | E | | | | | | | | | |
| | F | | -25 | -12 | -4 | + 2 | + 8 | + 16 | + 28 | |
| | F# | | | | | | | | | |
| | G | | -20 | -10 | -3 | + 3 | + 9 | + 18 | + 30 | |
| | G# | | | | | | | | | |
| | A | -45 | -15 | -8 | -2 | + 4 | + 10 | + 20 | + 32 | |
| | A# | | | | | | | | | |
| | B | -40 | -10 | -7 | -1 | + 5 | + 11 | + 22 | + 36 | |

**Table III Average Tuning Chart for Small Upright or Spinet Pianos**

ment octaves and stretching out from there by ear alone were tried. The results were then charted on a graph which seemed to prove time after time that the electronic tuner could more evenly divide the octave stretch between the notes of the ascending and descending octaves than could the human ear unaided.

Of special interest to the advanced piano professional tuner is the method by which Hale suggests the stretch per octave be divided exactly evenly note for note up through each octave. Used in this way, the other electronic tunings done with other manufacturers' instruments tended to give the same results. However, the Hale instrument does share with the Yamaha PT3 an extra advantage in that it is not responsive to notes very far removed from the notes for which it is set. There is a little more concentrated effort on the part of the piano man when he tries to do this with a stroboscopic unit, since he must choose from among a varied number of patterns in computing his stretch per octave. But it can be done and works out well after some practice. With the Sight-O-Tuner, much less practice is required in order to set an evenly stretched octave and to carry the proper stretch throughout the piano being tuned. Furthermore, the stretch is tailored to the piano under consideration in each tuning.

The claims made for this device are not exaggerated and the intelligent use of the Sight-O-Tuner, either for store tunings using the Chart method or for Concert and Fine Tuning using the evenly distributed stretch method, will turn out a well tuned piano, all other things having been done properly. The Sight-O-Tuner is the handiest tuner of them all.

# 9
# Electronic Tuning Is Better

The classic method of tuning a piano, as mentioned before, is based on beats. Obviously, it is impossible, or nearly so, for the human ear to differentiate in the matter of beats to the accurate point which may be reached by an electronic tuning device. This is not to say that tuning with the aural method by beats is not excellent and adequate. However, it is doubtful that the human ear by itself can differentiate down to .01 of a half tone per second.

The electronic instruments can make this accurate differentiation. When one is tuning with the beat method, which is the way that pianos have been tuned for years, the rapidity of the beats in the thirds as they progress up the scale is such that all are relative to each other within the temperament. That is to say, nobody is actually counting accurately to the exact beat in each interval. But in the long run, the aural tuner is able to make a relative spread of beats within his temperament that stands up well when the piano is played in all the different keys which are possible in the music as written in Western civilization.

Some craftsmen have gone so far as to use a pendulum in order to get training in measuring the number of beats per second that exist in a temperament. While this is certainly good training for the mind and ear, it is not feasible to use in a customer's home. And even when it has been imprinted in the mind firmly, the beat ratio within the temperament will still be relative to the beginning beats of the lowest third which is played in the temperament.

Some inventive people have devised a system of reeds similar to a pitch pipe into which one can blow and hear the exact ratio of 7 beats per second, 9 beats per second, etc. However, the accuracy of this method is subject to the temperature of the room at the time the reeds are being played, the volume of air that is being projected through a small set of tubes in the reeds, and the density of the air that is being breathed out of the lungs of the individual, that is, whether it is warm, moist, or cold air. So in the long run, all these methods still rely on a relative spread of beats between intervals.

With the advent of the electronic tuning devices which are now available to an accuracy of .01 of a semitone and precise vernier controls for easy calibration, it is possible to reach a high degree of proficiency. Many have found that their confidence in achieving a good temperament every time is significantly increased by using electronic instruments. Even well-established, older tuners who have always used an aural method find that such instruments are a real advantage. After all, our main concern is not to defend one method of tuning over and above another. Our objective is to make sure the American public receives the best tuning possible on any given instrument when a tuner performs his job. With this as our main goal, it makes sense to include the use of electronic tuning instruments in our temperament setting and throughout our range of piano tuning.

Many tuners over the years have found that violinists, especially, prefer to have clean fifths, with a small beat in the fifth. When one is using the old temperament method and setting a circle of fifths and a circle of fourths, and then checking them out with thirds and sixths, the even beat in the fifths is not always possible to maintain. This is so because, in order to get a smoothly increasing beat ratio within his temperament from the bottom to the top when he is playing thirds, the tuner is likely to change a few notes by a few beats, and thus sacrifice the quiet roll which he had originally set up in his fourths and fifths.

Musicians by and large prefer quiet fifths. That may explain why tuners who use electronic instruments and methods almost always find that musicians compliment them on the temperament and that they are quite pleased with the fourths and fifths. At the same time, this may explain why aural tuners who test a temperament which has been set precisely by a Strobotuner or other electronic tuning device often find that the beat ratios within the temperament, as far as thirds are concerned, do not quite agree with what they are used to. I have found that it is possible to correlate all methods and to lead to concise beat rates and spacing of intervals.

Much of the correlation that should be required between aural tuning and electronic tuning is due to the fact that pianos differ considerably in the way in which temperaments can be set. In the case of a large concert grand, it is usually possible for the aural tuner, without any other assistance, to set a good temperament because the beat ratios, when properly set up in fourths and fifths, usually will lead to a near approximation of the third beat ratios he will need as he proceeds up through his temperament while checking it.

But as the length of the piano scale goes down and the tuner begins to tune uprights and then on down to smaller spinets as they are built today, he finds that there is considerable adjustment required on the fourths and fifths in order to make the kind of third beat progression that he desires. On some smaller spinets, many aural tuners set a circle of fourths and fifths and hope for the best, because they have given up in despair when they tried to ever get the precise beat ratio for the thirds and sixths in the temperament that they would like.

It has been found by most tuners who work with smaller spinets to any extent that what is required is that the notes below middle C be adjusted while setting up the fourths and fifths in the temperament. They especially find this to be true at the lower G# and the G, F# and F below middle C. A glance at the table of piano tuning calibration, which is included with the Yamaha instrument, or at the table which I worked out over a period of years, reveals clearly that there is, in fact, a slight deviation below standard pitch or an evenly divided temperament at G# and G and F# and F below middle C. As a matter of fact, from C52 above middle C on down, the deviation begins to occur at the G or G# just above middle C, and it increases by ½ of .01 of a semitone as one proceeds downward through the temperament.

Fortunately, there is a good side to this whole operation. The advantage here is evident. Suppose one has begun to set a temperament at C52 with an electronic instrument, for example the Yamaha, following their table. As he moves downward through the next octave into middle C and then down through the next octave to the C below, he discovers that he has set up a beat rate within the temperament which closely approximates that beat rate for thirds and sixths—the ultimate goal for the aural tuner.

If one were to use any of the stroboscopic tuning devices described in this book and if he were to adjust the vernier control according to the Yamaha table, he would discover that he could set up precisely the same temperament with these instruments. Perhaps this is the best of all possible methods; that is, to know what you are looking for as a result of aural tuning experience and to adjust the evenly-divided intervals which were electronically set up in the tuning instruments. In this way, one has the accuracy of electronic tuning, and in the case of stroboscopic instruments, the ability to see the upper harmonics which will determine the amount of stretch put in the piano as one proceeds out of the temperament. In addition to that, one has the advantage of knowing how much to adjust G, G#, and like notes which are not evenly spaced in smaller pianos, to a degree that will enable him to end up with a temperament which has the proper aural beat ratios within it. Thus, we have a table in the temperament octave which offers us an exact spacing and a satisfactory beat ratio to please those who have trained their ears aurally.

The remainder of the piano, of course, can be completed in two ways. Either the tuner can space out in octaves from the temperament as set by the electronic methods and make his necessary adjustments in slightly increasing the pitch as he goes up into the treble and decreasing it as he goes down into the bass, or, he can if he wishes rely on the instrument's indication as to how much stretch is needed in the next octave by sounding the octave he has already tuned.

The stroboscopic devices, by and large, offer an advantage illustrated by this example: they will indicate, when one is tuning C40, how much stretch will be needed in C52. And at C52, they will indicate by the movement of the upper partials to the right, or sharp, how much stretch will be required to make C64 sound correct. It is quite an advantage, especially if one uses his ear as well, to check the octave range after he has set it to the approximate stretch he thinks will be required and to make sure there is no objectionable series of beats in the octave.

On the other hand, the Yamaha tuner offers another advantage, one which many tuners will find quite unique. Mainly it is that when one is using the Yamaha tuner, all frequencies other than the one he is trying to tune at the moment, and to which the dial is set, are, for all intents and purposes, eliminated. That is, he will see the note he is trying to tune, but the note two or three ranges away, or harmonics, do not appear on the screen of the cathode ray tube. This makes for less confusion as to which band to use, since no bands are used on the Yamaha while tuning a particular note.

Of course, the tuner must adjust the octave range to octaves 3, 4, 5, 6, and so forth, depending upon what octave of the piano he is working on. But the Yamaha does reject all spurious sounds over, above, and below the note one is actually trying to tune. This makes for a clear single frequency standard for each note of the piano and enables one to tune with a degree of accuracy seldom encountered in most instruments.

### *Compromise Methods for Electronic Instruments Tested*

I have found that by using the Peterson strobe, with its much larger dials, I can exactly duplicate the setting which the Yamaha instrument instructions require. In fact, I found that the Yamaha tuner and the Peterson strobe may be used side by side on top of a piano and if, for example, the Yamaha setting from the Yamaha table is used on both tuners for any given note on the piano, both instruments will agree as to the proper sound and setting of a particular string. This, of course, makes it clear that one can compromise in his tuning and deviate from the precise mathematical division of the temperament octave (which sometimes unjustly is considered the curse of an electronic instrument). By adjusting the vernier control in degrees of ½ of .01 or more, the tuner has a precision available to his work which is not possible with other methods alone.

It was noted that the Conn Strobotuner did not have a vernier dial in the upper left-hand corner by which one could calibrate to the precise .01 of a half tone. It might be a good idea if the Conn people were to include a more precise vernier in that position rather than a pointer which swings from zero to .10 and then to .20 of a half tone either sharp or flat. Of course, one of the reasons for the way the Conn control is set is that it can be calibrated to the 60 cycle AC line which is feeding the voltage to the instrument itself. Once the calibration is done in this manner, the user can then move the pointer to the exact place where the instrument is properly calibrated to the 60 cycle AC line, and vary the knob thereafter approximately .01, .02, .03, .04, or .05 of a beat sharp.

However, it would be possible to calibrate the Conn with the tuning fork or other standard, which would no longer require a constantly variable zero point in the upper left-hand control. After that, a large vernier dial could easily be affixed to the control knob. The tuner using the strobe could then proceed to calibrate it exactly, note for note, as he would the Yamaha tuner or the Peterson unit, using the table of piano stretch I suggested and also given by Yamaha.

As a matter of fact, pursuing this idea, I removed the small knob from my Conn Strobotuner, replaced the small pointer used for basic calibration purposes with a longer pointer, and then installed a large vernier knob with zero point and 50 degrees on either side of the zero point available. With the use of this large knob, which I purchased at a radio supply store, I was able to calibrate the Conn in precisely the same manner, note for note, as I could any of the other electronic instruments while tuning the piano.

Those who have an electronic tuning device (it may be a Conn if it is old) need not give up on the idea of the compromised temperament as I have set forth. All that is required is that they calibrate the shaft on the Conn so that a large vernier knob fitted to it will read zero when the instrument is on pitch. Of course, if one should want to tune to a pitch which happens to be higher or lower than the standard that is presented by any of these instruments, he has the privilege of

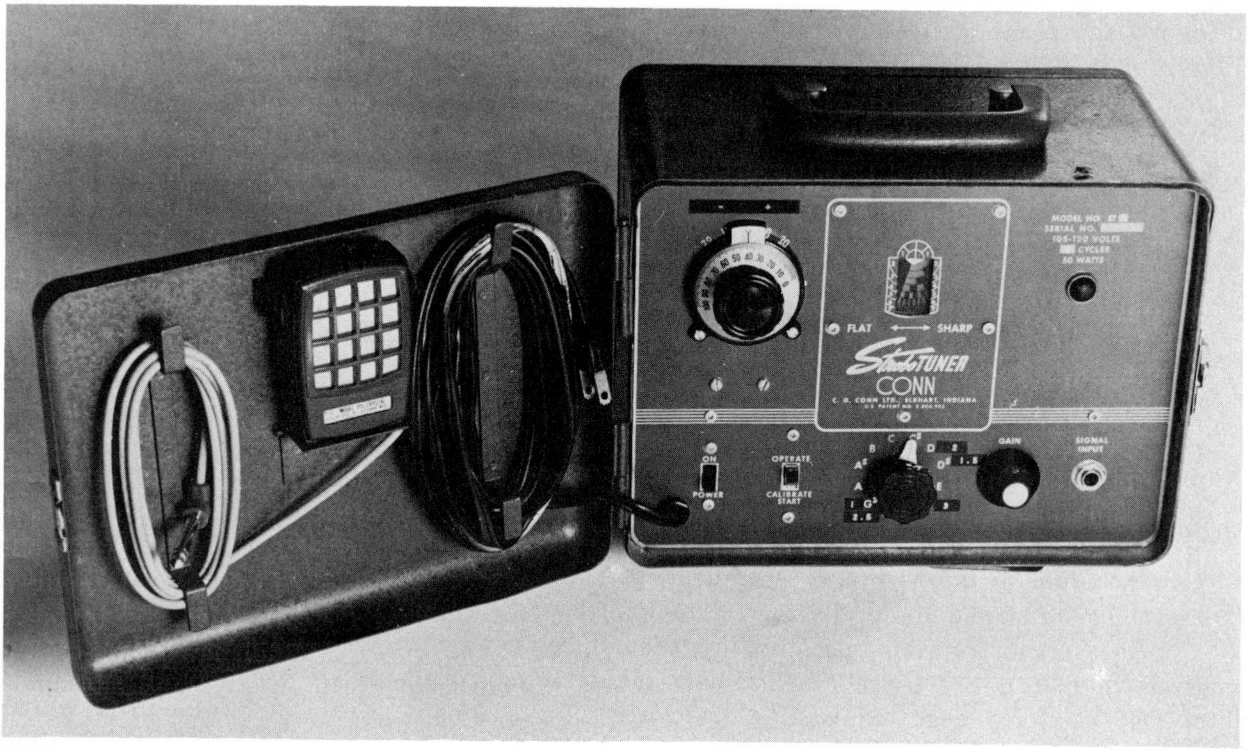


*Figure 9.1*

Conn Strobotuner with vernier control installed by the author. Note specified deviation points marked on instrument for tuning with compromise method for temperament.

| | | | |
|---|---|---|---|
| C52 | = 0 | D42 | = ″ .02 |
| B51 | ″ | C#41 | = ″ |
| A#50 | ″ | C40 | = Minus .02 |
| A49 | ″ | B39 | = ″ |
| G#48 | = Minus .01 | A#38 | = ″ |
| G47 | = ″ | A37 | = ″ |
| F#46 | = ″ | G#36 | = Minus .025 |
| F45 | = ″ | G35 | = ″ |
| E44 | = ″ | F#34 | = ″ |
| D#43 | = Minus .015 | F33 | = Minus .03 |

striking a tuning fork and calibrating the zero point of the instrument to that particular fork, adjusting the vernier control 5 or 10 degrees, even 20 if necessary, either flat or sharp, to suit the standard of pitch he intends to use.

It is not possible in tuning a piano to satisfy everybody, whether one uses the aural method or electronic methods. I would not insist that my method alone is the right method. But it is more nearly possible to suit most people, including fine musicians, by using a combination of electronic accuracy and the aural musicality that the tuner possesses. In order to make such a circumstance possible, I have written this book and provided tables of piano stretch. Furthermore, while it is not possible to please everybody in tuning a piano, it is certainly possible for a person to tune better, and sooner, if he intelligently uses the electronic aids that are available to him. No doubt, many who are now tuning pianos are doing excellent work without the use of an electronic instrument. It is equally true that many who tune with an electronic instrument would tune better if they were more experienced in listening for beat ratios in the temperament.

It is difficult, however, for the person who tunes with an electronic instrument to induce a tuner who tunes strictly by ear to use the instrument in such a way as to arrive at a temperament which would suit the most discriminating aural tuner. At this point we should make one thing clear: pianos are not ordinarily tuned so as to suit aural tuners and their fraternity. Pianos are tuned for students who are studying piano, for families who have a piano in the living room, for musicians who are playing for the public, and for schools and churches where they are used as an adjunct to other music.

Certainly it would be better if all tuners could tune in such a way as to please each other. However, it is the owner who pays the bill for tuning. He is entitled to the best tuning we can give him. That tuning usually can be done better, sooner, and with more accuracy with the intelligent use of electronic instruments. Those who are now tuning aurally but have not mastered the aural temperament as well as they would like should certainly be using an electronic instrument to guide them and to avoid mistakes.

Yet, tuners who are tuning with electronic instruments should not be slaves to the instruments. They should be aware of the fact that there is a certain beat ratio within the temperament which is the goal of all good tuners, and they should be striving to get that while using the accurate indications offered them by the electronic instrument. There is a method for arriving at this compromise, and it's a solution to a problem which exists in the tuning profession today.

New tuners who go into the business feel that if they have an electronic device they automatically will be able to make money sooner tuning pianos. Often they are correct in this assumption. However, they are never quite sure that there isn't something missing in their tuning unless they know more about *aural* tuning. Old tuners who are tuning strictly by ear often feel that they need an easier method, one which would accomodate itself to cheaper pianos or smaller ones which do not lend themselves well to setting up an even temperament in a hurry.

To new tuners relying on the electronic devices and to older tuners relying on a well-trained ear, I offer a method which will enable them to do their work more easily, more accurately, and with less wear and tear on the nerves. In addition to this, the compromise method, as described in this chapter, makes it possible for a man to tune a piano using an extension of the slow beat rate which can be easily heard in fourths and fifths throughout the piano; and which, if amplified by an octave, will produce a seventeenth that can be heard by anybody.

If we are checking out temperament by ear and sacrificing the accuracy of our fourths and fifths so as to get the kind of thirds that we want to hear, there will come a place as we move outward from the temperament octave where we find that the rapidly beating thirds are beyond our comprehension. Then we will be forced to add an octave to the thirds and still listen to a beat which is most rapid all the way up and down the piano and increases in its speed the farther away from the temperament we go. But if we use the compromise temperament I have provided, we find we can listen to the slow roll in the fourths and fifths all the way up the piano, and if necessary, add an octave to our fifth and still be listening to a slow beat which is easily identified and readily discerned by even a beginning tuner. It is also much easier for an older tuner to hear.

Of late, there have been statements in print deploring the fact that many beginners buy electronic tuning instruments and start careers. Naturally, this is resented by experienced aural tuners who spent years learning their craft. However, the situation is not as deplorable as some of these older men seem to think it is. A book like mine is intended to make it possible for the beginning tuner to do a satisfactory job *before* he gets years of experience.

First of all, there is little chance for a new man in this business to get years of factory experience. Factories now utilize special machinery to do many operations which were formerly done by hand. Multiple drilling rigs take the place of the laborious craftsmanship which was the rule in bygone days. There are fewer schools for learning tuning and repair than there were some years ago. To compensate for a lack of schools, I have written this book as well as my previous work, *Complete Course in Professional Piano Tuning, Repair, and Rebuilding.* A new man who starts in this craft will not necessarily do work that's worse than the old-timers do. With the aid of modern texts and an efficient use of modern instruments, he can do good work and need offer no apologies.

The public is not interested in whether a man tunes one way or another as long as the end result is good. However, modern electronic tuning technicians must master their instruments with a thorough knowledge of how they work. In addition, they must constantly seek to use every new mode of operation which will perfect their tuning.

Practice is required to be proficient at anything. Piano work is the same in this regard. And skillful use of the tuning hammer is especially necessary when one is dealing in units of .01 of a half tone. But there is no mystery to this. It can be mastered, and often the use of electronic tuning devices will enable a man to concentrate on his tuning hammer techniques more closely, since he is not worried about his temperament; nor is it constantly in need of correction.

Once in a while, you will encounter old, experienced tuners who have made a close study of electronic tuning devices and used them in their work. Almost without exception, you will find that they regard modern tuning devices highly. Their only worry is that someone will try to use one without a sense of craftsmanship. Otherwise, their opinions of electronic tuning aids will be favorable.

Remember what has been stated before: we do not tune pianos to suit other piano tuners—we tune them to please the public. And we are not paid by other piano tuners. We receive our fees from our clients. This is important to keep in mind.

# 10
# Ethics and People

In the tuning profession, as in others, there are problems that center around relationships with people. Fortunately, the competent tuner finds fewer of these problems than are found in other fields, but still they must be handled when they come up. Among these is the matter of giving the customer an opinion of his piano if he requests it.

When the instrument is a name brand of good reputation, you can often take refuge in stating that such-and-such a make has been known to be a fine one. Often this is true, but not always. Due to the limitations of mass production machinery, many companies today are floating on a past reputation which no longer fits the products they now make. In such cases, to perpetuate the myths which are extant regarding the superiority of one brand over another is somewhat misleading.

Perhaps the best way to cover this situation is to use the

question mode rather than volunteering your opinion without reservation. For example, you might ask the client the purpose for which he bought the piano. If the answer is that it was purchased because it was a beautiful piece of furniture, compliment the client on the design of the case, and let it go at that. A great many people today buy pianos on the basis of how they look rather than on how they sound and perform.

If the answer is that the piano was purchased to teach a child to play, the answer is that it is a good beginning piano indeed. Most pianos are excellent beginning pianos. Furthermore, you must inform the client that all pianos must be kept in proper tune if one is to learn to play correctly, since a child's ear is being trained with every exercise or small piece of music he is learning to play. Obviously, if the piano is out of tune, a pupil is learning to hear the wrong notes when he plays the right ones.

But the answer may be that the client purchased the piano because he wanted to have a fine musical instrument in his home. If such is the case, assure him that a properly tuned and regulated piano of any manufacture is far superior to the seldom-tuned or poorly-tuned instrument of the highest technical excellence. In each case, you are working on the basic frame of reference that "the tuner alone preserves the tone." And, since this is true, you do not mislead.

But avoid tearing down some makes to the detriment of their reputation and, usually, at the risk of your own. Give an honest opinion, that is, if you are informed enough about the piano under consideration to know what you are talking about. Still, tend to your own business. Your business is not selling pianos of any one make; it is making sure that pianos receive the proper care and the proper frequency of tuning.

Once in a while, you will run across a piano so poorly made and so obviously overpriced that you will wonder why anyone would pay so much for so little. When this happens, you are still ahead of the game by explaining that this particular piano will not sound as good as you would like for it to sound even after proper tuning, because the scale is not as evenly spaced and designed as you would like.

This puts the onus of scale design in a realm of subjective opinion, mainly your own. That is probably where it belongs, since given the same amount of money to use in manufacturing, shipping, and selling a piano, you might not have the ability to do much better. A doctor seldom says to his patient that he has badly shaped legs if he complains about arthritis. There is no reason for tuners to complain that a piano sounds differently than he would like to have it sound. Your job is to make it sound as good as possible. If you persist in complaining about certain makes of pianos, you will be dismayed to find that another tuner, who is perhaps less critical, has developed a manner of tuning a particular piano so that it sounds pleasant.

As a last resort, you can always do what a doctor friend of mine does when he is shown a newborn infant by proud parents. He looks long and hard at the scrawny, toothless infant, and says, with great emphasis, "Now that's a baby!"

### *Don't Criticize Other Tuners*

Sooner or later, the client will mention another practitioner of the fine art of piano tuning. The reasons behind this may be many and varied. Either he is a cousin, or he is cheaper than you are, or some friend recommended him. In any case, keep your opinion of the inferior qualities of other tuners to yourself. First of all, when you criticize another tuner, you belittle the profession in which you are engaged. You cannot disparage another man without doing some injury to others in your occupation.

In the second place, you are going to be discussed by your clients, either among themselves or among their bridge-club friends or acquaintances. When you are mentioned, your unfavorable opinions of other tuners will be the first topic of conversation. It will not be to your advantage to have it known that you are quick to find fault with the other fellow, since clients may start to wonder how much you talk to your wife and others about them. After all, you see things in the home that might be interpreted critically, and you are also aware of what they spent on their piano and what they got for their money. You will lose business by censuring other tuners. If you can't say anything good, say nothing. When you can praise, by all means do so. Praising another man shows that you are respectful enough of your own abilities that you don't worry about his taking any of your business away.

There is a psychological fact of life to be considered here. It boils down to the idea that everything we see, we see in a frame of reference. This means that if we establish a negative frame of reference toward a particular brand of piano, piano dealers, or manufacturers in general ("they don't make them like they used to"), the negative attitude toward one aspect of our profession is likely to be carried over into the next area, and soon we look through dark glasses. In fact, more men have been driven out of more businesses by their negative thinking than by any other factor. You owe it to yourself to think kindly thoughts about others in general and the piano business in particular.

Now and then you will meet tuners who tune by a method so completely different from your own that you assume it must be wrong. Before you decide that this is so, ask yourself if your method is the *only* way a piano could possibly be tuned. You will find, if you are honest, that it is not the only way. Then ask yourself if you could do a better job than he is doing, provided that you were equipped with his intellect, his mechanical dexterity, and his sense of musical intonation. Usually, you will find, given his gifts, that you could not do better than he does. Thankfully offer up a prayer that you have been better endowed than he, and let it go at that.

A man once considered the world's finest operatic tenor was appearing in Germany where he was severely upbraided by the critics. Their main argument was that, if he were the world's greatest tenor, why didn't he sing in German, since their own tenors could do it and were not as highly touted as he. His reply was that he found the German language hard to sing and difficult to intone; therefore he did not sing in it. He observed that those who did so must have a better understanding of the technique of singing German than he. And that was all he said on the matter. History still accords him a place as the finest operatic tenor of many decades.

# 11
# Building an Image and a Business

Many technicians are so engrossed in developing a fine tuning technique that they forget they must build a business. The first step in building a business is developing a public image. An image is often presented to the public by accident, without design on the part of the tuner. A little advance planning can make it possible for us to appear as we would want to appear and to present an image we can live with and build a business on.

Your first contact with clients can be through the medium of printed matter. It is wise to arrange for a continuing ad in the local newspaper and the Yellow Pages. The space need not be expensive or large. In fact, one good, small advertisement placed in the same medium over a long period of time has a cumulative effect which is far better than several large expensive ads.

A neat and well-worded sign placed in the back of your

car will bring results. It is important to have a sign in your car, or attached to the side magnetically so that it may be removed when you are not using the vehicle for business purposes. Such a sign should carry a brief message, and be conservative. It will bring you business for weeks after people have seen it. Also, it will keep neighbors from calling the police when you enter the home of a client who has told you to "go right in" if he is absent.

In our business, the best advertising is the kind you can afford. Try to keep your advertising budget within 7% of your gross income. But remember, word-of-mouth advertising costs nothing and is always effective.

It is important to keep your tools, equipment, auto, and clothes, in clean, eye-appealing condition. Never be seen without the attire befitting a professional man in your community. Do not carry the fewest tools possible, but instead, take along the proper tools for the job, without stinting. People notice these things and remember them.

When tuning with an electronic instrument, use it as an advertising advantage as well as an aid to fine tuning. Allude to the scientific accuracy of which the device is capable and to the fact that you will use it to get the best possible tuning.

Some tuners give away gimmicks such as a shower cap, a match book with name imprinted, dust cloths, etc. You will find that gifts work well for some people, but others wonder if they aren't paying for them through the fee for the tuning job.

I don't believe in gimmicks. Why not exert the same effort to promote your scientific and precise service, and by action, word, and deed present the image of a mature, conscientious craftsman, intent on doing his job very well?

When you are through tuning, in a client's home, you should leave one business card on the music desk of the piano, and another with the date of tuning and service, in the piano bench. Do not paste cards *inside* a piano. They will not remind anyone but another tuner of your service.

In addition, you should hand a pamphlet on piano care and on how often a piano needs tuning to the customer. Don't just leave it randomly where no one will notice or read it. Try to envision what kind of man you would like a tuner to be when he comes to your house and act accordingly. Quite often, in business, and that includes the musical arts, the impression made by the craftsman will do much to establish the atmosphere that carries the tuning performance sailing along to its victorious end. For this reason, and the others mentioned, proper attire, good looking tools, tool case, and equipment do much to quiet the client's anxiety when first you meet at the door.

When you have completed a tuning, there are two important things you must do if you are to expect more business in the future.

1. Demonstrate the piano by running arpeggios from the center temperament area up to the top of the treble, and then dropping in the bass note that complements that chord. If you are unable to do this with ease, be sure to get acquainted with a music teacher or church musician who can show you the 12 basic chords in music and how they progress up the piano. There is no doubt in a customer's mind that you have tuned the piano properly if you play chords in all 12 keys all the way up and down the piano. There is no doubt in your mind, either, since you came to tune the piano so that it could be played in all possible keys without discord. The major chord for each key is shown here to help you with this demonstration.

Use the sustain pedal; if there are still any keys that are sluggish, you will surely run into them. This will also avoid a call-back. (More on call-backs later.)

**The Major Chords**

| | | | | | | | |
|---|---|---|---|---|---|---|---|
| F | A | C | F | B | D# | F# | B |
| F# | A# | C# | F# | C | E | G | C |
| G | B | D | G | C# | F | G# | C# |

| | | | | | | | |
|---|---|---|---|---|---|---|---|
| G# | C | D# | G# | D | F# | A | D |
| A | C# | E | A | D# | G | A# | D# |
| A# | D | F | A# | E | G# | B | E |

2. Arrange the next tuning with this client for six months or one year later, whichever suits him the best, according to the use he makes of his piano and the amount of dependability you think may be counted on in this particular household. At this time, explain that you use a file system something like that which the dentist uses and that his name will crop up on the week agreed on for the future tuning. At that time, your employee will call and arrange a definite time and day for the tuning.

Do not rely on mail alone to get you the business, since many things are sent in the mail today and most people don't read everything that they receive. But make the appointment firm, if you possibly can, and then use the rotating file system to follow up. This way your tunings accumulate and within a short time you should have more business than you can handle. For more complete and detailed information as to how to set up a good repeat card and business system, refer to my previous book in this field, *The Complete Course in Professional Piano Tuning, Repair, and Rebuilding.*

One thing more needs be said: be sure to have professional-looking invoices or sales slips printed or order them from your supplier. There is nothing as likely to destroy the image of professionalism you are trying to convey as a shoddy sales slip.

Your appointment book should be placed by the phone in your home or office, with plenty of paper and pens handy, so that customers don't have to wait while you hunt for them. A duplicate of the appointment book should accompany you on your calls, so that you can make the next tuning appointment while you are at the client's.

Do not hesitate to quote your tuning and working fees.

Some tuners are reluctant to view themselves as professionals and hesitantly mention their fees when asked. First, do good work—and don't go on calls until you can do them right. Then charge the prevailing fee, or higher, for your area, since you are bringing to the job a new dimension in that you are a user of the best of both methods in tuning. Also you are carrying with you an instrument which cost many dollars in order to be more precise and accurate than most tuners care to be. So often, when we are finished at a doctor's office, and ask the fee, the girl will sweetly say, "That'll be 20." Usually, I ask her if she means 20 jelly beans, 20 safety pins, or 20 what? She then firmly states that she means $20. But the way she puts it at first, it seems she is a little ashamed to ask for so much. That's probably how it would seem to your clients too, if you went about it deviously. If your fee for tuning is $20, and if you are personally satisfied that you have given all you can to tuning that particular piano, why be ashamed to speak frankly? People will respect you more for doing so—if you did the job well, that is.

### *Working With Dealers*

Among my friends is a farmer who once said he wished he had a million dollars. When asked what he would do with it, he replied that he would "keep right on farming until it was all gone." A lot of dealers think piano tuners feel that way about the business of tuning. Because a good tuner brings intense concentration to his work and seems, therefore, to be happily engrossed in it to the exclusion of mundane things, dealers think we aren't really interested in money. They are wrong. We are.

Usually, dealers will come in three sizes, listed with the larger sizes first. There is the temporizer. He needs all the pianos on the floor tuned at lower rates than charged for outside tunings. He must have them tuned in order to sell them and to show off their tonal qualities. So, he asks you to tune them. Then, because he is involved and his money is tied up in the pianos in the store, he expects you to wait until he sells them before paying you for the tuning.

Over and above the fact that floor tunings are troublesome, and often interrupted by customers and salesmen talking, lies the salient fact that you are not making the profit on the pianos when they are sold. Therefore, you must make the dealer understand that your fee for tuning *must* be considered a part of his inventory for pianos. And he should pay you upon completion of the work. Otherwise, you will likely find that the passing of weeks and sometimes months will bring significant changes in the tuning of the floor pianos and the dealer may ask you to "touch 'em up" periodically; he considers this "touch up" as part of your original tuning.

Then there's the dealer who "glad hands" you with grandiose promises that, if you will make an exception by lowering your fee, he will see that you get all the tunings he can find for you. This arrangement will continue until you jot down on paper the amount of fees you've lost while doing cut-rate work for him. You also will find he controls an amazingly small number of tunings outside of his store. At that time, you will note that you have been subsidizing his operation with no tangible benefits whatever accruing to yourself. Usually, this dealer will also want you to kick back a small percentage of the outside fees, if and when he gets you any tunings. Often, he will give the impression of a "hail fellow, well met." Generally, he will be prone to break the arrangement before you do, since he will be looking for another patsy to take your place. The time will come when this fellow, like his peer, whose description follows, will use you only for "emergency" calls, at odd hours, and in distant places which are unprofitable to you.

Last, and definitely least, there's the dealer who shops around. He wants you only if you are cheaper than the tuner he has now. He tries out every tuner in town, and some from out of town, trying to get the cheapest tuning jobs possible. He is a danger to both you and his piano sales customers. None of his customers are likely to be satisfied with their pianos, since, if a good tuner tunes them, he will not stay with this dealer long. The piano will sound poorly after the next man, who is both cheap and inept, tunes it. This dealer will inform his salesmen that tuners will work for next to nothing; he undermines his employees. If this happens, and it usually does, the salesman will tell the prospective customer, who may or may not buy a piano, that "pianos don't need tuning often, but when they do, we've got a guy who is real cheap." Then, when you confront the customer in his home, and state your fee, you will find that you are "too expensive." Furthermore, you will find that the customer will tell his friends that you are high priced and that the dealer won't use you because you charge too much. Tuners who connect with a dealer like this are committing financial suicide.

There is only one answer to these problems: Contracts. At the outset, the terms of contract tuning for dealers should be set and signed between dealer and tuner. Then, as business conditions change, the contract may be altered with mutual permission. It establishes a business basis for your continued association with a dealer and enables you to accept your money with dignity. Furthermore, it enables the dealer to know with certainty that he has a good tuner at hand for all his pianos.

### *Rebuilding Old Pianos*

Within my files is a letter which reads as follows:

Dear Mr. Stevens,

I will be in your city in about two months and would like for you to give me an estimate on rebuilding and restoring my mother's piano. I teach music here and I have several friends who want me to O.K. your workmanship.

So, let's see what you can do for the piano I learned on. (It needs some new ivories.)

Sincerely,

____________

Among the devotees of the old upright are those who, for sentimental reasons, want to have an old piano restored. The cost will usually be prohibitive if one is to do a complete rebuilding job. And if the technician tries to do a half-way job, the complaints within a few months or years will keep him explaining why he didn't do better.

Based on the above letter, my first impression was that:

1. This is a music teacher; she thinks I will be eagerly seeking her approval of my work. The fact is that few music teachers are in any position to intelligently evaluate a piano technician's work, because, not knowing much about restringing a piano, repairing a sound board, regulating the 6,000 parts of the action, or adjusting the touch, their approval is practically meaningless. They do have a sense of musical tonality (although not nearly as good a sense of it as most people think), but know little about the beat ratio within a temperament.

2. An upright old enough for her to have learned on will be old indeed. And such a piano will require painstaking work in repairmanship, with the certainty that the hammers will need complete replacement, and the action parts, being made of wood, will be brittle and break regularly.

Without looking at the piano, I am able to visualize the condition of felts which probably are 50 years old, hammers which are flattened on the ends, and keys which have been played thousands and thousands of times.

I responded to the above letter as follows:

Dear Mrs. ________,

Thank you for your note concerning my services. Before we go any further, perhaps we should consider what we are getting into. First of all, my fee for estimating on repair work is $15, payable at the time of estimate, and allowable in full on the bill if the repair work is done within 30 days thereafter.

It is understandable that you want to O.K. my workmanship, but it is not absolutely necessary that you do so. Over the years, the hundreds of pianos I've repaired and the tunings I've done for my regular clientele assure me that my work is good.

There are as many parts (about 6,000) in an old piano as there are in a new one. Unfortunately, old piano parts are usually in need of replacement, and this can cost a great deal. Furthermore, the pin block, strings, and their associated friction areas are, if more than 25 years old, in complete need of replacement. While a technician can do enough work on an old piano to make it "get by" for a reasonable sum, to do the amount of work really needed to put it in first class shape will cost about what a new spinet piano costs.

Many people desire to have old uprights rebuilt, nevertheless. For sentimental reasons, they will gladly invest to have a resonant, full-sounding upright put back into first class shape. If this seems to be what you had in mind, I will be glad to discuss the matter further. If not, it would probably not be wise to invest only a little money and get only a partly restored piano. Thank you for your note.

Sincerely,
Floyd A. Stevens, Ph.D.

An exception to the above case is when a tuner is called only to tune an old upright and to do some action repair to make it work. Many people, understanding that the instrument can never be as good as new, will gladly pay for each tuning to get it working for another year. Another exception is when the tuner can buy an old upright cheaply, and when he can take the time during odd hours in his shop to put it back into playable condition, perhaps refinishing the case as well. He will then sell the piano at a good profit for the hours he spent on it after his day's tunings are over.

At this juncture, let me emphasize that there is only one way to rebuild a piano, and that is to rebuild it completely, replacing whatever is worn, weak, or unregulatable. No short cuts here. Rebuilding pays well, and, when well done on a quality instrument, will make a piano sound better than many do when new. Complete rebuilding instructions are given in my earlier book.

No tuner can be in this profession long before meeting a client who had called another tuner but who had been flatly refused. Usually, the piano was an old upright model, badly in need of repair. Sometimes it was an old grand piano with a loose pin block or split sound board. Whatever the situation, you must realistically appraise the work required to make the instrument tunable and operable, and then get a definite agreement with your customer as to exactly what repairs are to be made and what the cost will be. For this purpose, the best answer is a contract. (A sample contract is included at the close of this chapter.)

Not a little of the trouble which comes to many tuners can be avoided with the use of contracts which state exactly what is being agreed to between client and technician. After all, tuning is a business, and we should conduct ourselves as businessmen. No one questions the ethical position of a man who has stated his agreement in writing.

After the appraisal is made and the contract agreed to, your ethical position is quite clear. First, you receive a one-third payment from the client before beginning the work. This enables you to make progress in getting the parts, etc., and saves some trouble. Second, you complete the work in the time agreed upon, and upon completing it, you add an extra finishing touch to do more than what the contract called for. Then, upon inspection, at your shop, the client pays the balance due, and you deliver the piano. Every step of the way you are protected, and so is the client. The best way to handle problems with people is to handle them in advance.

### *Be Your Own Man*

There is an infinite variety in piano work. Some pianos are easier to tune than others; and the others, if we depend on the unaided human ear, present a real problem. Further, some older tuners are so sure they excel other tuners that they don't bother to compare their work with them. As a result, they exude a false sense of authority which can be overpowering to a newcomer in the field. It also is depressing to an experienced man, if he pays attention to them. Therefore, mind your own work, and learn to think carefully about what you are doing with the electronic aid you are using. Make it a practice to ignore the pompous opinions of self-appointed experts.

Not all tuners you meet will try to gain an upper hand. There are many fine tuners in this business who remember what it was like to be young and to want to learn. Many of them have known discouragement. In time they discovered that customers are amazingly loyal. Eventually old timers will fade away and their places will have to be taken by young men who are starting right now.

It is our duty to become excellent practitioners in the art of piano tuning. For this reason, we are wise to include in our learning the most modern and accurate methods and devices available for the purpose of tuning. That some may object to these "new-fangled gadgets" is to be expected. Electronic tuners must show the same high standards of craftsmanship that older men have come to associate with piano servicing.

*A Full-Time Career*

You are unlikely to become the kind of piano technician and tuner you should be unless you aim at getting into piano service full time. Over the years I have known a goodly number of men who took up piano tuning as a moonlighting job. While a few learned to tune well, most did not.

In truth, even the few who learned to tune well did not become piano technicians, for they had not learned the other part of their craft: they could not rebuild, and from this lack of a foundation, they were not strong on repairs, either.

It is difficult to learn the many and varied interactions of piano components and structural elements which definitely affect the way in which a piano is tuned and the way in which it will lose its tune, without going into this business full time. To repeat, I have never heard of a man who did the best tuning ultimately, unless he also was earning a living at this business full time.

It would seem highly unlikely that anyone would employ a part-time doctor or attorney. Yet piano work requires the same exacting attention to detail and to interacting elements that other professions require. Men who have to go to college in order to learn the rudiments of their profession somehow manage to survive and then go on to do well in their chosen fields. While a college degree is not necessary in piano work, it certainly doesn't get in the way of it either. In any case, the man or woman who desires to set up in business for himself as a piano craftsman should be willing to join a professional association, read the pertinent books, and perform the necessary fundamental tasks and experiments in order to perfect his craftsmanship.

There are small comforts in piano work for those who try to hold down two full-time jobs. The time can accumulate to 70 or 80 hours per week, and the same amount of hours put into piano work alone, once you are qualified to do it well, will offer a better income than both jobs put together.

If one tries to work a full-time job, and then tune pianos, he finds that he cannot put the hours, especially fresh hours, into it that it requires. He cannot follow up leads for new business, and he cannot take more than two or three days a week to do piano work.

Then, too, he cannot take care of the minor customer complaints which are likely to come up, since he is already losing time by simply getting ready to go to work in his regular job. He loses good will on every side, and he loses the image he once had of himself as a professional, competent craftsman who aimed at being a master tuner.

Also, if he should try to work only in the shop, he finds that he hasn't the time to think out his problems properly. He runs into many time-consuming jobs which would have been really easy if he had been doing the work every day in the field. Worst of all, he is not faced with reality in the piano field, and so, he charges prices that undercut all responsible men in the business. This makes them his enemies and keeps him from sharing in their good ideas and worthwhile meetings and educational seminars. He may not actually hurt their business, but he hurts the image of what a real craftsman is in the eyes of the public.

If he is a teacher, or other public employee, he is resented by those who are laboring ethically at their own professions, whether they be in law, medicine, or piano craftsmanship, since they are paying part of his salary in taxes. Finally, and worst of all, he hurts himself. He will never be paid what good work should be paid. And it will all be due to the fact that he just isn't confident enough to go into the tuning field and do good work day after day, because he hasn't taken the time to become a full-time professional.

The day of the "little old man who came around" and tuned the piano is gone, never to return. And the day of the man who "has a wonderful ear, and can tune any old piano" is on its way out as well.

Piano tuning and technical work have become a worthwhile profession. Using textbooks, some colleges and universities are offering a full sequence of courses in the field. National and international associations have formed for the betterment of piano craftsmen and the pooling of knowledge.

With the advent of electronic tuning devices and the careful application of space-age accuracies to the well-proven methods already in use, the business can only prosper. We can offer to the public better piano service than was possible years ago, and we can also accept what was always good in piano tuning and care.

But we will have to be professionals to do it, and we will never get it done if we are not. Dedicated tuners have brought piano craftsmanship up from the days of the "travelin' tooner" with his "chaw" of tobacco and his ramshackle car or buggy. They have studied their craft assiduously and applied their knowledge conscientiously. We are benefiting from their gradual public recognition today. And we will benefit still more tomorrow.

To these men, some of whom are still tuning and repairing, we owe much. They made it possible for modern tuners to become proud and independent men. The debt can be paid only by conscientious adherence to the better ways of tuning and servicing pianos. We should not make obsolete the tried and true aural methods. Instead we should blend the craftsmanship of the past with the new techniques now available through electronic devices.

**Typical Contract for Reconditioning a Piano (Front Side)**

**(Tuner's Name, Address, and Phone Number)**

**Ref**......................**Grand,** **Serial Number**................

**Ref**....................**Upright,** **Serial Number**................

*It was a pleasure to check your piano recently. Thank you very much for the opportunity. Following our conversation, and in accordance with my usual custom, I am presenting the following proposal for your consideration.*

*I agree to furnish the labor and quality materials for the repairing of your piano as follows:*

| | |
|---|---|
| Restringing Bass Treble | |
| Cleaning | $ ______ |
| Mothproofing | ______ |
| Bridge repairs | ______ |
| Soundboard repairs | ______ |
| Pin block repair | ______ |
| Pin block replace | ______ |
| Ivory keys | ______ |
| Ivoriene keys | ______ |
| Replacement of keys | ______ |
| Bushing repairs keys | ______ |
| Bushing repairs centers | ______ |
| Bushing repairs fronts | ______ |
| Backchecks | ______ |
| Refelting of action | ______ |
| Flanges | ______ |
| Wippens—new | ______ |
| Wippens—repair | ______ |
| Tightening of flanges, etc. | ______ |
| Hammers | |

| | |
|---|---|
| Resurface | ______ |
| Replace | ______ |
| Repair | ______ |
| Bridle straps | ______ |
| Leveling of keys | ______ |
| Regulation | |
| Complete | ______ |
| Partial | ______ |
| Dampers Felts | |
| Replace set | ______ |
| Repair | ______ |
| Damper guide rail repairs | ______ |
| Pedal system repairs | ______ |
| Pitch lowering & raising | ______ |
| Voicing hammers | ______ |
| Tuning to concert pitch. . . A-440 | ______ |
| Refinishing | ______ |
| Moving piano (both directions) | ______ |
| TOTAL ESTIMATE | $ ______ |

**Acceptance Contract** (Reverse Side)

**DATE** ..........................

*I (We) do hereby accept the proposal for repairing our piano and do hereby authorize you to proceed. Accordingly, as requested, we are enclosing our check for $.......... as the down payment, and the balance of $.......... is to be paid upon inspection of the piano when finished, in your shop, before delivery.*

**SIGNED** ..................................................................

**SIGNED** ..................................................................

**SIGNED** .......................... **Piano Technician**

## ORDER BLANK FOR YOUR CONVENIENCE

Dear Sir: Date ______________________

Please call me at your earliest convenience. I am interested in:

☐ Tuning or Repairing ☐ Installing a DAMPP-CHASER® in my Piano to prevent sticking keys, sluggish action and rust ☐ Advice on purchase of new or used piano

Name ______________________

Address ______________________

City ______________ Zip ________ Phone ______________

Directions (or name and address of a friend who wants tuning):

______________________

______________________

**"A PIANO IS ONLY AS GOOD AS THE CARE IT RECEIVES"**

(Front Side)

Promotional mailing piece with return card to increase your tuning business (available through Dampp-Chaser Co., Box 1610, Huntsville, N.C. 28739).

## HOW OFTEN SHOULD I HAVE MY PIANO TUNED?

As a wise piano owner you are interested in protecting the investment in your piano.

Most manufacturers recommend two to four tunings a year because dampness and daily temperature changes seriously affect the soundboard and delicate action parts. These changes are also the usual cause of sticking keys, sluggish action, and rust, which can be greatly reduced by installing a Thermo-Electric DAMPP-CHASER® Dehumidifier. Ask us about installing this low cost protective unit in your piano. For information on any of these services, use the convenient order blank attached.

If there has been a change of season since your piano was tuned then it is in need of tuning. (Date of last tuning ______________________________)

**(Tuner's name and address)**

---

From ______________________________

______________________________

______________________________

PLACE
STAMP
HERE

**(Tuner's name and address)**

(Reverse Side)

# 12
# Developing Your Full Potential

Recently I was surprised to find that an idea I had developed and used, but had then neglected to document for my tuning comrades, was being propounded as something brand new by a speaker at a regional meeting of tuners. Most of us have found ourselves in this position at one time or another.

Many of us could be wealthy, or at least more respected, if we took the time to evaluate our own ideas properly and refine them along with the related skills they require to work. There are happenings in the experience of every tuner-technician that he fails to capitalize on. He grieves in the bitter memory of what might have been when he should be tasting the fruits of success.

The following story illustrates this fact. Quite often you may be called upon to service a new piano which has been delivered to an owner's home by a dealer. More often than not, the keys will seem to be a little sluggish and especially difficult to operate well in a quick repetition of a particular note. This will lead you to examine the action; usually you will find that the jack fly is not reseating rapidly under the hammer butt when the key is released. Perhaps this will be because the factory allowed for no lost motion whatever when the action in the piano was regulated. Again, it could be due to a gradual loss of clearance, which is the result of humidity swelling the action components and filling up the small clearances usually allowed.

Whatever the reason for this condition, it must be remedied. The apparent remedy is to adjust the key capstans slightly downward so as to arrange for some lost motion between the top of the jack and the hammer butt. I have done this in the past. Then I had to readjust on the next tuning, after the piano had dried out in the customer's home, so as to remove the *extra* clearance which had developed in the action and the slightly excessive lost motion which had existed. This meant that, in the first instance, the dealer was charged for the complete adjustment of all capstans on an 88 key piano. In the second instance, the customer was charged for the same operation being performed in reverse. Somebody was paying when he shouldn't have had to. Further, the tuner was in an unfair position. He did extra work for which he was not amply remunerated, because he felt that he owed it either to the dealer or the customer to discount a service which was performed at one time and then, a few months later, ''unperformed,'' so to speak.

To solve this problem, all that was needed was to insert a small piece of felt under the hammer rail rest felts at each of the four points. This insertion, for all intents and purposes, cut the hammer distance from the strings by less than a 32nd of an inch, without reducing the tone to any discernible degree. But it did have the effect of lifting the hammer butts off the high jack tops and allowing for rapid repetition in the action.

Then, on the next visit for tuning, if the action had developed additional clearance due to drying out in the home, it was a simple matter to remove the small strips of felt to bring things to normal again. The dealer was charged for the original adjustment, but much less than he would have been had all capstans been adjusted. The customer was not charged for removal of the felt. Still, the tuner was rewarded with an extra half-hour's fee for doing what had formerly been a 60-minute job.

Trust your own thoughts as you do your work and develop them to their ultimate proficiency. That is the basic reason why we are learning to use highly sophisticated electronic instruments to simplify the accurate setting of temperament. It is also the mark of a conscientious craftsman that he try a better and more time-saving way to do everything.

Many times, we are prone to develop more trouble and tribulation for ourselves than is necessary, and in the process, we are likely to lose out on considerable cash which we could have had with little trouble. For example: once I was called to a farm home and asked to tune a piano. Upon my arrival, the family proudly showed me an old grand piano which bore a famous name. Unfortunately, it had borne the name for 60 years, and no one had ever done anything to improve its condition as it slowly deteriorated over the years. An examination of the instrument revealed that the action was completely out of regulation, some keys were unworkable, the hammers were not striking the proper strings, and the dampers seating was in various twisted positions due to dusting or bending by someone not familiar with pianos. In addition, the upper treble section showed much abuse, with several broken strings. Some were rusty, and that promised that others would break as soon as one began to tune the piano. Furthermore, the instrument was down in pitch a full tone.

Obviously, the piano was in need of complete restringing and a full damper job, with attendant action work, which would bring the total repair figure to ten times the present value of the instrument.

This family thought they had made an excellent buy when they paid $90 for their instrument. But they were not in a financial position to invest another $900 or so to get it in playable condition. This fact was made clear to me.

In such a case, some tuners would state that they would not work on the piano unless a full overhaul would be done, they would pack up their tools and leave. I, too, was tempted to do the same thing. But it was obvious that the family held me in respect. Also, they were so ignorant of the facts of piano care that they seemed certain I could get the instrument in fine condition without major surgery. This seemed nearly impossible to me, at first glance, and yet it was obvious that some middle course might eventually please everyone.

With considerable care, I explained to the family just how many tunings would be required before the instrument would be anywhere near proper pitch. Further, I pointed out that these tunings might be carried on over a period of one full year (and at the same time spread the repair cost to more nearly fit their budget).

The need for action regulation was immediate. A price was agreed upon for the work to begin at once, especially the first tuning, which would be aimed at lifting the pitch approximately one fourth of its distance toward concert pitch.

With agreement on these operations, the action was removed, regulated, and replaced, with some light filing of the worst hammer shapes to approximate their proper configuration. The piano was tuned, leaving the missing strings on the upper unisons just as they were. And an appointment was made for a tuning two months later, at which time the missing strings would be replaced and the worst dampers repaired. Some slight damper realignment was done at this first tuning in order to provide a practice piano, at least.

On the next visit to the farm, I was agreeably surprised

to find that they appreciated my matching the repairs to their budget and that the family had set aside a little money to afford a few more repairs. The second tuning was completed, the pitch raised a little more, and the dampers replaced and aligned properly; but the family had decided to pay for the full damper job and to let the upper treble alone until they could replace all the weak strings in that section. An appointmend was made for three months later for another tuning and replacement of the complete upper treble string section.

Upon the next visit, the things were done as agreed to, and the instrument was brought to proper pitch. At this time I suggested that we forego further repairs until such a time when they could afford a new pin block and restringing job in my shop, since we could tune the old piano every six months now and still have a good piano for the kids to learn on. They went along with this. The piano was tuned every six months thereafter.

Recently the piano was brought into my shop. The harp was removed, the sound board was refinished, a new pin block and new strings were fitted, and at the family's request, new key coverings were installed. The dampers were fine and reuseable and the action was still in good condition, requiring only that the hammers be reshaped in the shop.

Here is a case in which a family got use of a piano from the first day I arrived. It was able to afford the gradual repairs, and was so pleased with the payment method that it finally was able to afford the bulk of the remaining cost. How different from being summarily told they had bought "a piece of junk" with the resultant loss of confidence in the tuner. Furthermore, every call to this home paid me well, and helped my business. Potentially, the first visit suggested a profitable deal with this family and their piano. It was not possible to get my fee in one lump, so to speak, but it was possible to develop this potential.

Many years ago, a dealer sold a used grand piano to an

acquaintance of mine at a very low price because it had a split sound board. My friend, who had little money, asked me if I could stop the rattling of the sound board edges and make it look presentable without removing the strings and doing costly repairs. Being much less experienced at this profession than I am now, I cudgeled my brain to think of some way to accomplish this minor miracle. Finally, I resorted to the use of a hot melt glue gun and filled all the creaking cracks with hot melt glue, then leveled it down with a hot spatula. The repairing was successful, my friend was pleased, the cost was reasonable, but I avoided telling anyone about this job, since it seemed too "backyard" to boast about.

During the years since then, I have repaired many sound boards. I used the tried and true method of clearing the area of work, opening and enlarging the cracks, tailoring shims of sound board material to fit the cracks and grooves, and then sanding and refinishing the board. From time to time, I have wondered if subsequent contracting and expanding of the sound board might not dislodge the shims or lift them somewhat. I have seen such things happen to boards repaired by the best tuners in this business.

Lately, I have read reports by men who are able and qualified in the field of piano technology that espouse a new method for repairing sound boards. They had been looking for a filler that would not shrink at a different rate from that at which sound board grains compress the crack; also, they sought a filler that would not remain inactive when the sound board spread, but would spread with it. It turns out they began using a hot melt glue gun, filling the cracks with hot melt glue, and finishing the surface by heating a burn-in knife or spatula and making all things level.

The reports reveal good success thus far, with little reason to expect any dislodging of the glue from the cracks. Since the repair of sound board cracks is primarily cosmetologic and only for appearance in many cases, there is no reason why this stretchable glue should not work satisfactorily. Should repair be required because the edges of the crack are rubbing against each other and causing a buzzing sound, the glue is a good solution to the problem.

Here is an idea which deserved further development on my part when first I used it. It could have saved me much time. Instead, it was neglected and the potential was not developed. But, at least, I did discover that you can melt hot melt glue and remove it from any surface by an application of rubbing alcohol. A person is indeed shortsighted to conceal his ideas!

Every tuner who has been in this business long knows that the ideal goal is a completely quiet unison with no "wirey" sound and no pulses within it. Also, every tuner should know he cannot always attain the ideal in his unisons. But here's one tuner who learned that attaining a "wirey" sound can make you money.

The dealer in a nearby city mentioned one day that he was trying to sell a piano to a man who had been the church organist. Also he was an old pipe organ tuner. However, he did not like the tone of any of the pianos on the dealer's floor.

Further inquiry elicited the fact that the old man was in his late 70s, and, although hale and hearty, somewhat prone to speak in a loud and booming voice. It was suggested to the dealer that he select the console or studio piano which the old man had shown the most interest in. Then the dealer was told to arrange a demonstration for the elderly gentleman for the following afternoon after "our best tuner has just tuned it." Here's what was done.

The piano was tuned to proper pitch and temperament. The octaves were stretched to the proper amount, and then just a little bit more stretch was added. This resulted in the arpeggios becoming somewhat sharp. Such an adjustment appeals to violinists and guitarists. The result is a high, ringing sound which is a little more than most piano tuners like to put into the piano treble stretch. This tuning brought the top octave up to a full 30 cents sharp above pitch, which is the probable optimum amount of stretch you can put into a piano without having double octaves sound funny. Then, as he tuned each unison to the center string, the tuner lifted the pin to 2 beats above perfect unison, let it lower the normal 1 beat, and pressed the pin just lightly downward to kill off the last small beat before perfect unison. Upon release of the hammer, the outside string on the right side was allowed to have that slight "wirey" sound which indicates the string rose slightly after pin setting. The unisons were left that way, producing a piano in tune, but one which had a tendency to accentuate the high harmonics in each unison.

On the following day, the old gentleman came in, heard the piano, played it, and bought it. He bought it because years of tuning pipe organs and listening to them, plus the attenuation of the upper hearing ranges at advanced age, made it almost impossible for him to hear upper frequencies unless there was an edge to them, or a slight beat within them. Thus, the tuner did something "wrong" to enable this old man to hear the piano tones in the upper treble. Of course, the dealer was grateful and made that clear to the tuner.

Since then, this piano has been tuned by the original tuner and sometimes by the customer. Both are tuning it for precisely the same sound because that is the sound the organist bought, and that is the sound he is paying for. Personally, I think that a man who wants his steering wheel on the curb side of the automobile has every right to have it placed there if he is buying the car and driving it. People who cannot hear the tones that result from normal professional tuning are entitled to hear the tones they want to hear from their pianos. Sometimes it is better to do something differently from a standard if it pleases the customer who, after all, pays for the job.

At the turn of the century, some piano tuners would make

their calls attired in a swallow-tailed coat, wing collar, morning trousers, and gloves. They carried canes with gold knobs. No doubt they commanded as high a price and respect as their style denoted. Such an attitude would not hurt our business today, either. Certainly they were far less likely to forget to develop their potential than someone who dressed inconspicuously.

Once I encountered a piano which I had taken in a trade. This piano was in bad shape. The hammers were flattened throughout the range, the keys were scruffy, with half of the ivories missing and key buttons split from moisture.

The dampers were devoured by moths, and the upper pin block was pulling away from the back of the case in three or four places. After a careful examination, I decided this old upright was not worthy of restyling in my shop and that the best thing to do with it was to burn it. However, a few days later, a local dealer in decrepit pianos stopped by and offered me $15 for it. Using a large file, I made an X mark on the harp above the treble and helped him throw the various pieces of the case into his truck.

Some months later, while tuning pianos hundreds of miles away in Florida, I made a call to a sand trail which had been beaten down by wild cattle, bears, and whatever else had to get through to the high, scrub palmetto in the Great Gulf Hammock. About a half-mile away stood the home of a client who had called me to tune her piano. I drove to the house where I was met by pugnacious dogs. She called off the dogs and I carried my tuning kit into the house. There, in the front room, stood a piano which had been carefully sanded, antiqued, and cut down. A mirror had been affixed across the top. It had new keytops and a generally handsome appearance. After carefully removing the mirror and the top, I removed the panel which served as music rack. In the upper right-hand corner was a large X mark. Closer examination showed that the split key buttons had been replaced. The bolts which had run from the front of the pin block into the back of the piano had been removed, larger holes reamed, and long stove bolts with giant washers installed in their places, with nuts countersunk in the back beams. Broken strings had been replaced, and the hammers filed.

In the course of the tuning which followed, some action repairs were required, but they were minor. The piano took and seemed to hold its tune rather well, and the whole job was not onerous.

With some amusement I realized that I was tuning the piano which had been thrown out of my shop and which now taunted me some 1,000 miles from the place where I had last seen it. I asked the client what she had paid for the piano. She named a price which was $150 more than it would have sold for if it had been completely gone over and restyled in my shop in Ohio. Someone had seen the potential which had escaped me and had developed it for a greater profit than I would have thought possible.

While tuning and repairing in Florida, I developed a new potential. It happened that a large Baptist church contracted to have all their pianos serviced on a regular basis. Since this was a new church, the pianos were new as well, and of a fine quality, studio type. While tuning them, I had a chance to talk with the church music director. He explained that they were having a great deal of trouble with their recently acquired organ. It seemed to him that the sounds were beating against each other on certain chords. The local dealer was unable to correct the defect. He had replaced the suspected defective speakers and even some of the controls in an attempt to make a satisfactory adjustment. Incidentally, this large and expensive instrument had been made by the same manufacturer who provided the fine pianos in the church.

I listened to his playing of the organ and noted that every stop worked as designed, and that all tones seemed even and true, without warbling in the divider circuits or oscillators. The addition of the tremolo while playing the organ intensified the beating sound of which he complained, but the movement was not stopped when tremolo or vibrato was turned off. After finishing the piano tunings, I decided to check the tuning of the organ with the Yamaha Tuner Scope, since it seemed to me the beats he was hearing were dependent upon which fifths he was playing. Sure enough, once the organ was checked against an absolute standard of pitch for each note, it was clear that the organ was out of tune within itself. Subsequent tuning of the oscillators to standard temperament with the steady aid of the electronic instrument eliminated the beats both in the keyboard and in the pedals.

Here was an instance in which just having possession of an electronic tuning device gave me a ready potential for additional satisfaction for the client, and the ability to be absolutely certain that the tuning I did on that organ was accurate. When I asked the music director who had tuned the organ, he said no one. They had spent many hours removing modular sections and replacing them with new ones in an attempt to stop the trouble within the organ. Finally, he did remember that the dealer's man had turned a few things while blowing on a pitch pipe. Thus the potential that exists when a man becomes expert in the field of electronic tuning is worthy of considerable thought and development.

For a long time, salesmen have been telling people that organs never go out of tune. With the exception of the Hammond tone wheel organ, this is not true. And in fact, the Hammond tone wheel system is not in perfect tune itself. For your information, especially when tuning other instruments to the Hammond, here is the table of frequencies which exist in the Hammond as originally designed and manufactured with the 60 cycle sychronous motor tone generating system:

| Hammond Scale | | Tempered Scale |
|---|---|---|
| 440.000 | A | 440.000 |
| 466.163 | A# | 466.086 |
| 493.883 | B | 493.714 |

| | | |
|---|---|---|
| 523.251 | C | 523.076 |
| 554.365 | C# | 554.146 |
| 587.329 | D | 587.397 |
| 622.253 | D# | 622.222 |
| 659.255 | E | 659.200 |
| 698.446 | F | 698.181 |
| 739.988 | F# | 740.000 |
| 783.991 | G | 784.000 |
| 830.609 | G# | 830.270 |

Organs other than Hammond should not be tuned to the Hammond scale, since various stops are built into them. These make it possible for their output to sound similar to a Hammond, and tuning them to a frequency scale other than tempered will mean then they will not sound properly in tune. Only the Hammond has this frequency setup.

In developing your potential, remember that your public image can be enhanced and your business brought to favorable public attention by your constant identification with the musical field and its activities in your area. Attending concerts and becoming acquainted either as a member or a speaker at musical clubs in your area will do much to add to your potential. Not only will this bring you favorable public notice, it will also give you a sense of self-worth—the prime requisite for increasing your readiness and potential in all situations.

However, some of us may not feel that we could speak or perform well in public. For those who are in this frame of mind, the alternative of sponsoring performers is a happy one. For example, regularly I appear as a musician and singer at public gatherings, especially those with sponsorship underwritten by musical or church groups. This has led to instant identification of me and my business with the field of music. The music teachers and public school music staffs in the county are familiar with my ability as a piano tuner and technician.

Recently, we have sponsored, as a part of our business, the auditioning of singing and playing groups for a series of gospel music festivals in which I play a purposely minor role. The main idea is to encourage musicians, both young and old, who wish they were on the stage. These people come as trios, quartets, etc., and are integrated into an evening show which is open to the public. Usually it is best to rent the local high school auditorium, which is a neutral place without commercial or religious connotations, and arrange to have the performance there.

The good will engendered by these nights of music and opportunity for talent to be heard cannot be measured. But we are sure it has something favorable to do with building our piano business. Brief information in the newspaper advertisements that announce the auditions and performance mentions that the event is sponsored by our firm. This, we think, helps to develop our potential with clients living in this general area.

The nice thing about this idea is that it is applicable everywhere and is reasonable in cost. It provides much publicity for people who ordinarily are not heard in public. Local music dealers will usually be willing to help you do this and will often furnish instruments or public address units as needed. You are building up some of the potential in other people in this way. If this does not result in also developing a greater potential in your own business and abilities, it will be surprising. Variations on this idea are endless, but you will find that you will profit in many ways you least expect with every enlargement you can make for someone else's life.

Respond to challenge because in your toughest problems you will usually find the greatest growth. And remember to trust your own thinking, since no one else on earth understands it quite as well as you do. Each of us brings to every situation a unique preparation which has been developed through our life. No other person can bring to a situation exactly what you can bring to it. If your solution or answer seems different from others, do not be surprised.

There is usually more than one right answer to any problem, and waiting to find a general consensus of opinion means the problem will never be solved in a creative way. Instead, it may be solved committee fashion, in the most regressive and dull way possible. You will develop your potentials when you start valuing them precisely because they are yours. And only then can you develop them fully.

Sometimes it pays handsomely to break the mold of established practice and to take the simple steps through a problem or situation which seem logical to you. Too often, we lose opportunity because we are wondering what someone else would do in a like situation. It doesn't matter what someone else would do, since you alone will profit or lose from a particular condition. When other people start paying your bills, they might have something to say about your decisions. Until then, you have the best answers, since you are the one who will profit or lose.

Lots of trouble could be avoided in this business if tuners took their work seriously and themselves less so. All too often, those who undercut new ideas in their field become insulated from reality. They begin to think they alone know what is right and sound. Such insularity of personality leads to a plodding, method of going about their profession which makes new ideas and fresh insights impossible. We owe our profession our finest efforts and concentration. But we cannot realize our potential when we are constantly thinking about the impression we are making or how important we are personally. There is a stiffness which results from this that makes us impervious to new thoughts and ideas. Such an attitude is not properly called self-assurance, since to be truly self-assured, we must know what other ideas are available. We can develop our potential only as we share in the development of other men and their ideas. Taking oneself too seriously does not enable us to profit from the developments and mental abilities of others.

Human beings, when faced with a new situation, can apply what they have learned from a careful evaluation of past situations. Each new fact, every new technique, must become a part of our thinking if we are to make an objective evaluation of why we succeeded or failed. To proceed through a new situation, using old aversions or preconceived opinions, simply means we won't profit from either experience or opportunity.

The field of piano tuning is wide and bright with promise for the man or woman who will take the extensive technical expertise which grows from the past and build on it with the modern sophisticated attitudes and methods which are available today.

# Index

## *C*

## About the author

Rated a master craftsman among professional piano technicians, Dr. Stevens has been associated with the world of music almost all of his life. He teaches piano tuning and repair, is educational director of a guild, and operates shops in Ohio and Florida where he tunes, repairs, and rebuilds pianos. He is also an electronics expert, which serves him well in the repair of electronic pianos and organs.

Well known as a singer for many years, Dr. Stevens has given numerous concerts throughout the East and Middle West. He still composes and arranges music for his daughter, Sandra Lee, a professional organist.

Dr. Stevens began his musical studies at the Cincinnati Conservatory of Music, and continued through Ohio Northern University. He lived for a time in Great Britain, where he attended St. Andrew's College, and earned a Ph.D. at the Free Protestant University.

Dividing his time between Ohio and Florida, Dr. Stevens states that his Florida visits are not vacations, as he spends most of his time tuning and repairing pianos. "Fixing pianos is so pleasant and relaxing," he says, "that it's a vacation wherever you live!"